Political Fiction and the American Self

Political Fiction and
the American Self

JOHN WHALEN-BRIDGE

UNIVERSITY OF ILLINOIS PRESS

URBANA AND CHICAGO

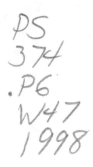

This book is printed on acid-free paper.

Library of Congress Cataloging-in-Publication Data
Whalen-Bridge, John, 1961–
Political fiction and the American self / John Whalen-Bridge.
p.   cm.
Includes bibliographical references and index.
ISBN 0-252-02388-9 (alk. paper). — ISBN 0-252-06688-x (pbk. : alk. paper)
1. Political fiction, American—History and criticism.
2. Politics and literature—United States.
3. National characteristics, American, in literature.
4. Aesthetics, American.
5. Literary form.
I. Title.
PS374.P6W47   1998
813.009'358—dc21   97-33737
CIP

All is dross that is not Helena.

自己を
習ふといふは
自己を
忘るなり

道元訓

[In studying the self, we forget the self.]
—Dōgen

Contents

ACKNOWLEDGMENTS

Once when Lord Mitsushige was a little boy and was supposed to recite from a copybook for the priest Kaion, he called the other children and acolytes and said, "Please come here and listen. It's difficult to read if there are hardly any people listening." The priest was impressed and said to the acolytes, "That's the spirit in which to do everything."
 —Tsunetomo Yamamoto, *Hagakure: The Book of the Samurai*

I thank, as sincerely as I know how, those who made it possible for me to write this book by reading drafts along the way. Jay Martin and Milton Stern read the entire manuscript in early and late stages, and Ron Gottesman and Robert Ellwood read early versions and pushed me to clarify my claims. Louise Schleiner, a.k.a. "Mrs. Hun," helped me with problems I encountered in the first two chapters. Eric Paul Shaeffer and Josiah Bridge also read drafts and made useful suggestions, and I should also mention that the main ideas of chapter 3 were first suggested by comments made by my father. Alexander Pettit, Pamela Gilbert, and Kathryn Hume heard me moan about this book and everything else for years, and I also learned a lot by hearing them moan and groan about my writing. Alex, Pam, and Kit: I also thank you for several years of good e-mail. Michael Kowalewski and Tobin Siebers gave me some of the sharpest criticism and thus made me work harder than I intended to, for which I am indeed grateful. Jay Williams, Erica Briscoe, and Jacqueline Tavernier-Courbin aided and abetted chapter 4. In addition to having a review copy of *Harlot's Ghost* sent my way, Norman Mailer read a draft of chapter 5 and responded with genuine kindness. J. Michael Lennon, John Abbott, Leo Braudy, and Lothar Cerny also gave me advice and encouragement on chapter five. At the University of the Ryukyus in Okinawa I received advice and encouragement from Tony Jenkins, Peter Petrucci, and Ikue Kina, and then, when he thought I'd gotten an introduction or conclusion just right, Bill Mihalopoulos told me it was "bitchin,'" for which I am warmly grateful. Sean O'Grady refused to read this manuscript, but I forgive him since he's almost totally bald.

Ann Lowry of the University of Illinois Press has been extremely helpful, and thanks also to Theresa Sears and Louis Simon. I am especially grateful also to the anonymous readers who made me go the extra kilometer. Sections of chapters 2 and 4 appeared in *Studies in the Novel* and *Thalia*, and a portion of chapter 5 appeared in *Connotations*. Two books in particular were helpful. R. W. B. Lewis's *The American Adam*, written during the beginning of the cold war, and Tobin Siebers's *Cold War Criticism and the Politics of Skepticism*, written at the cold war's close, helped me gather my thoughts toward the latter end of this project.

I can't remember seeing anyone thank a critical adversary before, but without the prior writings of Irving Howe, Joseph Blotner, and Gordon Milne; the recent theoretical interventions of Donald Pease and Thomas Schaub; or the nonfiction of Toni Morrison I would not have been able to define my own position very well. Anyone who has practiced a martial art knows the difference between a well-executed technique and an outburst of spleen. I hope those with whom I have taken issue will recognize in my writing much of the former and none of the latter.

And now for family. Hatsuko Machida (a.k.a. "Okāsan") made the calligraphy. Helena Whalen-Bridge read, and talked when I couldn't write, and helped in all the myriad ways. Thomas Josiah Menla and William James Sokei Whalen-Bridge didn't do anything to help, but it sure didn't hurt to have them to play with after a long day's work. Finally, I'd like to acknowledge my debt to my grandfather, John Bridge. He died in 1984, even before I knew I was going to write about political fiction, but his example has been most important. As I sit here, happily naming names on this cheerful occasion, I remember with pride that he did not name names when told he must do so, though it cost him his career as a Classics professor. I am told he once said, "Oh, you *can* say 'No' to city hall. But there's a price." I never actually heard him say this nor complain about anything else. I believe that his uncomplaining action is also "the spirit in which to do everything"—but must confess that I complained ten thousand times during this writing.

Thank you all very much.

Political Fiction and the American Self

The Problem of the American Political Novel

We are by our occupations, educations and habits of life divided almost into different species, which regard one another for the most part with scorn and malignity.
—Samuel Johnson

Thus spake Dr. Johnson, and he wasn't even thinking about politics. We are divided by our educations and our jobs, but we are especially alienated from one another by political attitudes and affiliations. Of course, political culture brings people together just as much as it divides them, and yet it is more usual to give culture (casually understood as erudition, breeding, manners) full credit for creating solidarity among people, and to blame politics (carelessly ascribed qualities such as partisanship, factionalism, bureaucratic maneuvering) for dividing people against one another. This habit of thought, in which Culture is the great "lumper" and Politics the great "splitter" of human sympathy, tends toward notions of community that can do little to nourish democratic politics.[1]

In America politics is frequently regarded as an inherently negative activity, perhaps because in conversations and writings that are predominantly cultural in concern, politics is understood as the crude realm of "us vs. them."[2] The best lack all conviction while the worst are full of passionate intensity precisely because political struggle at any level inevitably disrupts the humanistic and utopian ideals of Art. We are educated to assume that art has the power to unify people. Literature, in contrast to partisan politics, is "disinterested."[3] However flattering such an aesthetic ideology may be to those who praise literature as an alternative to the degraded language of election-year promises, politics is hardly limited to deception or unpleasant divisiveness, nor is divisiveness a trait only of political activity.

In everyday language it would be difficult to confuse "politics" and "aesthetics," but, now that we find ourselves in an "ideological age," the confusion has become all but unavoidable. Literary scholar Robert Alter suggests in *The Pleasures of Literature in an Ideological Age* that we honor "the difference of literature" if we intend to approach literary fiction nonreductively. To respect such a difference means that we must not slight the various aesthetic choices an author has made and focus on ideological significance alone, but by the same token we should grasp the difference of *politics* when we read literature, especially political fiction. Prose with any social resonance can be read politically, but the kind of story that "gets its hands dirty" with actual political struggle and affiliation, that which is deemed likely to inspire readers to take sides in a political controversy, is frequently given sub-literary status by critics, scholars, and other taste-makers. This reduced literary status stems entirely from the difference of politics.

Political activity, which is widely reviled in the United States, is generally something we wish would be done by other people. It is often those who manipulate others for personal benefit who get yoked with the tag "political." Some would argue that this scorn for the politician is unfair. Political scientist Steve Buckler focuses on the moral complexity of political action in his description of what he calls "the dirty hands problem," arguing that we need to assess political morality differently from the way we assess individual morality: "The disturbing fact that, in a political context, one might frequently have to act badly in order to act for the best marks out a key sense in which political morality may be seen as a distinctive and problematic area" (2). If Harry Truman soiled his reputation by choosing to drop atomic bombs, historians after the fact may argue that he saved many American lives. Let us assume for the moment that Truman sacrificed more than 100,000 Japanese lives in order to save perhaps half as many American lives. If we divorce the action from its political context, the morality of the decision is questionable. But if we judge Truman's decision in political context, we must at least consider that it would have been highly immoral for him (given his direct responsibility to American soldiers) not to have dropped the bomb.[4] As a human being Truman had a duty to other human beings, but as America's commander in chief, he had a particular duty to American soldiers. These two duties cannot be reconciled (in this exact scenario), and so Truman is seen by some as having done his sworn duty as commander in chief but by others as having sacrificed Japanese civilians out of racist disregard or because he wished to intimidate the Soviet Union. The politician, it would seem, dirties his or her hands no matter which decision he or she makes.

Just as Buckler does not wish to argue that there is *no* way to assess morally a political decision, I do not wish to divide absolutely the way we read a political novel from the way we read other novels. Still, there is a particular challenge to the political novel, both for the writer and for the reader, and specifying the nature of that challenge is worthwhile. The New Critics—defenders of the aesthetic faith while they held sway— treated political activism in literature as an impertinence, as though politically engaged literature ought to be disqualified on the basis of a conflict of interest.[5] The conflict is certainly real, but it is not grounds for disqualification, especially since the New Critics prized "conflict" and "tension" in the evaluation of literary art.

While there is no absolute difference between political and literary language, many people involved with literature continue to believe that politics is a disagreeable business. In *The Nature of Politics*, J. D. B. Miller has written that "The essence of a political situation, as opposed to one of agreement and routine, is that someone is trying to do something about which there is not agreement; and is trying to use some form of government as a means and as protection. Political situations arise out of disagreement" (14). So the New Critics were correct, in a way, to find political literature "disagreeable." Whether or not one believes political engagement to be grounds for aesthetic dismissal, the perception that political enthusiasm promulgates divisive sentiments within literature has affected the production and reception of literature at all levels. Critics concerned solely with the aesthetic qualities of literature rather than the diurnal hatred arising from mundane political skirmishes have named such "impurity" so that it could be tossed aside, and critics who accept the validity of political art have had to defend that art against its accusers. Its advocates have mainly had to defend political art against reductive presuppositions in which literature has been oft-enlisted in the army of love, whereas political mercenaries who are legion serve the cause of hate.[6] By writing about literature as if it were only an aesthetic concern, the strict formalists hedged out sociological, political, and other concerns.

The formalist understanding of art has often been blamed for depoliticizing literature, but to conclude that the reactionary demons of New Criticism have de-clawed poesy of its politics is far too simple. E. L. Doctorow, author of the indisputably political novel *The Book of Daniel* and outspoken opponent of the Reagan administration's foreign policy, claimed that "political diction and aesthetic diction are always antithetical" (89). In the interview in which he made this statement, Doctorow also looks askance at the politician who "has to appeal to prejudices, symbols, biases, fears—all the ways we have of not thinking. But the artist is always saying, 'Wait, this is too simple [. . .].' His diction is more like the texture of real life. Politics scants reality" (89). Neither a New Critic nor a cold warrior, Doctorow scanted reality in this passage, the reality of his own best writing. His too-clear division of politics from aesthetics is belied by many finer passages from *The Book of Daniel*.[7]

Aesthetic language and political language are not mutually exclusive, but for much of American criticism the two kinds of language have come to seem like two magnetic poles with the same charge, each repelling the other. Because of the belief that politics and aesthetics are strange bed-fellows, the New Critics objected to the intrusion of "extraliterary" concerns into literary discourse (which was believed to engage universal concerns rather than temporal struggles), and, largely because the New Critical hold on postwar American literary criticism was so strong, aesthetics and politics *became* opposites within the context of literary criticism.[8] One response to this complete aestheticization of literature is to be fastidious about the distinct differences between categories such as "literature" and "aesthetics." If we assume that a literary work has both aesthetic and political capacities, we may respect the differences between political and aesthetic motivation and at the same time allow for their intermingling within a work of art.

The study of political fiction also requires that we resist the equally erroneous and now prevalent equation of politics and literature. According to Miller's previously quoted definition of a political situation, conflict alone is not sufficient: a political situation is one in which someone "is trying to use some form of government as a means and as protection." We may argue that literature is inherently social, but not all literature is equally political. From beginning to end, Doctorow's *Book of Daniel* measures out as much justification as possible for the excesses of the New Left. Robert Penn Warren's *All the King's Men* presents the metastasis of moral corruption within American history (Cass Mastern, slavery) and politics (Willie Stark's journey from naiveté to proto-fascism). Both of these books present individuals in relation to government, and both make recommendations to readers-as-citizens about how to regard government. We might individually feel encouraged to change our attitudes about government after reading J. D. Salinger's *Catcher in the Rye* or Jack Kerouac's *The Dharma Bums*, but the relationship between these two novels and government is far less direct than that of the novels by Doctorow and Penn Warren.

Even so, Doctorow's statement about the difference between aesthetic and political diction expresses a general truth. Perhaps it would clarify matters if we substituted the word "motive" for Doctorow's "diction": literary and political texts are not easily distinguished from one another by diction, but we regularly recognize a writer's motive as aesthetic or political. "Political" writers are often accused of "grinding an axe." Writers know this and deal with such rhetorical problems accordingly, as Doctorow did in *The Book of Daniel*. There is a proverb saying that one cannot chase two rabbits, yet this is in effect what a political novelist must do, at least when political and aesthetic diction are so commonly assumed to be "antithetical." Under such conditions, the political novel must move an audience both politically and aesthetically. However tempting it may be to deconstruct the claim of a difference between political and aesthetic discourse, writers often complain about the difficulty of performing in these two different capacities simultaneously. In his preface to a collection of essays on topics ranging from the Watergate break-in to the stylistic differences between Henry Miller and Ernest Hemingway, Norman Mailer finds he is torn between his "literary ghost looking for that little refinement of one's art which becomes essential as one grows older, and the cry of the street debater, front and center, who always speaks in the loudest voice" (*Pieces* x). There *are* two rabbits, and they run in various directions, but the cleverest of political novelists traps them both.

But two rabbits in a trap can quickly become four or eight. When we move from generalization to specific description, the simple abstract division of motivation into political and literary categories becomes anything but simple. If political and literary motive are the first two rabbits, among the first offspring we also find production and reception aesthetics. The last quarter century has witnessed the Revolt of the Reader; reader-response criticism, broadly understood, would have us know that politics, every bit as much as beauty, is in the eye of the beholder. Did Salinger and Kerouac write political novels? Allen Ginsberg has suggested at public talks that Kerouac's irreverent attitudes toward Harry Truman in novels such as *On the Road* were, to him, politically enlightening. Henry Miller is a counter-cultural hero, and one even encounters him in the counter-cultural meditations of Deleuze and Guattari.[9] In these days of readerly hope and rage, it has become less easy to say precisely what a political novel might be.

Political novels are fashioned out of different and even conflicting motives, and they are often read in similarly divided ways. A book may move one group of people politically while it is read by another group for entirely different reasons. If a genre is to be recognized by its effect on readers, and if it affects different groups variously, we must ask which audience defines a political novel: its original audience, or one born a hundred years later? Did *Uncle Tom's Cabin* cease to be a political novel after the Emancipation Proclamation? After the Civil Rights Act of 1965? Defined in relation to *specific* audiences, a novel cannot offer a single, permanent political essence.[10] Rather, it has a history, or even several histories, since its various audiences may overlap, coincide, or never meet.[11] We may select audiences variously to suit our purposes. A novel may have a purely "local" ambition, or it may address much larger communities. As you cannot run for president without being hated by 40 percent or more of your would-be constituents, so do those novels that address national or international political issues arouse and organize the largest communities of resistance, and this generation of resistance is partly what has led many critics to demand a separation of Art and State.

However indeterminate designations such as "the political" have become in the parlance of today's cultural criticism, in the language beyond academe it still seems to mean something specific, such as when a reviewer of *Mao II* begins with this sentence: "During the past 20 years, American author Don DeLillo has received critical praise for his intelligent political novels about the paranoia, corruption and dislocation at the heart of contemporary life" (Kucherawy). This reviewer and many others have prized perceptive ironists such as DeLillo, but political fiction of the more activist sort has, for the greater part of this century, been something of an embarrassment in America. Many American literary critics admire political fiction by writers such as Allende and Llosa from Latin America, Coetzee and Gordimer from South Africa, Havel, Kundera, or Milosz from Eastern Europe, or Canada's Atwood, but the American political novel has tended to suffer a critical curse whenever it has been discussed in reviews and academic criticism in the United States.

Few scholars now accept the dogmatic division of politics and culture, and yet the obsessive linkage of politics and culture in today's academy is better understood as the eclipse of culture by politics than as the rich intermingling of two areas of human activity. There can be no reconciliation where there has not been a sundering, as Stephen Dedalus would put it, but the current modes of political criticism overreach one another in efforts to attack any such distinction. The notion of politics as the Fallen realm and culture as the Unfallen has not really been rejected by those who practice ideological critique, cultural studies, and so forth. Rather, the taint of politics has extended into the realm of culture. Culture has become politics by other means.[12]

An approach to cultural studies in which the truly various interrelationships between political and aesthetic motivation could be respectfully grasped is as appealing as it is necessary.[13] To make such an approach, we would need to recognize the degree to which the political writer develops alternative personae to answer the needs of very different vocations.[14] The Politician and the Artist may come together on special occasions, but these two roles require very different kinds of comportment, and often the roles are in direct conflict.[15] For this reason, the mythological division of political from aesthetic concerns will continue to structure this inquiry, since the duality of politics and art has been a subjective reality of fiction writers and literary critics. The non-Manichean approach to political art must avoid acquiescing to the notion that politics and art are metaphysical opposites. At the same time, such a nonreductive approach must continue to witness the artificial divide between politics and art, especially since this imaginary boundary continues to shape our experience in innumerable ways.

Trends blurring the boundaries between politics and literature have led scholars and critics to shy away from or even attack terms like "political novel." The term can mean any novel or almost none, depending on one's orientation, and so it has become preferable to theorize the political potential of the "carnivalesque" or to situate rebellion within illusive abstractions such as "the postmodern." Subversion in such accounts is always praiseworthy since the word invariably implies freedom and autonomy, or at least resistance to something bad. There is, however, little or no discussion within most criticism of this ilk about what political situations are worthy of affirmation, or of the possibility that subversion could ever be anything but a public blessing.[16] The "theorization" of resistance has substituted itself for the discussion of political songs, poems, plays, and novels; it has translated vernacular struggle into the bombastic argot of a privatized intelligentsia.[17]

Very little is said in contemporary criticism about political literature in the old-fashioned sense of the term, by which I mean literary art that is overtly concerned with political themes and that may even take a political stance in a contemporary public controversy. Given the inflationary value attributed to literary indeterminacy in recent decades, this reticence to designate a "political literature" is understandable, as it has become impossible to say that politics and literature relate in any given singular way without adopting an ideologically chauvinistic viewpoint. Some, claiming that "everything is political," dissolve differences between political and literary discourse, while others yet maintain that politics and literature are separate and dissimilar kinds of language that usually cannot be mixed advantageously. The pages that follow differentiate the political and aesthetic motives operating within literary fiction without surrendering to any notions of a fundamental difference between art and politics. Flavors can be mixed well or poorly, and mixing them well certainly does not make them identical. It is possible to recognize the differences between a political event and aesthetic object in ways that improve our enjoyment of—rather than invalidate—political literature.

The chapters that follow are presented in three parts. Part 1, "Politics vs. Literature in America," examines American cultural resistance to the union of politics and literature, a marriage many believe has been made unworkable by the particular characteristics of the American self. Part 2, "The Range of the American Political Novel," develops this presumed impasse and discusses contrasting strategies by which American novelists have confronted the problem. Part 3, "Individualism and Political Power in Contemporary America," discusses postwar American novelists who, recognizing that American selfhood has hindered a continuous tradition of American political fiction, contextualize American selves so as to reveal the connections between the mythical American self and American political realities. Our myths are written rhetorically and—the writers in part 3 suggest—ought to be read that way.

Chapter 1 extends and supports my claims that the political novel in the United States has been cast in an adversarial role by academic critics and literary reviewers. "Political Fiction as Impurity in American Literary Criticism" stages key moments in twentieth-century Americanist criticism to show how exaggerated differences between politics and literature have affected the critical reception of the genre.

After looking at critical resistance to political literature in its various historical contexts, the chapters in part 2 delineate the main choices available to political novelists. "Submerged Revolution in *Moby-Dick*," the second chapter, maintains that Melville's novel is political in all sorts of ways but is a book that, ultimately, subordinates political revolt before the needs of a quasi-political, highly literary practice of interpretation. In his mysterious chapter "The *Town-Ho's* Story," Melville confesses his retreat from the sort of political fiction that overtly celebrates mutinous revolt. "The *Town-Ho's* Story" is the only chapter in which Ishmael speaks directly to an audience that is represented within the story. Melville uses metanarrative to reflect on the politics of storytelling, and to reveal to readers of the larger fiction *Moby-Dick* how humor and genre are used to balance political and aesthetic effects and thus make politically un-popular themes palatable to presumably hostile audiences.

If Melville tried in *Moby-Dick* to work within the system of readers as it existed in mid-nineteenth-century America, Jack London revolted against the notion that the managers and owners of the middle class were the only people for whom one could write. Chapter 3, "How to Read a Revolutionary Novel: *The Iron Heel*," discusses London's dystopian novel as a political novel that does not try to charm readers of the present regime into liking it, but instead gambles on the development of a socialist audience.[18] Unlike Melville, who sublimates revolt, London challenges his would-be censors directly. We need not suppose that the book is without literary merit even if London subordinated literary effect to political purpose, as I argue he did. London unmistakably marks his story as an intervention in political struggles of the moment, though he also uses literary devices skillfully, including, surprisingly, humor, to make his story speak beyond the events of the day's newspaper headlines. Novels critical of the American system of government typically face less resistance during those periods in which many Americans fear that the government has failed in its duties. The years after the Great Depression were boom years for Marxist-oriented literature, and political writers who were active during the time of Vietnam and Watergate also faced less critical resistance. Even so, the most politically serious postwar writers have, upon examination, had to steer a course between the Scylla of literariness and the Charybdis of political engagement.

Chapter 4, "Adamic Purity as Double-Agent in *Harlot's Ghost*," discusses Mailer as a political novelist who critically envisions the political meanings of American literary mythology. *Harlot's Ghost* combines London's unrelenting focus on politics with Melville's penchant for plurality of meaning to analyze the Central Intelligence Agency, the government agency that attempted to make of itself, in Mailer's fictional history, "the mind of America." Since his first novel, *The Naked and the Dead*, Mailer has attempted to work within and to alter American literary mythologies such as the "American Adam" narrative described by R. W. B. Lewis. Many critics have suggested that America has produced few great political novels precisely because American literary mythology and American individualism divide American writers from social issues, but American writers, fully cognizant of mythological and ideological obstacles to political engagement, have also adapted literary mythology to suit political purpose. Mailer's CIA novel *Harlot's Ghost* provides an excellent focal text for a discussion of the politics of American literary mythology, a more politically ambidextrous novel than most of its critics have been willing to admit.

Mailer can cloak his political dramas within American innocence, but American innocence is not an equal-opportunity form of literary entitlement. For African-American authors, American innocence appears more frequently as an awful lie, an ideological effect in need of deconstruction. Whereas a white author might have to guard against seeming too political, a black author writing in the same city and the same year might come under an equal-and-opposite pressure. A black author whose work is cloaked in innocence is instantly liable to charges of Uncle Tomism, such as when Ralph Ellison (creator of the most naive protagonist since Ford Madox Ford's John Dowell) was reprimanded by both black and white critics for not being more politically engaged. Whether political engagement or literary innocence is the stigma, the literary and the political continue to have marital difficulties in African-American fiction. Chapter 5, "Invisible Prophet: Sula Peace, 1965," compares rhetorical strategies in novels by African-American authors Ralph Ellison, William Melvin Kelley, and Toni Morrison to show how authors maneuver tactically between overt and covert ways of expressing political ideas. The three African-American novels I have selected (Ellison's *Invisible Man*, Kelley's *A Different Drummer*, and Morrison's *Sula*) restage the comparison between Melville and London to show how specific racial issues inflect authorial decisions about how to balance political and aesthetic materials. Each author strikes a slightly different balance between literary and political purposes, and so the moral with African-American fiction, as with Melville and London, is that we must concede that the political novel has more range than critics and scholars have typically been willing to admit. Contemporary critics have been racing, as it were, to find America's political unconscious within African-American fiction, but this practice is not as flattering as many critics would like to think. Race does not relate to the writing of political fiction in any single, general way, though it is often assumed that African-American fiction must be inherently political because of the history of race relations in America, a way of reading that robs the author of personal and artistic choices.

Each chapter of *Political Fiction and the American Self* recommends that we interpret political novels as art forms while at the same time making a place within that interpretation for the political aspects of the work. Allowing for the political aspects of a work means more than admiring an author's political intelligence or ability to connect the political and the personal within a tapestry of themes; it also includes the possibility that authors, like politicians, can work with power structures in realistic and pragmatic ways. We need to get beyond the habit of always seeing ourselves in pure opposition to the powers that be. Manichean views of political power offering a false choice of totalitarian Ahab or innocent Ishmael—with nothing in between—embody a particularly American refusal to acknowledge the real complexity of social struggle. To one degree or another, "we" are the power. This Will to Simplicity is a benefit neither to American politics nor to American literary culture, but it is as popular in the vernacular of election-year politicking as it is in the postures of literary criticism.

Notes

1. Kenneth Burke once split philosophers into "lumpers" and "splitters." Robert Putnam warns of a sharp decline in American civic engagement in his now-famous essay "Bowling Alone."

2. Des Pres dichotomizes politics and poetry along the lines I have been describing in the opening pages of *Praises and Dispraises:* "The poetic impulse," he writes, "arises to fulfill itself in praises and in blessings" (xiii). "Politics," on the other hand, shall be recognized "as the play of impersonal force disrupting personal life" and "as a primary ground of misfortune" (xvi). Des Pres is certainly not opposed to political poetry in his study of Yeats, Rich, Breytenbach, and others, but he does occasionally succumb to the literary reduction of politics to its worst features.

3. "Disinterested" is, paradoxically, a fightin' word. The entry on Matthew Arnold in *The Johns Hopkins Guide to Literary Theory and Criticism* notes that the word "disinterested," if often misunderstood in relation to Arnold, has nonetheless become the focus of many a critical dog-fight. Arnold's idea that "a disinterested effort to learn and propagate the best that is known and thought in the world" is, author Joseph Carroll notes, "now the most violently disputed word in the Arnoldian lexicon. Marxist and new historicist critical ideology, for example, make a good deal of epistemological heavy weather over this term" (45). Carroll himself prefers to understand the word to mean a generosity that allows one to appreciate more than one otherwise would.

4. Buckler argues that we must judge political morality by different criteria than we use for other ethical situations: "Politics, when it disappoints our moral expectations and offends our moral sensibilities, does so for reasons other than mere malpractice: it may do so, that is, for good reasons from a political point of view. The agent with dirty hands is different from the one who engages in evil for its own sake and from the criminal. This indicates the manner in which at least some of the moral offenses committed in politics are not contingent but are related to the character of politics itself and to the nature of its claims" (2). Buck-

ler charts a course between the view in which there is no possible morality where politics is concerned and the opposing extreme in which political exigency offers no exemption from other moral standards.

For a full-length argument about the relationship between the Battle of Okinawa and the decision to drop the atomic bombs on Hiroshima and Nagasaki, see Feifer's *Tennozan*.

5. See Barbara Foley's chapter "The Legacy of Anti-Communism" in *Radical Representations* for an interpretation of New Criticism as a politically engaged form of criticism in denial about its own engagement (3–43).

6. Henry Adams explains why politics has tended to upset the spirit of literature when he writes that "politics, as a practice, whatever its professions, had always been the systematic organization of hatreds" (7). Tobin Siebers has commented on hatred as a nasty side-effect of genuine politics in *Cold War Criticism and the Politics of Skepticism:* "Whenever we question the objection to a political use of literature [. . .] we can expect to hear an appeal of some kind to a higher ideal, most likely to the ethical ideal demanding that we respect diversity and individuality. The political has been tainted by human violence, and 'literature' is supposed by many critics to be the cure for violence" (73). Siebers cites a specific example of hatred as an unavoidable cost when discussing Hannah Arendt's *Eichmann in Jerusalem* in his chapter "The Politics of Storytelling": "That Arendt chose to tell that story and not relinquish her Jewishness is a tribute to both her courage and her foolishness, for some may doubt whether the story was worth all the personal woe that befell her. The tranquility of her work was invaded by hatred" (133). Political activity includes a social cost that we frequently misunderstand when we find it in literature.

7. Political novelists often attempt to stay engaged with political problems and maintain at the same time the illusion of detachment. To get caught being "too political" is to risk one's status as a *writer*. A political writer, particularly those who create activist political novels, will often be regarded as a hack rather than as an aesthetic technician. Writers who keep their fiction politically neutral are considered"storytellers" rather than "liars." But to engage in a rhetorical struggle is, as Kenneth Burke puts it so bluntly, to enter the "lugubrious regions of malice and the lie" (*Rhetoric* 23).

8. Politics increasingly came to be seen as an impurity in the world of literary art. In reaction to the New Critical exclusion of politically programmatic and activist points of view, subsequent varieties of criticism have attacked the New Critical division of aesthetic and political discourse, and some critics would have us believe that the category of the aesthetic is, itself, political to the core. Alternatives exist. Des Pres places Yeats within an Irish bardic tradition in which the public power of words, ritually expressed, was *not* considered an intrusion of politics into art (33–98).

9. As we learn in *Anti-Oedipus*, stream of consciousness writing is an acceptable substitute for class struggle: "Strange Anglo-American literature: from

Thomas Hardy, from D. H. Lawrence to Malcolm Lowry, from Henry Miller to Allen Ginsberg and Jack Kerouac, men who know how to leave, to scramble the codes, to cause flows to circulate, to traverse the desert of the body without organs. They overcome a limit, they shatter a wall, the capitalist barrier" (132–33). Miller is discussed more than half-a-dozen times in *Anti-Oedipus*. One person's hero is, however, another's demon. The *locus classicus* of Miller demonization is Millet's *Sexual Politics*, which argues that writers such as Lawrence, Miller, and Mailer are sexual counter-revolutionaries. So: is Miller a liberatory hero or a domineering misogynist? One problem with too great an emphasis on cultural politics (as opposed to political literature that thematically takes up the burdens of government and policy) is just this sort of muddle.

10. *Uncle Tom's Cabin* was one kind of political novel for abolitionists, but it is more often used by contemporary critics, such as Jane Tompkins, who wish to fight against the canonical exclusion of sentimental and popular fiction as much for reasons relating to gender politics as to abolition. In its earlier incarnation, the novel was active in an important political struggle between divisions of American government and society. This book is currently used to teach about gender, race, and class, but the "political" effects of this latter-day activity are much more tightly circumscribed. When discussing such a political novel, we may have to specify exactly what audiences and social conflicts we understand the novel to be addressing.

11. The political novel can exist in two places at one time: it can enjoy celebrity at a political rally where it functions as a totem or standard; simultaneously it can bring together readers who form around it solely to discuss its "purely literary" merits. There may even be persons common to both groups. Activists I met at Pro-Choice rallies certainly enjoyed a sense of approval from *The Handmaid's Tale*, but no one was very interested in the subtleties of Offred's word play. I knew the book had a political effect because it is what initially led me to get up at 5:00 A.M. to engage in demonstrations and counter-demonstrations, but once I arrived at the actual meetings and protest sites, everything about Atwood's novel except its celebrity was widely regarded as beyond politics in much the same way that the New Critics deemed politics an extraliterary concern. On such early mornings in Los Angeles, I would regularly experience a dysfunctional relationship of sorts between political activism and what I thought of as literary insight.

12. In *Politics by Other Means*, Bromwich describes the "culture wars" as a set (Left and Right) of puritanically extreme moral positions.

13. Cultural studies: the academic criticism resulting from a suspicious approach to boundaries separating the concepts formerly known as highbrow and lowbrow art. Cultural materials of all sorts (art, pornography, law) are considered worthy of explanation and are capable of mutual elucidation. Usually the term effectually signifies political dissidence, but one book review used the term in this way: "Readers familiar with Rawson [a scholar of eighteenth-century British lit-

erature] will not be surprised to find him agilely incorporating sources as diverse as Flaubert's prose, Yeats' and Ted Hughes's poetry, and W. J. T. Mitchell's work on media coverage of the Vietnam and Gulf Wars. This is cultural studies of the highest order, although Rawson might jib at the term" (Pettit 512). Thus, cultural studies is predicated on the mixture of materials studied: it is the refusal of an intellectual caste system in which certain materials (or discourses) are deemed sub-cultural, while others receive the honor of critical attention. Another review in the same journal issue raises a concern similar to my own, noting that "ahistoricity is a problem [. . .] in much of what passes for 'cultural studies' today. If all material culture is fair game, if exempla may be drawn from novels as easily as from shopping malls, from propaganda leaflets as easily as from historical archives, how do we know what to foreground?" (Perloff 522). A middle way would be to proceed as though aesthetic and political practices can and should be mixed, but this does not mean that we must slop them together as though there were no differences between them; cultural *analysis* demands that we distinguish and clarify the objects of study. For an example of cultural studies that does not mire itself in neologism and that consistently refuses to flatten political questions into Manichean melodrama, see Dyson's *Making Malcolm.*

14. As I demonstrate in chapters on London and Melville, the assumption that political struggle is one thing while literary art is something very different creates an either/or choice for the author. The writer can either mute expressions of political dissent and thus maintain proper "universality," or risk losing status as an aesthetic innovator by engaging in that other endeavor, politics. Literature, when conceived solely in aesthetic terms, "otherizes" politics.

15. In an article discussing Simon Schama and Natalie Zemon Davis, two historians whose work challenges the border between "storytelling" and "history," Diana Solano uses "comportment" to describe the conduct or behavior of the writer in adherence to the requirements of either role. A writer may be, as I shall soon discuss, political in any number of ways, but a political novelist is for my purposes one who must comport him- or herself both as an artist and as a politician.

16. Hutcheon defines the postmodern as a mode of "complicitous critique" stemming from a "compromised politics" (2); this definition exhibits the dual tendencies toward subversion and against affirmation. Maltby discusses Pynchon, Barthelme, and Coover to define a less compromised mode of political activism.

17. Jacoby insightfully describes the flight of intellectuals from public language, quipping in one chapter that "For many professors in many universities academic freedom meant nothing more than the freedom to be academic" (119).

18. *The Iron Heel* has also been described as a "radical novel" in the words of Walter Rideout, and it could probably be described as an "authoritarian novel" in the sense defined by Suleiman.

PART 1

Politics versus Literature in America

1

Political Fiction as Impurity in American Literary Criticism

A whole history of art in our century, not too badly distorted as such histories go, could be written as a grand competition for the position of chief purifier, artists and critics catching each other out for failing to expunge lingering impurities.
   —Wayne Booth

I think the word *political* tends to be weighted in the United States in a way in which it is not in other countries in the world. [. . .] It got shoved over to the side as something that didn't belong in art, and if you started putting it in your work, you were somehow sullying yourself.
   —Margaret Atwood

The political novelist may therefore have to take greater risks than most others, as must any artist who uses large quantities of "impure" matter.
   —Irving Howe

The old-fashioned response to the idea that the political element of literature is an impurity was either to exclude the impurity or to apologize for it. Since the vogue of New Criticism, critics have attempted to deny that politics is an impurity by arguing that all aspects of literature—its aesthetic components, psychological presuppositions, sociology, and so on—are inherently political. This attempted defense of political literature tends, actually, to smuggle in the premise that "literature," "politics," and the "aesthetic" would all be the same, were it not for the ideological shell game that is played with these categories. Buying into this idea, the new-fangled advocate of political literature once again undermines the status of political literature, this time by voiding its political rather than aesthetic qualities. What we need instead is recognition of the differences between political and aesthetic motives within literature; this recognition cannot acknowledge either motivation merely as a contamination of the other.

Margaret Atwood, Nadine Gordimer, and other writers who work outside of the American literary context have suggested that politics is regarded as an intrusion within literature more frequently in America than in other countries. Frederick Karl argues that America lacks developed political fiction mainly because of the apolitical-pastoral tradition that has largely dominated literary criticism in this century: "The persistence of the Edenic myth has, I believe, dissipated our seriousness about politics" (254). Karl does not at all claim that American political fiction is impossible, but he does assert that American myths of innocence *deter* the political novelist. According to this mythological view, the American narrative is one of a constant fall from innocence, followed by a constant return to innocence. The national self-conception does not encourage one to make a home near the tree of (political) knowledge, and so the myths of a "fixable imperial America" (as Joan Didion has put it) or of "political virginity preserved" (as Frank Lentricchia has put it) continue to shape American literary culture.[1] Lentricchia in fact proposes that the main traditions of American literature have always been politically active, and yet influential literary ideologies have made American literature seem like a world elsewhere, away from political conflict.

Mythical innocence and political experience wrestle with one another like Jacob and his angel: the heavenly generalization goes to war with the utterly secular particulars. That political problems have been excluded from the discussion of American literature through the invention and constant refashioning of mythical innocence is an intricate matter, and so we must underestimate neither the power of generalization nor that of the unwieldy particulars that are so ready to foul our theories. The "Edenic" cause in American history and identity has its limitations, but I believe that the rush to deny the validity of complex cultural patterns is an extension of American innocence, not its rejection. A too-hasty rejection of American mythical modes bespeaks a desire to be untainted by American mythical innocence—a continuity, not a rupture, in American intellectual tradition. As I will argue below, the New Americanists who emerged in the late 1980s are just as "American" in their procedures as the myth critics who in many cases bypassed history through a concern with mythical pattern. Both roads rhetorically purify the critic.

For the moment, historical particulars have the upper hand over mythical generality, but we cannot understand the history of American political writing adequately without recourse to the grand narrative of America's (decidedly mythical) innocence. This innocence is a crucial element in the story of how, for many readers, politics and literature became separated in principle, as "Church" and "State" are within the American legal system. The presumption that there is a vast impasse separating matters political and poetical was championed by critics reacting against the combination of political and cultural energies in the decade after the Great Depression. For Marxists and fellow travelers, literature became a weapon within a larger class struggle. A decade later the cold war, which was not only a holding-formation against international Communism but also a means to suppress dissidence within the United States, influenced both the composition and critical reception of postwar literature. When we notice the ways in which the concept of the political novel has shifted in meaning before, during, and after the cold war, we see that the political novel, at least as it ventures to express dissident ideas, has had to work around or against the dominant trends in American literary culture.

The cold war was waged and is here conceptually deployed semi-mythologically. Though I will be demonstrating that soft pressures on literary critics influenced their discussions of political novels, I am also fully aware that the tension between politics and aesthetics can be traced back to Sidney or to Plato—but I am not writing a history of Western civilization, and so I must streamline and simplify. I will offer a variant of the cold war myth. My account works toward the present moment, as I believe critics are now attempting to see through cold war dualisms (false alternatives) that have largely structured our approach to literature. A critic with a different telos would very likely choose a different pivotal moment.[2] The presumed and illusory difference between politics and literature (*not* aesthetics) has been used to give the political novel a bad name, and so any attempt to review the status of the political novel must appreciate the vicissitudes of this distinction. To make *my* case, the cold war story works best.

The Political Novel, 1924 Model

The academic study of the political novel begins confidently in 1924 with Morris Edmund Speare's founding study *The Political Novel*. He wrote about both English and American political novels but was concerned to show the differences between these traditions as well as their similarities, and he argued that a specific genre, the political novel, had been introduced by Disraeli and developed by subsequent authors such as Anthony Trollope, George Eliot, Mrs. Humphrey Ward, and H. G. Wells, as well as by Americans such as Henry Adams, Winston Churchill, and Paul Leicester Ford. While there were numerous book reviews published condemning the mixture of political activism and literary technique by the time this study was written, Speare's book itself does not describe the political novel as a fallen form. Speare never apologizes for exploring the political novel, a form that soon becomes inherently questionable.

In *The Political Novel*, Speare points to the connections between this form and such English didactic literature as Daniel Defoe's novel *Moll Flanders* and Samuel Johnson's novelistic parable *The History of Rasselas*. To understand what Speare means when he claims that the political novel develops from didactic literature, we must recall that, in the decades before Joyce's *Ulysses* (1922), it was just as often a defense as a criticism to describe a book as didactic or moralistic. We have become used to thinking of didactic literature as a crude evolutionary stage, like the morality play that had to be borne before Shakespeare's morally variegated art became possible; however, according to Speare, Defoe does not divide moral intelligence from psychological insight, as though one were the primitive and the other the mature form. In reading *Moll Flanders* through Speare's eyes, "we watch the infinite misery of a sinner who, after arriving at Newgate, gets no satisfaction from repentance when she knows that it has come after the power of sinning further has already been removed from her" (360). Literary movements that became powerful during the cold war such as modernism and New Criticism have been quick to dismiss just this sort of didacticism.

In emphasizing the didactic function of literature as he did, Speare unknowingly left himself vulnerable to later critics, who could blame him for defining the political novel in an anti-literary or anti-aesthetical way. Completely lacking in foresight what we in the age of political correctness now know to be true, Speare would define the political novel as

> a work of prose fiction which leans rather to "ideas" than to "emotions"; which deals rather with the machinery of law-making or with a theory about public conduct than with the merits of any given piece of legislation; and where the main purpose of the writer is party propaganda, public reform, or exposition of the lives of the personages who maintain government, or of the forces which constitute government. In this exposition the drawing-room is frequently used as a medium for presenting the inside life of politics. (ix)

As we can see from this quotation, Speare's definition is flexible yet specific; he discusses the political novel in terms of its tendencies rather than any rigidly defined characteristics. Speare's is a civil and useful definition that subsequent readers have invariably faulted.

In his introduction to *Political Fictions* (1980), Michael Wilding arraigns Speare for the narrowness of his definition, which, Wilding claims, "corresponded with the narrow social elite that peopled the drawing-rooms of those novels" discussed in Speare's study (1). In complaining about the "elitist social assumptions" underlying Speare's definitions, Wilding is in effect blaming the messenger. While social, political, and literary historians have successfully challenged the "Great Man" approach to the telling of history, this was certainly not the case in 1924.[3] Wilding, in thus disposing of Speare, reads the definition clearly but does not consider the practical consequences of Speare's definition as demonstrated in his introduction or interpretations. Wilding's account would lead one to think that Speare was unquestionably advocating a literary form that justified the privileges of the upper classes. This is not the case. While Wilding appears to criticize Speare on political grounds, the difference between them is political only in a trivial sense: in his introduction to *Political Fictions*, Wilding is more radical than thou, and he uses Speare's bludgeoned definition as a foil for his own. The greatest weakness of today's political criticism is that one need only claim a more radical position than a predecessor in order to be recognized as "political." Wilding's own study is valuable for its willingness to question overly certain boundaries between political and supposedly nonpolitical fiction (he discusses *Huck Finn* alongside conventionally recognized political novels such as *The Iron Heel* and *Nineteen Eighty-Four*), but the need to present himself as a literary liberator has distorted his reading of previous critics.[4]

While Speare has been faulted both for his inclusiveness and his exclusiveness, his definition requires the political novelist to do much more than merely represent the various movements and sub-movements of political history. His enthusiasm for "the pageant" and the "canvas" of history may very well have the recognizable feel of the men-only parlor room, of smoking jackets and civil banter, but Speare's privileged liberal tones should not distract us from more significant matters such as his basic demands of the political novel: "In this sort of pageant men take sides on great national and international issues. Whigs, Tories, Conservatives, Liberals, Unionists, Chartists, Anti-Corn Law Leaguers, Utilitarians, Utopians of every type and color—they crowd upon your canvas and demand a hearing" (26). Inclusiveness may not by itself be a satis-factory defense against charges of elitism. To proceed within the herme-neutics of suspicion properly, we should also ask: Does Speare merely demand that the political novelist include token characters from various rag-tag political parties? Or, if he were writing today, would he say that the political novelist must include representations of all genders, races, and classes? One of the most pleasing aspects of Speare's definition is that he never seems to be making a show of his own moral superiority.

The political novel in 1924 is a large and contentious collection of voices. One might suppose that the novelist need only acknowledge ideo-logical variety in such a work, but Speare does not rest his case for the political novel on superficial inclusiveness and argues instead that the political novelist faces a tougher standard. As old-fashioned as Speare may at times sound, his demands of the novelist in some ways parallel Bakhtin's prerequisite, the "dialogic" aspect of fiction. For both Speare and Bakhtin, the political novelist must be more of an artist than the nonpolitical writer, not less. Speare writes:

> To portray these diversified beings dispassionately, to let each man have his say and none the entire platform, to treat all fairly and truthfully and succeed in steering between the Scylla of partisanship and the Charybdis of tractarianism, requires the most delicate craftsmanship on the writer's part, and a scholar's knowledge of the arguments, but withal an artist's delicate fancy and power of creation, if the result is not to be a creed dis-guised in the garments of a novel, a political platform hidden by a moun-tain of decoration. (26)

Though few would today agree that a novelist must be dispassionate or objective, most of the instruments agree that a single-sided presentation of a political controversy is just as deadly for the political novel as for other kinds of literature.

For Speare the political novel is a unique genre, and the American political novel has its own individual character within the class of po-litical novels. He was the first to insist that we *not* use the English or European political novel as a yardstick to measure the American politi-cal novel, since they were each working within different traditions, ap-pealing to different readerly expectations. The American version, claimed Speare, has a more activist-pragmatic aim than the English: "A compari-son [. . .] of the American with the English political novelist brings out one striking fact: that whereas in England the writers have often enough been interested in presenting the political panorama for the sake of panorama,—shall we say, for art's sake?—American novelists have been mainly concerned with Reform" (334). Some political novels lean toward political activism, some toward art for art's sake. Speare observes that American novelists in particular were distinguished by their zeal for reform. This activist difference could help to explain why the prejudice against political fiction is stronger in America than in other countries.

Speare's recognition of the partisan nature of political fiction is presented in a disarmingly direct fashion. Contemporary readers who are so quick to find in Speare quaint signs of class privilege overlook the ways in which this reader from 1924 is ahead of today's culture contests, wherein it must be continually reasserted that political struggle is an appropriate end of art. The demand for an absolute separation of politics and aesthetics is today rarely voiced as an imperative, but occasionally we happen upon it whole cloth. In the section of its booklet entitled "What the Endowment Does Not Support," the National Endowment of the Humanities makes it clear that it will support no projects that "Are directed at persuading an audience to a particular political, philosophical, religious, or ideological point of view, or that advocate a particular program of social change or action" (6). This policy gives us a negative definition of the political novel to complement Speare's positive description. His judgment that the American political novel is engaged in the business of Reform has become a much more controversial position since he first wrote it, and the reason is found in critical standards and even government policies that attack works of art that "advocate a particular program of social change." Art must affirm the status quo to receive NEH funding.

The political novel exposes itself to economic and critical perils that are somewhat more focused than those faced by other novels; its author will receive fewer government grants, or it may be singled out for reproach in reviews.[5] This condition has not always obtained to the same degree, and there have been moments in this century when challenges to the idea that politics and literature are unmixable discourses were particularly strong.[6] Speare's study is, nonetheless, the last one published in the United States to speak of the political novel without apology.

Reading Red in the Cold War

Speare's 1924 study does not express the anxieties or suffer the deformations that have typified American criticism of political fiction in the decades following World War II. The prejudice against mixing politics and literature began to receive a great deal of support from 1930s anti-

Communist critics, chiefly the Agrarians, who would later become the New Critics. The New Critics began to rise in the 1930s but became ascendant during the period known as the cold war, which cultural historian Stephen J. Whitfield claims has had a traumatic effect on American culture as a whole.[7] In *The Culture of the Cold War*, a study of the ways in which anti-Communism politicized American culture to an unprecedented degree, Whitfield sums up the atmosphere of the cold war this way: "Unable to strike directly at the Russians, the most vigilant patriots went after the scalps of their countrymen instead" (9).[8] Left-of-center writers and free-lance critics in the 1950s became the quarry of McCarthyism, as did those actors and professors who could in any way be associated with the Communist Party.

However tempting it might be to blame vigilant patriots on the Right for censoring literary expressions of dissent, the anti-Stalinist Left (composed of Trotskyites, former Communist Party members, and radicals of other stripe) also played an important role. Critics who wished to discuss dissident fictions certainly could not ignore such signs of the times, as we see when we look at writers who went against the grain by celebrating Communist or otherwise politically radical writers.

The cold war tempered the writing of Walter Rideout's 1956 study *The Radical Novel in the United States, 1900–1954* and also Daniel Aaron's *Writers on the Left*. Literary historians of politically engaged fiction such as Rideout became more than a little defensive about the supposed incompatibility of politics and art, and Rideout prefaced his study with an ominous note: "Doubtless some readers will find this book unsatisfactory. The general reader may be put off by the subject matter, for nowadays in the United States the mention of anything having to do with radical politics is likely to be met by suspicion or anger" (vii). Rideout also suspected disapproval from various professional fields: "The strict literary historian may object to finding some literary analysis and evaluation here, while the formalist critic will surely be unhappy over the very large amount of what he would call 'extrinsic' material. Likewise, if the literary critic may object that the book contains too much talk of politics, the political scientist may feel that it contains too little" (vii). Just as the phobia of political impurity abroad (the Red scourge) justified a foreign policy of containment, so too did Rideout's sense of his audience's "suspicion or anger" at the impurity of his writing (Is it political science? Literary history?) bring him to worry about leaks in his own container.

The difference between politics and literature was an obstacle in Rideout's path, but he handled it in the best possible way: he conceded that some readers might refuse to acknowledge that politics has a place in literary art but quickly added that this refusal would not stop novelists from writing political fiction, nor would it prevent him from appreciating their work. Rideout discerned that there were differences between the aesthetic and political uses of language, but he refused to cooperate with any sort of categorical apartheid. The cold war climate did not prevent Rideout from completing and publishing his study, but he had to work against the anti-political prejudice constantly to fashion his book: the radical element in fiction is "extrinsic" to the pure matter of literature and perhaps ought to be "contained" elsewhere. Since "strict" literary history would effectually gerrymander the political novel out of existence, the study of political fiction itself became a kind of impurity.

Irving Howe's discussion of political fiction apparently was haunted by no specters of readerly suspicion or anger, perhaps because of his belief that the American ground was unable to produce a novel of first-rate political intelligence. In his 1957 study *Politics and the Novel*, Howe did not voice discomfort at any cold war harpies tormenting his text, conceivably because he envisioned the political novel in a more purely literary way (as it were) than did Rideout. Howe waved away the problem of precise definition as something for rigid scholastics to quibble over, opting, instead, to define the political novel in this way: "By a political novel I mean a novel in which political ideas play a dominant role or in which a political milieu is the dominant setting. [. . .] Perhaps it would be better to say: a novel in which *we take to be dominant* political ideas or the political milieu" (17). Howe incorporated his own uncertainty principle into this definition, and we may as well grant him that the study of audiences is a rather uncertain business. Still, he provided no particular insight about why the political novel should be harder to define than other genres. He may have avoided precise definition in order to circumvent the pressures that Rideout clearly experienced: by refusing the "academic" problem of definition, Howe freed himself to select novels of undeniable literary quality. However, he found very little worth mentioning from the United States, and his commentary on this deficit is disappointing.[9]

Perhaps as a strategy for avoiding the bias that political literature is by nature inferior, Howe consistently aestheticized politics, thus transforming the object of his criticism slightly. Trotsky's *History of the Russian Revolution*, for example, "is history in the grand style and like all histories in the grand style, also the work of the literary imagination" (203). Marxist "praxis" or connections between aesthetic form and political content had no place in Howe's analysis, as we see in this comment on the writing of Leon Trotsky: "Apart from its claim to being a faithful record and true interpretation, Trotsky's book is one of the few in our time that is able to sustain the kind of stylistic scrutiny now reserved for Shakespeare's plays, James' novels and minor poets" (203–4). Politics as style, then, became the premier way of enjoying politics in a literary way while subtracting the social conflicts that give extraliterary political struggles meaning. The purely aesthetic approach to political fiction introduces brief references to political conflict in order to inoculate the reader. This kind of criticism looks out upon the impure world from the realm that values Beauty above all.

Although it must be said that he in no way intended *Politics and the Novel* to be a comprehensive study in the manner of Speare, Milne, or Blotner,[10] Howe nonetheless shortchanged American authors. His explanation was that Americans love to hate politics, that "neither as public activity nor intellectual pursuit is politics to be regarded as quite legitimate" (159). Howe summarized Anthony Trollope's *Autobiography* as registering the American belief "that public life is a thing of ugliness, a source of corruption which every honest man does his best to avoid" (159). What kind of political novel *could* be written in a culture where such views prevail? In answer to this question, Howe offers his only full-length treatment of an American author in his chapter on Henry James: "When he came to write about nineteenth century revolutionary politics in *The Princess Casamassima*, his own opinions were neither risked nor challenged; the book presented itself to him as an experience in craft and imagination" (140). Howe criticizes James's novel for its "too easy acceptance of second-hand impressions," such as the cartoonish depictions of conspiratorial anarchists. Howe's American political novelist turns out, upon inspection, to be more of an *anti-political* political novelist.

The chapter on James as an anti-political political novelist is followed by Howe's chapter on isolated political impulses. Earlier books such as *The Blithedale Romance*, Henry Adams's *Democracy*, and modern examples such as *U.S.A.*, *All the King's Men*, and *The Middle of the Journey* can all be thought of as forming a tradition of American political fiction, one organized around a "politics of isolation." While there is no mention of the utopian or dystopian fictions of the 1890s, or of literary revolutionaries such as Jack London, Howe mentions Ben Compton, Dos Passos's shattered revolutionary; John Laskell "waiting alone in a train station to begin the middle of his journey"; and Jack Burden, "asking himself how he could place his trust in a puny dictator like Willie Stark" (200)—but these sullied men are hardly the whole story of American political fiction. In fact, there are many novels and stories concerning those who strive against all odds for connection. *The Jungle* is one such story, as is *The Iron Heel*. Howe neglected these books, but it was only through such selective reading that he could claim that political fiction is improbable in America. Political fiction in which political activism and aesthetic risk are felt to intermingle was an aesthetic embarrassment to most critics during the cold war, and the politically engaged socialist critic from New York was no exception.

In an epilogue completed in 1986 entitled "Politics and the Novel after *Politics and the Novel*," Howe continues to read political fiction without truly acknowledging the necessary impurities of political fiction or the pressure of politics upon interpretation. He suggests that postwar literature in general has suffered from a lack of the "wrenching conflicts" (254) that buttress all great political novels: "One thing, I believe, can profitably be said about [contemporary political novels]: they constitute a literature of blockage, a literature of impasse" (252). Predictably, he discusses Gordimer, Solzhenitsyn, Latin Americans, and East Europeans in glowing terms but does not mention an American. American novels in which politics and aesthetics are inextricably linked, such as *The Book of Daniel*, might have been the basis for a nice three-to-five page discussion. Howe's 1986 afterward, like his 1957 study, contributes to the critical trend toward apolitical ambiguity: "There is no conclusion. We are charting paths here which twist and turn each day, and sometimes come to a halt in the pain of impasse" (273).

In the Sixties: Taxonomy or Taxidermy?

After Rideout and Howe's approaches, many studies of the American political novel became taxonomical outlines in which the messiness of the political novel was fairly well defined out of the picture. Gordon Milne's *The American Political Novel* begins by acknowledging the rudeness of the genre (which has, since Stendhal's bon mot about the pistol-shot in the concert hall, been the opening ritual in most studies). Milne attempts to redeem the political novel from the limitation implied by Speare's emphasis on ideas alone. The political novel, according to Milne, is an emotion-laden form: "I quickly came to agree with the astute Stendhalian comment that 'politics in a work of literature is like a pistol-shot in the middle of a concert, something loud and vulgar, and yet a thing to which it is not possible to refuse one's attention.' Quite willing to grant my attention, becoming intrigued by the diverse political points of view of writers of this type of fiction, [I became] astonished by their emotion-laden tones" (vii). It should not be necessary to add that Speare hardly decreed boredom as the necessary reader-response to the political novel. Perhaps to exonerate the genre from charges of inherent dullness, later critics such as Milne question the difference between the political novel and the nonpolitical novel. This is done through an approach that is in some ways similar to Howe's: the political novel is aestheticized completely. The political novel can be emotional and exciting without seducing readers into actual political activity if we regard it as a kind of opera rather than as a form of activism. Milne's political novel is purely a spectator sport: "Whether aesthetically pleasing or not, political novels usually make fascinating reading. [. . .] Although most Americans no longer hang around the cracker barrel in the village store, they go on discussing political issues and political candidates with considerable avidity. They talk, they watch conventions on TV, *and* they read; witness the tremendous success of *Advise and Consent*" (6). That no political engagement is essential makes the political novel a perfectly safe thing to talk about, but what conclusions about the genre are likely to follow from an opening that claims political fiction is interesting "whether aesthetically pleasing or not"? Milne is one of many critics to complain about how much muck one must go through before finding adequate fictions.[11]

Joseph Blotner published a comprehensive study of modern American political fiction in 1966.[12] Blotner's definition in *The Modern American Political Novel* is more sensitive than Milne's to post–cold war uncertainties, though it attempts to recuperate the nonrelativist sense of the genre that has become difficult if not impossible when approaching postwar American texts: "In order to keep the study from extending to all outdoors, 'political' is here defined in a very literal and functional sense. The subject of these works, apart from a few on the fringe noted as such but illustrating particular themes, is also primarily political" (8). By this standard the political novel has a disadvantage as art. Blotner's "functional" definition actually excludes a number of interesting novels that are about politics and that function politically in the senses outlined in my introduction. It frequently excludes books considered to be of greater literary value for reasons that may seem to us to be arbitrary. When he explains these exclusions, his explanation compounds our difficulties:

Sociological novels such as Sinclair's *The Jungle* (1906) and proletarian novels such as Steinbeck's *The Grapes of Wrath* (1939), for example, are excluded. This definition excludes novels which do not deal primarily with political processes and actions, but concentrate instead on the conditions out of which political action may eventually arise. It also omits novels portraying actions and attitudes which can be regarded as political only after being extracted from a matrix of allegory and symbol—a highly subjective process.

To dismiss *The Jungle* as a "sociological" novel is perplexing. No one with any sense would claim that the novel is devoid of sociological interest, but to phrase the matter in such a way as to imply that "sociological" and "political" could be mutually exclusive categories leads to a number of puzzling omissions. Blotner's comprehensive approach resists definition without exact borders, and his resolution to approach art with "objective" criteria paves the way for a definition of the political novel that will in practice be almost procrustean.

Blotner and Milne obviously set out to praise the political novel, and in many cases they were able to do just that, and yet there seems to be a bedrock assumption in their approaches to political fiction that foreordains a woeful outcome for the form. Like many students of the political novel who attempt an exact and exclusive definition, Blotner asks, "Why are there so few modern American political novels of any excellence? Why are there so many bad ones?" This sense of almost unavoidable disappointment is the natural consequence of any attempt to describe the American political novel from an apolitical vantage point.

In the Nineties: Some New American Adams

The "political novel" per se is not a factor in contemporary criticism, though politics is supposedly more important than ever before. We no longer discuss the political novel, though there is a great deal of discussion about politics "in" and the politics "of." The political novel has disappeared as admissible evidence within the most prestigious journals of academic literary criticism, and for this we may thank poststructuralism and new historicism. Today's literary theory and criticism is a mode of discourse that offers psychic self-defense in a world of ideological oppression. Critical theory is favored as a doorway out of ideological prison-houses such as national identity, and so American literary critics after Vietnam and Watergate have immersed themselves in this discourse to enjoy the sense that they are "other" than traditional American literary critics. Conventional labels such as "political novel"[13] have been shunned, as they are, supposedly, tainted elements or even building blocks of the ideologically inscribed discourse of American imperial-ism—against which the critic is the latest incarnation of the Emersonian "simple, genuine self against the whole world."

Dedicated to challenging such ideological formations as American innocence, Adamic entitlement, and especially the absolute separation of political and literary discourses, this language is in one sense thor-oughly political, but ideological criticism usually works at a greater dis-tance from the literary work than do other kinds of criticism, and so there has been a divide in literary studies between those who think we should read literature and those who think we should *read the way we read litera-ture*. The weakness of ideological criticism is that it often scants the par-ticulars of individual works in pursuit of the politics of literary study, usually by focusing on primal scenes in new historicist fashion, which are in themselves interpreted with great thoroughness. Some of the most politically self-conscious American criticism has been termed New Americanism, a discourse in which the critic "otherizes" an Old Americanist to authorize his or her own position.

Donald Pease organizes various New Americanist ideas at the close of the cold war in his introduction to a special issue of *boundary 2* entitled, *New Americanists: Revisionist Interventions into the Canon*. In a time of dis-appearing enemies, to designate an Other is to authorize oneself, and so the New Americanists designate the previous generation of literary critics as the political Other. As in any name-calling situation, both sides accuse the other of having initiated hostilities and, thus, Pease begins his intro-duction to this collection by summarizing Frederick Crews's critical re-view of revisionist literary histories, "Whose American Renaissance?" (Crews first coined the term "New Americanist" when this essay ap-peared in *The New York Review of Books*.) Pease and Crews agree that there is something different about the New Americanists. Rhetorical opposi-tion is a highly visible element within new historicist criticism, but it remains a question whether this opposition is political in any genuinely public sense.

Notice how, in the days after "the death of the Author," the political identity of the critic has become much more significant than the views or influence of any practicing novelist. Supposedly reporting on Crews, Pease writes, "the New Americanists have returned ideology to a field previously organized by an end of ideology consensus" (2). The sentence is not an exact reproduction of Crews's meaning, since Crews (accord-ing to Pease) presents the conflation of ideology and literature as a very bad thing, whereas New Americanists regard the "new historicist return of the repressed context" (35) to be a very good thing indeed. Pease re-writes Crews's critique in order to reverse its polarity, such as when he quotes a few phrases from Crews to define the New Americanists: "the New Americanists' critique of 'slavery, "Indian removal," aggressive expansion, imperialism, and so forth' reasonably seems to Crews indistinguishable from the demands of academic special interest groups" (3). We are of course to conclude that the critiques of slavery or imperialism are hardly the demands of a special interest group—but not yet. We must first pause to ask who "we" are, for we are not necessarily of the same group. In political criticism, as in the political novel, the concept "we" is never as casual as it sounds.

That is to say, we must mind our Pease and Crews. Crews criticizes the younger generation of critics for not respecting the disciplinary boundaries that have given the study of American literature its meaning. According to Pease, Crews has not merely criticized the New Americanists, he has *rejected* them as followers in the path of American Studies. Pease embraces the claim that New Americanism is a bastard discipline (and he exaggerates Crews's "rejection" to do this) because the illegitimacy of the newer discipline is, paradoxically, the ground of its legitimacy—as a counter-hegemonic formation.

New Americanism—Call it Ishmael! To transcend the mob, to light out for the territory, or to maintain some connection to innocence—these are the marks of the American Adam, as described by Lewis. All New Americanists should take a dim view of such a naive ideological construct, and so we see that the description "Adamic" is often used as a pejorative word to describe a naive American false consciousness. While Russell Reising concedes that *The American Adam* was "not simply [. . .] a retreat from social and political turbulence," his need to condescend to previous theorists of American literature and culture clouds his view, and so Reising somehow fails to register that the epilogue to Lewis's book is entitled "Adam as Hero in the Age of Containment." As in the last chapter, the social function of the literary mythology is implied throughout the text. I will return to the political significance of literary mythologies, particularly that of the American Adam, in later chapters; for now it will be enough to note the self-serving ways in which many contemporary theorists make a straw man of literary tradition.

The irony of the New Americanist critique of Adamicism is that New Americanists are solidly in the Adamic tradition. To look at Pease through his own lens, we can see that the New Americanist is Adamic in the pejorative sense because of his or her need to "displace and dismiss": just as Pease charges Crews with a quasi-Freudian repression of the critical-theoretical Other, the New Americanist's insistence that he or she differs in kind from the "Old Americanist" can be traced to the newer critic's anxiety of influence. By seeing him- or herself as more ready to admit "historic national shames" than the previous generation of critics, the New Americanist undergoes rhetorical self-purification and is reborn as the simple, genuine self against the whole academy. Unable to bear the sins of traditional criticism, the New Americanist reinvents him- or herself, and in this respect the New Americanist is a most familiar specimen. New Americanism, as practiced by Pease, is a rhetorical mode of self-purification. It provides a way to see oneself in pure opposition not only to the national sins (slavery, imperialism), but also to earlier modes of criticism, such as those practiced by the depoliticized academy. Pease, then, arranges the mirrors so as to present himself as an anti-academic academic. However, to allude to Althusser in a sentence on "an ideological state apparatus complicit with aggressive expansionism, patronage politics, and slavery," (3) as Pease does in his discussion of Crews, does not really distinguish Pease from Crews. Pease's claim that the New Americanists are in a Somewhere Else unintentionally (or ironically?) echoes Poirier's claim that American writers seek "a world elsewhere," an Eden or virgin land beyond guilt (and thus history). The American Adam must ever be born again in flight from history, and the Adamic critic must ever "make it new."

There is an adventurousness to Pease's call for a political criticism, but we need not agree with him that New Americanism exists in pure opposition to American Studies as practiced by those who have not yet had a critical-theoretical conversion experience. I believe Pease to be guilty, as it were, of what Shelby Steele calls in *The Content of Our Character*, "seeing for innocence." Seeing for innocence is a form of seeing in which the object of one's perception is distorted so as to enable one to see oneself as "innocent"—and thus politically entitled.

New Americanist seeing for innocence is theorized in Pease's introduction-and-manifesto, and it is practiced in Thomas Schaub's *American Fiction in the Cold War* (1991). A study of novels written since 1945, Schaub's book is a good example of the way in which a focus on the politics of criticism displaces the reading of political literature. Schaub presents his *donné* with admirable clarity: "This book is about the discourse of revisionist liberalism—what was then called 'the new liberalism'—as it appears within the discussion and practice of fiction in the United States during the forties and fifties." In its unmasking of this liberalism, the book leaves us with a Foucauldian sense that the Revisionist Liberal discourse was somehow inescapable.

Each chapter develops the political consequences of innovations supposedly following the 'end of ideology,' but Schaub's critique of the postwar "anti-ideology" does not really operate from outside of that ideology. We can see this in a general way in the preferential treatment he gives to supposedly apolitical or anti-liberal writers such as John Barth and Flannery O'Connor, and his way of reading becomes especially cramped when he discusses an unrepentantly political novelist such as Norman Mailer.

Every Adamic narrative must have a Fall, and Mailer takes a tumble in the chapter "Rebel without a Cause: Mailer's White Negro and Consensus Liberalism."[14] In the first part of his study Schaub uses Mailer's writings to exemplify the position of "The Unhappy Consciousness," and Mailer is thus one of the good guys—except that in his chapter on Mailer Schaub dismisses Mailer's fiction of the fifties to discuss, instead, "The White Negro." Schaub is free to conclude that Mailer's novels are of little interest if he so chooses, but to quote from *Barbary Shore* to develop his view of the interrelations between politics and literary form in the first part of a book and to then ignore the novel in a chapter that should address Mailer's novels written under those difficult conditions is unusual. Cold war fiction is the ostensible subject, and Mailer's cold war novels, starting even with *The Naked and the Dead* (1948), invite discussion from a number of angles.

It appears that Schaub chose "The White Negro" for its excesses, for its latent and manifest racism, and for its sexism in particular. Mailer is discussed as a writer supposedly hostile to liberalism, but he is then shown to work within the discourse of revisionist liberalism. Or, to divide the doctor from the disease, Mailer is a good doctor in part one, but Schaub needs to purify himself of Mailerism in the second part. While writers in part 1 are at times considered to be perfectly conscious of the political discourses around them, the writers of part 2 are understood to express ideology unknowingly. When "the Author is dead," the critic may still pick among stony striations for veins of discourse, "which we may read as evidence of culture speaking through Mailer, just as a geologist may read the sedimentary striations of canyon walls to learn the earth's history, the canyon being merely a convenient point of access. To do this is to see 'The White Negro' transformed into an expression of culture inhabiting Mailer, who has, in varying degrees, thus lost the reins to his own thought" (138). Mailer is "merely a convenient point of access," indicating that Schaub has lost any particular interest in Mailer as a writer. Mailer certainly merits reading against the grain, and Schaub's argument that we must question the pure opposition Mailer offers between himself as a noble novelist and "the shits [who] are killing us" (as Mailer formulates the opposition in *Advertisements for Myself*) is well taken; but it remains a problem that Schaub discusses the novels of three writers who are interesting as novelists but then selects from Mailer's work a symptomatic *essay*. While Schaub appears to affirm a politically oppositional form of criticism, he is at the same time concerned to separate himself from the necessary messiness of politics. By presenting Mailer as a symptom of American culture, Schaub avoids all risk that he will contaminate himself with Mailer's expression of racialist theories, and by arguing that Mailer's existential hipsterism is really liberalism, Schaub thus purifies American literary radicalism of the sins of Norman Mailer. If the essence of the Adamic is that it separates one from the sources of guilt, Schaub's telling of American fiction in the cold war is an Adamic narrative.

Schaub happens to be right in many of his criticisms of Mailer's moral and political postures. Furthermore, the Adamic mode hardly makes *American Fiction in the Cold War* bad literary criticism (though I am unhappy with his geological approach to Mailer's prose). It just strikes me as a great hindrance to the project of combining politics and literature that today's ideological enthusiasts continue to avoid the risks of political interpretation. Schaub's study is in fact a useful and interesting study of the interrelations of political ideology and literary technique, especially the early chapters on postwar changes in fictional voice and form. Schaub and Pease both practice "seeing for innocence," which I argue is a predictable effect of American Adamic ideology, but this does not mean that the New American Adams are "wrong." It certainly means that their approaches are not as new as they claim and that their efforts to construct a perspective without moral liabilities is another one of those sins of the fathers that gets passed along to the sons and most of the daughters. It also means that the feat of accommodating the division between politics and aesthetic discourse is easier said than done.

Perhaps after the Cold War

Are we out of the cold war? The United States, without its old foe, the Soviet Union, presumably should have to go on its solitary way and leave the Garden in which it had been the world-savior of democracy, but if the desire for a national self-concept predicated upon "innocence" has not been vanquished (and it has not), then we may predict a reincarnation of sorts. The cold war has been a story with many sequels.[15] In the meantime, are we out of the *literary* cold war? Too much criticism continues rhetorically to position the reader in an imaginary Somewhere Else that is free from the compromises of politics, but the news is not all bad. Three books suggest ways to combine politics with literature in ways that do not make politics an impurity.

Barbara Foley's *Radical Representations: Politics and Form in U.S. Proletarian Fiction, 1929–1941* is a polemical, revisionist attempt to rescue the proletarian novel from the charges that political commitment on the part of writers affiliated with the Communist Party yielded only programmatic rhetoric rather than "literature" as the New Critics understood it. In this inclusive, remarkably well researched and argued study, Foley fights the remnants of New Critical faith tooth, nail, and footnote. Furthermore, Foley argues that literature is inherently political without discussing the Wall Street Crash as a "text." *Radical Representations* is skeptical about the radical skepticism of much postmodern literary theory, though it employs contemporary modes of interpretation judiciously, such as when Foley engages the complexities of narratology to show that the *roman à thesis* novel should not be regarded as "inadmissible evidence" in the court of literature. Foley's study defends categories such as "proletarian novel," thereby throwing the gauntlet down before today's literary fashions, especially when she argues that the neglect of proletarian fiction in postwar criticism directly parallels the disregard of proletarian realities in contemporary America. Her critical approach to the sense that political discourse is a sullied form is analogous to Jack London's response to similar prejudices against political fiction; her study combines wily argument with a damn-the-torpedoes regard for supposedly disinterested criticism.

T. V. Reed attacks the notion that we should distinguish between political and literary discourse in *Fifteen Jugglers, Five Believers*. Reed integrates "high theory" (which I take to mean poststructuralist, feminist, new historicist, and neo-Marxist writing that is very, very abstract) with close readings of a selection of socially engaged texts to "assist the project of convincing literary critics that their work is unavoidably political and needs to become more attuned to radically democratic social movements" (xi).[16] "Texts" is, of course, a slippery word, and Reed extends the boundary-challenging aspects of his study with a chapter on "Dramatic Ecofeminism" that interprets a political event as a symbolic construct just like *Let Us Now Praise Famous Men*, *Armies of the Night*, and *Invisible Man*.

Reed's is unlike the kinds of studies that "say" politics while merely doing literature: he claims he cannot distinguish between the two—and then proceeds to illuminate political novels (and other "texts") in very interesting ways. While I am never convinced that a march on the Pentagon or other sort of public theater should be confused with the text of an actual writer, his approach is fruitful and interesting. Hybrid forms such as *Armies of the Night* have to a large extent evolved precisely because they combine the modernist/New Critical penchant for innovation with an end-run around those discursive boundaries blocking political fiction. It makes sense to approach these novels through a criticism that also challenges discursive boundaries. Nor should we object to applying literary or otherwise deeply philosophical modes of analysis to public events—just as long as we can still tell event from text.

For many poststructuralists, cleanliness is next to fascism. Thus, individual works of political literature are not impurities for postmodern literary critics, but the notion that we make categorical distinctions between political and aesthetic experience is an impurity. Reed's suggestion that we not distinguish between politics and literature but instead interpret "politerature" is a nice attention-getting new historicist move, but since he never uses the "everything is political" approach merely to discuss fiction that is—theoretical disingenuity aside—unconcerned with social problems and social change, his approach is honest and unpretentious. Reed could have distinguished between political and aesthetic purposes to make the same arguments. Though his suppression of the patent differences between aesthetic and political motivation within a given piece of writing occasionally raises one or more eyebrows, his approach usefully draws attention to the intersection of cultural and political discourse.

The third book I wish to mention is not directly concerned with novels but is the best book on the interrelations between politics and literary criticism as they interrelate in the cold war era. Tobin Siebers describes the political causes and effects of "Cold War criticism" in his *Cold War Criticism and the Politics of Skepticism* to suggest ways out of the Somewhere Else of American innocence. Siebers is refreshingly direct about the interrelations between politics and literature, and about limits conditioning such interrelations. He finds a lack of true political connection during the cold war period, a time when the politics and aesthetics of "skepticism" have become de rigueur. Siebers on the politics of literary skepticism warrants a lengthy quotation:

To say that skeptical criticism is directionless is to assert its essentially apolitical nature, to expose its fear of taking political positions, and to explain that the dogma espoused by skeptical critics, where "everything is political," is primarily a means of fleeing from politics. Politics demands that we risk taking a position, that we stand somewhere, that we decide, and that we accept as part of the political process the possibility that our positions, stances, and positions may go horribly wrong, nowhere, or miraculously right. This is the only form of arbitrariness, a favorite term of skeptical criticism, worth talking about and with which it is important to live. The possibility of arbitrariness and risk in the political process is the only good rationale for binding ourselves to skepticism. (viii)

"Arbitrariness" for Siebers means much more than multiple interpretations. Skepticism about a book's meaning can be a fruitful way of opening up questions of interpretation, but when "arbitrariness" becomes the chief critical value, criticism and text alike are politically neutralized. Cold War skepticism has given literary critics a gamut of dazzling ways to flee political responsibility.

In attacking skepticism, Siebers criticizes a wide spectrum of postwar criticism. In brief, skepticism is "the project of opposing thought to itself" motivated by "the desire for logical purity in a political and social paradox" (3, 4n). The theorists have consistently sought more sophisticated (read "abstract") ways of ducking the moral messiness of genuine political engagement. In discussing such critics and theorists as W. K. Wimsatt, Monroe Beardsley, Stephen Greenblatt, Paul de Man, Jane Tompkins, and Barbara Herrnstein Smith, Siebers demonstrates the intricate and manifold ways in which cold war criticism (some of which refers to political struggle and claims to struggle politically) flees from genuine political risk. Politics depends on a sort of belief that has been ruled inadmissible by New Critics and poststructuralists of various stripes, critics who have all avoided the defining risks of political activity. "Social existence," writes Siebers, "depends on the tautology of belief in which our actions and ideas are risked, and politics is defined as that domain in which beliefs determine the interests, purposes, and actions that lead to these same beliefs, which explains why political choices are always dangerous, and necessarily so" (27). Arguing that skepticism can never be the philosophical basis of a politics, Siebers insists that skepticism must be qualified and limited if criticism is to be political in a way that is consequential—consequential "in the world," not only in the context of a university career. The most theoretically "rigorous" critics of the postwar period have, however, achieved impressive academic success under the banner of radical skepticism, usually without even trying to be politically consequential. To "adopt a resolute skepticism toward beliefs—to label them arbitrary constructions—is to move outside the hermeneutic circle of belief, the tautology, in which politics takes place." Political literary criticism must not seek "a world elsewhere" but instead must be faithful to what Siebers terms our "home in the world."[17]

Suggesting only a few exceptions to his claim that literary intellectuals flee political risk,[18] Siebers makes a final warning before offering positive suggestions. He knows that academic presses genuflect to authors who pray to one or more components of the current Holy Trinity, race, gender, and class (a group that replaces the old triumvirate Freud-Nietzsche-Marx) but are actually no closer to engaging in political risk. "The academic publishing world is in a fever. These books and essays all have political agendas, but rarely does the writer have the nerve to spell out the issues and make proposals." Because critical skepticism is so entrenched, everyone knows or seems to know that politically engaged writing is bad form, even would-be defenders of political literature.[19] Bad money drives out the good: counterfeit political engagement is positively harmful to the possibility of genuine political criticism.

Siebers concludes his polemic by demanding, albeit with wit and style, that skepticism be maintained as a means rather than as an end in itself, since skepticism as an end is only a form of critical self-fashioning. He also claims that "literary criticism needs to take account of what politics really is," that it must not resort to "reinventing politics as a trope of negative freedom," and that literary criticism involves life-affirming principles and, therefore, must respect our inner lives. This last recommendation is, for Siebers, very much part of making a home in the world: "Literary critics who abandon their fondness for storytelling, beauty, aesthetic pleasure, language, and human talk about them willfully estrange themselves from a large part of the world in which they live" (156–57).

As the work of Foley, Reed, and Siebers illustrates, there is no reason why American readers *have* to follow uncritically the traditional paths wherein the critic eyes political struggle from afar, even if the most enduring element of the American Dream happens to be that Americans continue to view themselves as individuals defined in opposition to the State—even when doing the State's work. To abandon our fondness for storytelling is to estrange ourselves from a large part of the world in which we live, but to deny or acknowledge only as "complicitous" our formative role in the world in which we live is equally stultifying. Americanist criticism of political fiction must combine aesthetic pleasures and a fondness for storytelling with the political motivations—sometimes pleasurable, sometimes risky and unseemly—that are essential to public life.

Notes

1. Lentricchia praises writers who do not limit themselves to the "new regionalism" of the Reagan eighties: "Unlike these new regionalists [. . .] DeLillo (or Joan Didion, or Toni Morrison, or Cynthia Ozick, or Norman Mailer) offers us no myth of political virginity preserved" ("American Writer" 241). About the 1988 Democratic convention Didion wrote "It was into this sedative fantasy of a fixable imperial America that Jesse Jackson rode, on a Trailways bus" (79). In an equally memorable image Didion describes eternal innocence at the Dukakis campaign: "I recall pink-cheeked young aides of the Dukakis campaign referring to themselves, innocent of irony and therefore of history, as 'the best and the brightest'" (56).

2. To locate the division of political and literary discourse in the Agrarian reaction to proletarian literature and in the ascendancy of New Criticism during the cold war period is a dashing and perhaps critically convenient move, but it is hardly the case that political dissent was expressed without resistance before the middle of this century. My second chapter presents ample evidence that pre-Depression era writers such as Jack London also were critically punished for mixing politics and literature, as almost every bad review of *The Iron Heel* makes clear. The way we currently divide discourses does, however, owe a great deal to anti-Stalinism, as Foley points out in *Radical Representations* (3–43).

3. See Zinn's *People's History of the United States* for a critique and an alternative to the Great Man approach to history.

4. Wilding's progressive gesture in including *The Adventures of Huckleberry Finn* has apparently become reactionary: novelist Jane Smiley has (rather late in the political correctness game) attacked the novel as racist in *Harper's Magazine*.

5. The attacks on Don DeLillo for the "bad citizenship" he displayed in writing *Libra*, a novel that flaunts the inconsistencies of the Warren Report on the Kennedy assassination, are recent examples. See Lentricchia's "The American Writer as Bad Citizen."

6. The thirties, the sixties, and the nineties—a thirty-year cycle seems to apply.

7. The term "cold war" commonly refers to the period from 1947 to 1960 in which political dissenters were demonized by the witch-hunt tactics of Senator Joseph McCarthy, but the term is also frequently used to describe the postwar period that may or may not have ended with the collapse of the Soviet Union. Whitfield finds the election of Kennedy to be the end of the cold war. While this event certainly marks a shift in American culture, it certainly does not mark the end of the period in which political progressives were demonized as potentially

communist—only a lull. Siebers remarks that the cold war has a "history of false endings" in *Cold War Criticism and the Politics of Skepticism* (29).

8. In *Why Americans Hate Politics*, Dionne does not see the politicization of American culture as the work of the American Right alone. The New Left and the evolving counter-culture were also, in Dionne's presentation, integral to the polarization of American culture. See especially his discussion of counter-cultural themes in Kerouac (38–39).

9. Boyers resumes Howe's approach to political fiction in *Atrocity and Amnesia*. Like Howe, Boyers expresses none of the embarrassment about political fiction that has characterized much criticism; like Howe, Boyers also finds American political fiction unworthy, and he gives almost identical reasons for its exclusion in his preface: "Had there been a dominant American political novel produced in the last forty years, a novel that would stand in relation to American culture in the way that *The Book of Laughter and Forgetting* stands to Czech culture, I would, of course, have included it." American authors such as Mailer, Heller, Doctorow, and Coover were rejected as "provincial," and Boyers complains that a focus on works by these authors would have to treat their "peculiar Americanness." If only American political novels were not so . . . American. In an interview with Bill Moyers, Doctorow compares American critics' preference for foreign political novels to President Reagan's fondness for trade unions—so long as they were in Poland (84).

10. Trivedi applauds Howe for salvaging the political novel but criticizes Howe's inattention to the American political novel: "It would seem [. . .] that Howe had, once and for all, redeemed the political novel from the impure fringes of literature to install it right at the centre, dragged it out of its circumstantial quagmire to stand it shining and whole on the prominence of significant art. And yet, as it turned out, his superb example held few lessons for a more enlightened study of the American political novel—for the reason that very few American novels were admitted to his select canon" (7).

11. Trivedi's review of this critical ritual is both thorough and witty. See "Defining the Political Novel" (3–15).

12. In 1955 Blotner published a broad overview of the political novel in a series intended for political scientists. *The Political Novel* has a brief section on "The Novel as Political Instrument" yet for the most part defines the political novel in purely aesthetic (that is, in part, politically nontransitive) terms: "Since its beginning the political novel has fulfilled the ancient function of art. It has described and interpreted human experience, selectively taking the facts of existence and imposing order and form upon them in an esthetic pattern to make them meaningful. The political novel is important to the student of literature as one aspect of the art of fiction, just as is the psychological novel or the economic novel" (1). Blotner seems ready to add a political component—until we see that the Political Scientist, and not the Politician, is the model. Like the political scientist, the political novelist is advised to create dispassionate analyses.

13. "The convenient working distinction between cultural texts that are social and political and those that are not becomes something worse than an error: namely, a symptom and a reinforcement of the reification and privatization of contemporary life" (Jameson, *Political Unconscious* 20).

14. For an excellent discussion of new historicist approaches to Mailer's essay, one which counts the losses in using Mailer as a critical straw man, see Steve Shoemaker's "Norman Mailer's 'White Negro': Historical Myth or Mythical History."

15. On "many sequels," see note 7.

16. Reed is fluent in the dialects of critical theory, but he also shows awareness of the political limitations of such arcane language. Like Siebers, Reed has some doubts about the value of pure skepticism, such as when he explains his peculiar title drawn from the lyrics of Bob Dylan: "I want to suggest that among those much-needed word and world *jugglers* we call postmodernists, there are and must be some *believers*, believers in political values and practical strategies for social change" (xi). Literature, with its theory-defying specificity, is the bridge between theory and politics, which saves literature from the bad guy position it must take in so much ideological criticism. Note the felicity with which Reed summarizes the carnivalesque attempt to levitate the Pentagon in *Armies of the Night,* calling it "the most literal enactment of *Aufhebung* in political history. Theory practiced, the abstract made concrete" (108).

17. Poirier's study of style in American literature is entitled *A World Elsewhere.* For Siebers, Hannah Arendt, source of "home in the world," is the political-interpretive exemplar because she is not scared by the scare-quotes that usually surround reality. Siebers writes, "Among the many ideas that Cold War theorists have refused to consider is the notion that literary criticism is out of touch with what in academia we like to call the 'real world.' Cold War criticism has every interest in remaining blind to this truth as long as it refuses to view itself with the same skeptical regard that it directs toward everything else" (x).

18. Edward Said and Noam Chomsky receive honorable mentions.

19. Lentricchia writes that the mainstream of American literature is indeed political, "but not in the trivial didactic sense of offering programs of renovation, or of encouraging us 'to do something'" ("American Writer" 244). At this point in his argument Lentricchia is as much a mandarin as Virginia Woolf, who despised the kind of book that made you want to write a check for some cause. As Lentricchia is also not shy about combining political invective with literary criticism, it would also be possible to argue that he is merely attempting to woo purely aesthetic readers in the comment quoted above. Even read this way the comment is an awfully large concession to those who would cleave art from politics.

PART 2

The Range of the American Political Novel

2

Submerged Revolution in *Moby-Dick*

What the White Whale was to them, or how to their unconscious understand-
ings, also, in some dim, unsuspected way, he might have seemed the glid-
ing great demon of the seas of life,—all this to explain, would be to dive
deeper than Ishmael can go.
—Herman Melville

Let us read *Moby-Dick* as a tale of class warfare and counter-revolution—
not something we find every day in American literature. That Melville's
epic novel has a political dimension has been frequently noted, but what
has not been adequately addressed is the way in which this muted political dimension continually shapes the identity of the novel as a whole,
even when political conflict is not overt. If we consider carefully the
matter of "The *Town-Ho*'s Story," we see the ways in which class antagonisms and political struggle continue to have a formative presence in the
novel even after the last worker-hero of the Pequod has been silenced.

Let us begin by recognizing the variousness of *Moby-Dick*, since the
novel's reputation springs from its richness of meaning. One interpretation discusses the novel's generic plurality to argue convincingly that
"The heterogeneity of *Moby-Dick* [. . .] actually reflects the narrative license of the times," which is to say that Melville may not have been so
very eccentric when he created his encyclopedia of styles and stories
(Post-Lauria 300). *Moby-Dick* is about many things, not just politics. Even
so, there have been a number of readers who have found *Moby-Dick* to
be political through and through. Critics such as C. L. R. James, Alan
Heimert, Michael Paul Rogin, Carolyn Karcher, and James Duban have
shown that Melville used political symbolism to express controversial
political views.[1]

Melville's novel, then, was certainly connected with politics, and its political representations are not merely background scenery. It alluded to explosive controversies that would, in a few years, sunder the nation, yet these allusions are buried beneath teeming references to the Bible, literature of the more secular sort, general history, American and world geography, as well as subjects cetological. My claim is that the political portion is not merely outweighed by these other matters; it is masked by them. The political content dives beneath an ocean of literariness. *Moby-Dick* is an exemplary submerged political novel: Melville's political design, like the white whale itself, is almost always submerged in the novel.

"The **Town-Ho's Story"** *as a Political Parable*

The fifty-fourth chapter of *Moby-Dick* is entitled "The *Town-Ho's* Story." The story comes to us with a dreamlike uncertainty because it has been told and retold several times under various conditions before appearing in the pages of Ishmael's whale-tale. It is first told to Tashtego, a harpooner on the *Pequod*, by sailors of the *Town-Ho* who make him promise not to tell anyone else: "For the secret part of the story was the private property of three confederate white seamen of that ship, one of whom, it seems, communicated it to Tashtego with Romish injunctions of secresy [sic]" (208). Ishmael first hears this piece of private property when Tashtego "rambled in his sleep, and revealed so much of it in that way, that when he was wakened he could not well withhold the rest" (208). The story *Moby-Dick's* readers get is not Tashtego's account of his own dream, though. Instead, Ishmael retells this already oddly framed narrative in "the style in which I once narrated it in Lima, to a lounging circle of my Spanish friends, one saint's eve, smoking upon the thick-gilt tiled piazza of the Golden Inn" (208). Ishmael imposes the Golden Inn frame on the *Town-Ho's* story as a whole, thus separating it from the developing narrative of the *Pequod*.

The chapter begins with a reference to the Cape of Good Hope, which, we learn in an earlier chapter of Melville's novel, once had a less inviting name: "Cape of Good Hope, do they call ye? Rather Cape Tormentoso, as called of yore; for long allured by the perfidious silences that before had attended us, we found ourselves launched into this tormented sea, where guilty beings transformed into those fowls and these fish, seemed condemned to swim on everlastingly without any haven in store" (201). The unpleasant name for a hellish place is displaced by a more inviting name, one indicating a good place. This sort of displacement makes us wonder about the "Golden Inn." Did it have a previous name? In ways that relate directly to the conflicts on board the *Town-Ho* and the *Pequod*, the Peruvian context and the use of various names illustrate the sort of displacement Freud found in dreams.

If "The *Town-Ho*'s Story" can be interpreted as a political dream, we must ask, What taboo desire accounts for the dream's obscuration? "The *Town-Ho*'s Story" narrates one sailor's rebellion against a corrupt authority figure, a story that can be further generalized into a parable about class antagonisms. Heroically presented class revolt will appear, upon analysis, to be the fundamental truth that Melville had to disguise in the presentation of his epic vision. "The *Town-Ho*'s Story" increasingly takes on the role of the unconscious as described, in semi-political terms, by Jacques Lacan when he writes that the "unconscious is that chapter of my history that is marked by a blank or occupied by a falsehood: it is the censored chapter" (*Écrits* 50). But in Lacan's formulation, the censored chapter is not permanently lost since "the truth can be rediscovered; usually it has already been written down elsewhere." The "elsewhere" of *Moby-Dick* is the fifty-fourth chapter, "The *Town-Ho*'s Story." The censored chapter, it will turn out, is an honorific treatment of class revolt.

Steelkilt, the rebel-sailor of the *Town-Ho*, is one of Melville's worker-heroes, an ennobled commoner who resists a corrupt authority figure. Radney, our evil authority in this melodramatic confrontation, is the chief mate of the *Town-Ho* and also happens to be part-owner of the vessel. The story begins with the *Town-Ho* cruising for whales, until the vessel springs a leak that Ishmael describes to his audience of Spanish Dons in tall-tale fashion: "They supposed a sword-fish had stabbed her, gentlemen" (209). The leak in the vessel triggers a series of events that culminates in Steelkilt's attempt to kill Radney, although Ishmael's manner of telling attempts to maintain good humor at all times. That the storyteller must not "rock the boat" is one developing theme in Ishmael's metafictional narrative. Freud stresses in *The Interpretation of Dreams* that dreams function to reduce affect: "We can thus plainly see the purpose for which the censorship exercises its office and brings about the distortions of dreams: it does so *in order to prevent the generation of anxiety or other forms of distressing affect*" (301). Dreamworker Ishmael distorts and displaces elements of his narrative to reduce anxiety among his listeners, the Dons.

Verbal interruption occurs when the storyteller says something that is somehow out of bounds, and the storyteller, according to the rhetorical guidelines of the Freudian dream, must maintain the connection with the (censoring) audience by binding the unruly elements in his tale.

Ishmael runs into stormy weather first when he points out that this "leak" should have been no great problem since the *Town-Ho* was equipped with "pumps of the best." The *Town-Ho* "had all but certainly arrived in perfect safety at her port without the occurrence of the least fatality, had it not been for the brutal overbearing of Radney, the mate, a Vineyarder, and the bitterly provoked vengeance of Steelkilt, a Lakeman and desperado from Buffalo" (209). At this exact moment Ishmael's narrative is interrupted by one of the Spanish Dons: "'Lakeman!—Buffalo! Pray, what is a Lakeman, and where is Buffalo?' said Don Sebastian, rising in his swinging mat of grass" (209). Ishmael, in addressing the aristocratic Dons, is confronted by audience shock and disbelief when he tries to present them with events outside their register of experience. Just as Radney fails to take an accurate measure of Steelkilt in the story Ishmael tells, the Spanish Dons frequently indicate their own disorientation. The developing correspondences between "owners" such as Radney and aristocrats such as the Spanish Dons of Lima tell us much about Ishmael's difficulties as a storyteller, since throughout his story he is sympathetic to the democratic hero Steelkilt.

After this and subsequent interruptions, Ishmael redirects his story in such a manner that his audience, the Dons, will not be disoriented or disturbed. Each interruption by one of the Dons, who are the censors in my dream analogy, is followed by Ishmael's narrative digression or substitution, making Ishmael the Freudian dream-smuggler. Ishmael calms his audience and makes it possible for them to connect with the kind of American reality embodied in Steelkilt by telling them a tale of wonder about America's inland oceans: "They have heard the fleet thunderings of naval victories; at intervals, they yield their beaches to wild barbarians, whose red painted faces flash from out their peltry wigwams; for leagues and leagues are flanked by ancient and unentered forests, where the gaunt pines stand like serried lines of kings in Gothic genealogies" (210). The medieval reference, the archaic vocabulary, and the various other exotic details blazon Romance. This excerpt from a much longer catalog of America's fantastic dimensions is the sort of fantasy-bridge that can connect Steelkilt's world of ships and work to the Dons' world. As we do not have "kings in Gothic genealogies" in America, Ishmael transforms pines and forests accordingly. The Dons, men of leisure and breeding rather than men who work for a living, are unable to fathom Steelkilt without Ishmael's help. The mere mention of Steelkilt is, however, hardly an insurmountable obstacle, and so, with an occasional helping of romance, the story continues.

Ishmael tells the Dons that some skippers on a leaky boat "might think little of pumping their whole way across" the ocean (210). On such occasions, crews take turns at the pump handles without worry. Ishmael reports a well-ordered work space in which the labor is divided according to rank, a world in which class divisions do not necessarily doom the society to civil conflict. When the chief mate Radney (who, Ishmael tells us, "was a little of a coward") becomes more apprehensive about the leak, "some of the seamen declared that it was only on account of his being a part owner of her" (211). Ishmael's direct moral judgment of Radney and his corresponding idealization of Steelkilt present his audience with a melodramatic alignment of sympathies not characteristic of *Moby-Dick* as a whole. The melodramatic form and the tall-tale style that align Ishmael with Steelkilt foreshadow the coming class conflict of the inner narrative that Ishmael tells the Dons. Conflicts within the story itself parallel problems Ishmael encounters when telling the story to the Dons, and so "The *Town-Ho*'s Story" also becomes a parable about the politics of storytelling: Ishmael certainly does not intend to alienate his immediate audience, and so he must shape his tale to make it suit those who are buying the drinks. Furthermore, in re-telling "The *Town-Ho*'s Story" in "the style in which I once narrated it at Lima," Ishmael gathers all of his various audiences including mid-nineteenth-century book buyers and present-day readers together at the Golden Inn. Insofar as this device unites people of disparate backgrounds by giving them a common imaginative experience, it fulfills the most utopian ideals of literature. The overall aim of his Golden Inn style appears to be the subtraction of political conflict whenever that conflict undermines the *communitas* created by stories. Melville, to extend this model, speaks through the mask of Ishmael to smooth over class conflict before it disturbs his audience, thus enabling himself to speak and speak again, despite frequent interruptions and embarrassing silences. If we pursue the implications of this broader conception of Melville's audience and imagine sailors and aristocrats uncomfortably together at the Golden Inn, we become instantly alert to how much Ishmael must scuttle back and forth like Ganymede, pouring out dollops of good humor or exotic detail to keep the peace. When the crewmen of the *Town-Ho* begin to make jokes about owners, the Dons will feel some discomfort, hence the recurrent tall-tale humor: "Such, gentlemen, is the inflexibility of sea usages and the instinctive love of neatness in seamen; some of whom would not willingly drown without first washing their faces" (212). This joke guides the Dons away from literal expectations created by the narrative, and it does so in ways designed to confirm their own self image, since every sailor is found to be a face-washing *gentleman.*

So long as Ishmael continues to reduce affect, to use Freud's term again, his auditors are easily calmed. With Ishmael as speaker, tall-tale humor smooths over class divisions. However, when we step within the various narrative frames and enter the world of the *Town-Ho,* the words that come from Steelkilt do anything but calm listeners. He is a different kind of speaker, a political agitator rather than an entertainer, and his words prod the sensitive areas of class conflict in America. If we are to understand Melville's parable about the politics of storytelling and the politics of interpretation, we must be sensitive to the way in which radically different speakers give identical words entirely different meanings. Put a frame around words and their meaning can be neutralized or reversed: context is all.

In Ishmael's account to the Dons, Steelkilt has been pumping away, doing his job, but he has also been antagonizing Radney with his tall-tale humor of a different ilk. After suggesting that below the ship there is a "gang of ship-carpenters, saw-fish, and file-fish [. . .] cutting and slashing at the bottom," Steelkilt says that Radney should "jump overboard and scatter 'em. They're playing the devil with his estate" (212). The owners and the workers have different interests, as Steelkilt's wisecrack makes uncomfortably clear. Just after the exhausted Steelkilt has left the pumps, Radney responds to the sailor's barbs by demanding that Steelkilt sweep pig droppings. Ishmael intimates that violence will result from Radney's insult: "Now what cozening fiend it was, gentlemen, that possessed Radney to meddle with such a man in that corporeally exasperated state, I know not; but so it happened" (212). Note that Ishmael's assertion that no one should meddle with an exhausted worker indicates a worker's view rather than an owner's. At this point in Ishmael's telling there are fewer tall-tale jokes and a far greater number of silences, ominous withdrawals of meaning, and other minor-chord variations. Steelkilt, angry at the insult, is said to be possessed by a "nameless phantom" (213). When Radney shakes a hammer in Steelkilt's face, Steelkilt is silent; Radney does not pick up on Steelkilt's "awful and unspeakable intimations" (213). The "unspeakable" in this narrative becomes the center of attention, until Radney grazes Steelkilt's cheek with the hammer: "the next instant the lower jaw of the mate was stove in his head; he fell on the hatch spouting blood like a whale" (214). Ishmael has arrived at the heart of his story, which is, since it offers such a strong indication about the symbolic significance of the white whale, also the heart of the novel. After Steelkilt hits Radney, he and his mates prepare to take over the ship: "'Ere the cry could go aft Steelkilt was shaking one of the backstays leading far aloft to where two of his comrades were standing their mast-heads. They were both Canallers'" (214).

A mutiny has begun—how will the Dons react? The Dons immediately interrupt and demand to know who (and what) "Canallers" are. Note that the Dons' interruption, which is integral to Ishmael's dialogic Golden Inn style, comes just at the moment when a melodramatic character conflict evolves into violent conflict with owners. Ishmael complies, just as he did after the previous interruption, and displaces his revolutionary story with a far-off, wondrous, mystical description. After asking one of the Dons to refill his cup, he says,

> "For three hundred and sixty miles, gentlemen, through the entire breadth of the state of New York; through numerous populous cities and most thriving villages; through long, dismal, uninhabited swamps, and affluent, cultivated fields, unrivalled for fertility; by billiard-room and bar-room; through the holy-of-holies of great forests; on Roman arches over Indian rivers; through sun and shade; by happy hearts or broken; through all the wide contrasting scenery of those noble Mohawk counties; and especially, by rows of snow-white chapels, whose spires stand almost like milestones, flows one continual stream of Venetianly corrupt and often lawless life." (214)

That is quite a sentence. I propose that the delay in the main narrative is not inserted merely for the sake of suspense. While it is tempting to slice off a part of this long sentence for discussion, all of the travel-guide details that come before "lawless" are necessary, because we must acknowledge that Ishmael is insulating his story with wads of noble nonsense. For Ishmael to tell his story, the real social conflicts at its heart must be submerged in a safer kind of language. The politically dangerous theme is submerged beneath encyclopedic details, travel-guide stuff, red-faced Indians, and other kinds of exotica.

When interrupted by the Dons, Ishmael, in all civility, asks that his cup be refilled before continuing his story. After the lengthy aforementioned stretch of noble nonsense, Ishmael proceeds to violate a number of taboos, such as when he says "sinners, gentlemen, most abound in holiest vicinities" (214). We know his irreverence has broached a taboo by the Dons' nervous reactions, for when Ishmael makes his observation Don Pedro responds by asking, "Is that a friar passing?" (214). Is "vicinity" in Ishmael's reported speech-act the church with which the friar is most often associated, or, since sinners like the blasphemous Ishmael there abound, is the Golden Inn, the place of Ishmael's story, among the "holiest places"? The Dons verbally acknowledge discomfort concerning Ishmael, the religious Freethinker, but the timing of their interruptions suggest a lower layer of meaning. The passing of the friar triggers a series of exchanges between Ishmael and his audience that deepens the problem of "the politics of storytelling." The pattern of substitution begins to quicken as the audience takes an active part in the narrative, suggesting that conflicting realities break through the surface of Ishmael's narrative faster than he can submerge them.

Although Ishmael places his telling of "The *Town-Ho's* Story" more or less firmly in Lima, by the end of his narration he may well wonder where Lima is. The difference or similarity between Lima and other worldly places becomes an issue in the foreground once again when Ishmael "gets caught" speaking of one place in terms of another. In response to Ishmael's "Venetianly corrupt" reference in the prior purple passage, a "Limeese" gentleman discovers that Venice is really Lima:

> "A moment! Pardon!" cried another of the company. "In the name of all us Limeese, I but desire to express to you, sir sailor, that we have by no means overlooked your delicacy in not substituting present Lima for distant Venice in your corrupt comparison. Oh! do not bow and look surprised; you know the proverb all along the coast—'Corrupt as Lima.' It but bears out your saying, too; churches more plentiful than billiard-tables, and for ever open—and 'Corrupt as Lima.' So, too, Venice; I have been there; the holy city of the blessed evangelist, St. Mark!—St. Dominic, purge it! Your cup! Thanks: here I refill; now, you pour out again." (214–15)

The banter is witty, often sharp, but never of the flighty sort, and so the displacement of Lima by Venice, happily noted by the man from Lima, momentarily silences Ishmael. Melville critics have often described the Dons as stupid, but here one is alert and good humored—and quite willing to go a layer lower. With St. Dominic's help and a filled cup, Ishmael is permitted, even encouraged, to continue.

The interruption about "Canallers" begins a complex exchange between Ishmael and the Dons that only apparently concerns "Lima." Melville readers such as Heinz Kosok have taken the Dons' questions at face value, but Melville gives us reason to scrutinize the meaning of "Lima" in *Moby-Dick*. We are told in "The Whiteness of the Whale" that "Lima has taken the white veil; and there is a higher horror in this whiteness of her woe. Old as Pizarro, this whiteness keeps her ruins for ever new; admits not the cheerful greenness of complete decay; spreads over her broken ramparts the rigid pallor of an apoplexy that fixes its own distortions" (168). The veil that obscures while nonetheless preserving, the references to the conquistador Pizarro, and the concern about earthquakes and apoplexy are all highly charged politically. If "All the world's one Lima," as one of the Dons exclaims, this world is a place of conquest, oppression, and perhaps of revolution. Melville makes the connection between universal whiteness and the worldwide system of racial oppression in the same chapter: "this preeminence in it applies to the human race itself, giving the white man ideal mastership over every dusky tribe" (163). The world is one Lima because every place on it, to generalize along Ishmaelian lines, supports one colonial gentleman or another, usually white, at the expense and suffering of local dusky tribes—a theme that is never far from the surface of *Moby-Dick.* Before he even goes whaling, just following his initial interview with the owners of the *Pequod,* Ishmael asks himself "Who ain't a slave?" This is a rhetorical question and we are to assume no one ain't a slave, but "The *Town-Ho's* Story" tells of a worker who refuses to be treated like property, and that refusal is predicated entirely upon the character's willingness to use force. In this willfulness Steelkilt is something of a challenge to the Ishmaelian world view.

If all the world is one Lima, Ishmael could also be discussing the United States. We may trace the displacements from Venice to Lima and then back to America. In evoking the Peruvian context, Ishmael several times mentions Pizarro, the archetypal Spanish Conquistador, while the Dons themselves are not said to be personally cruel or in any other way oppressive. Ishmael "craves courtesy" and always speaks in courtly language when addressing the Dons. Ishmael's direct addresses to the Dons, that is, "gentlemen," always point out a difference between themselves and the authoritarian manager with a Napoleonic temperament Radney, but the pattern of displacement in "The *Town-Ho's* Story" invites us to speculate: Is Radney a "dream representation" of the Dons? Is Radney the unmasked tyrant beneath the gentlemanly surface?

Several places in Melville's writing invite us to trace links between tyrannical domination and the courtesy one learns to expect of cultured people. One might object that the way Ishmael and the Dons address each other signals a clear and substantial difference between the Dons and such a brutal authority figure as Radney, but parallel moments in *Moby-Dick* also remind us to consider the common ground, as it were, between the tyrant and the gentleman. The description of Ahab in "The Quarter-Deck" chapter makes the link between authoritarian captains and gentlemen of leisure: "Ahab, as was his wont, ascended the cabin-gangway to the deck. There most sea-captains usually walk at that hour, as country gentlemen, after the same meal, take a few turns in the garden" (140). There is no "common ground" on ship or in a garden, as it has been enclosed and possessed by the ruling classes. Later in the novel Ahab makes the link between an imbalance in the possession of ground and tyrannical authority explicit: "But look ye, the only real owner of anything is its commander; and hark ye, my conscience is in this ship's keel.—On deck!" (393) Ahab's passing comments form the missing links between the seemingly benevolent world of gentlemanly leisure in "The Paradise of Bachelors" and the Marxian vision of the workers' world in "The Tartarus of Maids," but this uncomfortable link is not a matter of *direct* exposition. As the dream may circumvent the censor through displacement and thereby reveal uncomfortable messages, "The *Town-Ho's* Story" presents an uncomfortable image of owners to the Dons, as does *Moby-Dick* to its readers.

We have been following "The *Town-Ho's* Story" very closely, pausing to digress specifically at those points in the story where Ishmael is *forced* to digress. After the "Canallers" interruption, after the passing friar and the retort that "Dame Isabella's Inquisition wanes in Lima" (214), and after the impetuous exclamation that "The world's one Lima," Ishmael is interrupted one final time: when he mentions Moby Dick to the Dons.

Ishmael returns to his story by saying "I left off, gentlemen, where the Lakeman shook the backstays" (215). The captain and his men attempt to overtake them, "But Steelkilt and his desperadoes were too much for them; they succeeded in gaining the forecastle deck, where, hastily slewing about three or four large casks in a line with the windlass, these sea-Parisians entrenched themselves behind the barricade" (216). Ishmael, excited at this point in his narrative, bares the revolutionary moral that has been ascribed to his tale (as in Rogin's chapter "The American 1848").

Steelkilt, the reasonable chief of the sea-Parisians, insists that the men are ready to return to work, but they will not accept the blame for Radney's foolish actions: "treat us decently, and we're your men; but we won't be flogged" (216). When the captain refuses to promise any such thing, Steelkilt says they will not risk hanging by killing the captain, though they refuse to work until the captain promises not to flog them. Steelkilt essentially has declared a strike and has, for the moment at least, renounced outright mutiny. He and his comrades then endure a "lock-in" and allow themselves to be secured in the forecastle. After five days, three of the ten whalers originally locked in the forecastle have still refused the captain's offers to come up, but on the sixth morning Steelkilt's remaining two comrades betray him.

After this symbolic death, Steelkilt, our Worker-Christ, rises again and rejoins the crew of the *Town-Ho*. Though he warns both the captain and Radney not to flog him, Radney flogs Steelkilt anyway. After the punishment is dispensed, all seems to go smoothly on the *Town-Ho*, since "the Lakeman had induced the seamen to adopt this sort of passiveness in their conduct" (220). This is because Steelkilt had decided upon "his own proper and private revenge upon the man who had stung him in the ventricles of his heart." Steelkilt proceeds to knit a sling of sorts in which he intends to insert an iron ball. His plan is to shatter Radney's skull, and his borrowing twine from Radney to complete the sock displays his cold-blooded determination. The arisen Steelkilt will administer justice to sinners on a day to come: "In the fore-ordaining soul of Steelkilt, the mate was already stark and stretched as a corpse, with his forehead crushed in" (221). If any of the Dons are sensitive to the Christian cloak being draped over Steelkilt's shoulders in this revolutionary narrative, they say nothing. This is indeed striking—Steelkilt is about to revolt against the owner's law, and the Dons do not interrupt!

Steelkilt's murderous desire and Ishmael's sympathy with it could not be more clear, but this time the break in the story eventuates from within the inner narrative rather than from the narrative frame. Ishmael tells the Dons that "a fool saved the would-be murderer from the bloody deed he had planned" and that "a stupid Teneriffe man [. . .] all at once shouted out, 'There she rolls! Jesu! what a whale!' It was Moby Dick" (221). Note the ambiguity of "Jesu": the word is at once an interjection and the "christening" of Moby Dick that will be so interesting to the Dons. The whale, rather than Steelkilt, becomes the again-risen spirit of revolt. By making the Moby Dick interruption the punch line of his shaggy dog story of revolution, Ishmael-Melville conditions us to understand the displacement function of the great white whale in the *other* chapters of the novel as well. When Ishmael first mentions the name Moby Dick, he is again interrupted by his audience: "'Moby Dick!' cried Don Sebastian; 'St. Dominic! Sir Sailor, but do whales have christenings? Whom call you Moby Dick?'" (221). The whale substitutes for Steelkilt at just the moment when Ishmael's democratic hero was rapidly approaching the taboo of revolutionary violence, a taboo I take up in the two following sections.

The Dons shift to asking the same sort of questions about Moby Dick that they had been asking about the Canallers. Like the captain of the *Samuel Enderby*, Don Sebastian is struck that a whale should cross the threshold into the symbolic order in anthropomorphic terms. But the Don's apparently trivial question "do whales have christenings" is of some consequence. In his surprise the Don cries "St. Dominic," from L. *Dominus,* or "master." St. Dominic is the patron of the cathedral in Lima, which is appropriate to the Spanish *Dons,* masters in that place (Attwater). Don Sebastian, thus, cries out to his saint of domination at the mention of Moby Dick. "Moby," if we track it in the dictionary, resembles no particular word more than "mobile" or "mob." Though Moby Dick stands out from the mob of whales as Steelkilt or Bulkington do from sailors, a (Peruvian) mob is exactly what the privileged Dons most fear and must dominate.

The Dons are unaquainted with the Lakemen and Canallers of the world, the sort of men who overthrow aristocratic elites, and so Ishmael's story gives them narrative indigestion at key points. When Ishmael completes Steelkilt's story, Don Sebastian tells Ishmael, politely, that the story is incredible: "'I entreat you, tell me if to the best of your own convictions, this your story is in substance really true? It is so passing wonderful! Did you get it from an unquestionable source? Bear with me if I seem to press'" (224). Don Sebastian, we might suppose, is saying "Is this only literature?" or "Is this only a dream?" Though Ishmael's auditors fear the consequences of his next gesture, Ishmael demands "the largest sized Evangelists" that Don Sebastian can procure so that Ishmael might swear to the validity of his story. He would swear the truth of his tale (of rebellion against corrupt authority) on a Bible, and yet the tall-tale-scale demand for the "largest Evangelists available" gives an ironic cast to Ishmael's claims of absolute sincerity. "The *Town-Ho*'s Story" gives *Moby-Dick* its forgotten theme by highlighting Steelkilt as one of democracy's Invisible Men, lost on an aristocratic audience. Their social blindness signals their politically selective vocabulary and their inability to hear anything other than wholesale "good news" [fr. LL *evangelium,* fr. Gk *eu-angelos*]. What would these aristocrats, so nervous at a friar, make of the wicked book that Melville baptized so strangely—"Ego non baptiso te in nomine—but make out the rest yourself" (562). In a famous, elliptical letter to Hawthorne (29 June 1851), Melville voices his uncertain relationship to his larger readership, and even to Hawthorne: "When you see or hear of my ruthless democracy on all sides, you may possibly feel a touch of a shrink, or something of that sort" (556–57).

Heinz Kosok has argued that the Dons in "The *Town-Ho*'s Story" are there to satirize Melville's own readership.[2] The object of Melville's satire in "The *Town-Ho*'s Story" appears on the surface to be an obsolete class in a far-away country, but Melville's letters to Hawthorne indicate that Melville's anxieties about audience may even have extended to his most sympathetic readers, intellectual aristocrats like Hawthorne who, Melville feared, might "feel a touch of the shrink" at his unchecked democracy. Since Melville's "ruthless democracy" was potentially a source of discomfort even to his most sympathetic readers, "The *Town-Ho's* Story" offers itself as a parable on the politics of storytelling. In the fifty-fourth chapter Melville whispers how much he had to disguise to write *Moby-Dick*.

"The Town-Ho's *Story" and the Form of* Moby-Dick

If the "missing" theme of radical democracy were limited to the pages of "The *Town-Ho's* Story" it would be best understood as an oddity, but the political possibilities that surface in "The *Town-Ho's* Story" are apparent in other parts of *Moby-Dick* as well. The missing theme shows up at key moments, in fact. The most famous of these eruptions coincide with the descriptions of Bulkington (who disappears strangely in "The Lee Shore") and in those sections of "Knights and Squires" that I will be referring to as "the democracy prayer." By looking at the way Ahab's entrance dramatically submerges floating remnants of the democratic theme, we can see the difference between the novel that *is* and the novel that *might have been*. The novel as it is written, mainly as Ahab's story, only comes into being by displacing a different story. Any novel is the displacement of innumerable possible novels, but *Moby-Dick* is different since it suggests so strongly what that other novel would have been: the story of a democratic hero's repudiation of tyranny. "The *Town-Ho's* Story" is, once again, the novel's censored chapter.

Melville famously complained that dollars damned him and that the writing he most wanted to do was "banned," which tempts us to suppose that Melville *could not* write an overtly political novel, or that, because he believed he could not, he instead wrote a submerged political novel (557). This approach fails, since we need only mention Melville's overt political protest in his earlier novel, *White Jacket*. Our concern at any rate is not what book Melville could compose or what sort of writing he could legally publish, but rather what audiences he would probably attract if he were to write as he claimed he wanted to. Could he maintain his democratic populism and still satisfy his aristocratic appreciators? In another famous letter to fellow intellectual aristocrat Hawthorne, Melville describes the forces that require him to suppress material, especially when he writes that "Truth" conspires to silence the would-be writer: "It is but nature to be shy of a mortal who boldly declares that a thief in jail is as honorable a personage as Gen. George Washington. This is ludicrous. But Truth is the silliest thing under the sun. Try to get a living by the Truth—and go to the Soup Societies. Heavens! Let any clergyman try to preach the Truth from its very stronghold, the pulpit, and they would ride him out of his church on his own pulpit bannister" (557). How odd that "nature" and "Truth" should be mutually exclusive, but it is less odd when we factor in the church as context and implied audience. Libraries, courts, and churches all have very different speech rules. "Truth"—even the democratic truth enshrined in the American Constitution that George Washington and a jailbird are created equal—is thus inadmissible evidence in the court of public opinion, much to the disadvantage of democratic cultural reformers like Herman Melville.

Melville's solution is to use humor to "smuggle" his intolerable message past the censorious public. If one is going to make a forbidden representation, one had better make the idea tolerable by making it "ludicrous"; thus, Melville's audience would be more likely to accept such a representation if they considered its source to be Ishmael. He is a ludicrous and at times a self-mocking candidate for the Soup Societies, but his playful pantheism is not a satisfying substitute for a personification of radical democracy in the form of Steelkilt or Bulkington. Still, he is the last spokesman for radical democracy among all those who sailed on board the *Pequod*. He is the novel's sole survivor, and so his existence testifies to both the weakness of radical democracy and to the possibility of its endurance, in spite of tragic disappointment. He is a ludicrous hero because he is at once hardly a solution to the political problem represented by Ahab and at the same time the *only* remaining solution. Ishmael embodies a rather desperate faith in democracy.

The desire for radical democracy appears, significantly, just before the chapter introducing Ahab, the key agent of political repression within the world of the novel. The democracy prayer in "Knights and Squires" that concludes with the passage appealing to "thou great democratic God!" is a trace left behind, an unrepressed fragment of the radical democracy repressed in the narrative organized around Ahab's monomania. The content of the prayer bespeaks the real social possibilities inherent in democratic sentiments, and yet the prayer form also implies that such things are not to be had in this world. The prayer, then, appropriately takes the shape of a paradox by foreshadowing the unsayable: "were the coming narrative to reveal, in any instance, the complete abasement of poor Starbuck's fortitude, scarce might I have the heart to write it" (104). Of course, the novel *does* narrate Starbuck's failure. The subjunctive "were" of the prayer grammatically represses the truth of Starbuck's lack of fortitude, and this repression is, Ishmael implies in the democracy prayer, necessary for Ishmael to write his novel. This repression bespeaks the novel as a whole. As the truth of Starbuck's cowardice must be temporarily denied for Ishmael to continue with his narrative, so also radical democracy (personified by Steelkilt and Bulkington) must be submerged before the narration of Ahab's monomaniacal quest will proceed.

The rhetorical form of the prayer allows Ishmael to give his political wish a purely imaginary existence. As the democratic equivalence of George Washington and a cannibal can be expressed through humor, so can the hope in a democratic resistance to Ahab's usurpation of power be expressed in "prayer" form—if and only if we understand this prayer to be rhetorically excessive. Ishmael has said he might not "have the heart to write" his story if his protagonist turns out to lack the necessary fortitude, but his hero (Starbuck) fails, and Ishmael tells his story nonetheless. Ishmael could not tell his story if his discourse had to be realistic rather than rhetorically inflated in a way we sometimes call "Romantic." Ishmael does not pray to save democracy on the *Pequod*, since without a Steelkilt or a Bulkington democracy does not, Ishmael's prayer implies, have a prayer. Ishmael prays for the impossible just so that he may tell his story.

We can look to Melville's rhetorical arrangements and style, or we can see the same principle at work in terms of dramatic character substitution. The hopeful possibilities of Bulkington (he, like Steelkilt, with a name to advertise his bulk and strength; he who also disappears mysteriously) are displaced by the ominous appearance of Ahab. With the loss of Steelkilt/ Bulkington, there is a power vacuum on board the *Pequod*. Ishmael will certainly not fill it. George Washington-like Queequeg in no way imagines himself to be a player. The theme of radical democracy is momentarily embodied by Starbuck, but Ishmael develops his democracy prayer away from Starbuck, an insufficient object of this "unrealistic" desire.

As the prayer will demonstrate, the radical democracy that Ishmael values can exist only in increasingly abstract forms. Though presented in the context of romantic fiction, an allegorical struggle composed of heightened tones and stylistic flourishes is taking place; the struggle between the deck and lower levels of the *Town Ho* is the struggle at the center of American ideology: radical democracy fights for life against the degraded forms of this value system, forms that have clearly been usurped by owners. No specific audience member at the Golden Inn or other variety of censor silences the novel's democracy theme, and yet Melville's rhetorical arrangements and dramatic juxtapositions show how radical democratic hopes are squeezed out of the realm of the possible. The democratic hopes are silenced not by an incarnate politically interested censor, but by the evanescent spirit of *realpolitik*, with the result that the Ahabs of this world are considered "real" and therefore worthy of attention, while utopian urges and democracy prayers are merely distractions from these real dangers. This distinction between "realistic" and "unrealistic" political desires has a numbing effect on the sort of philosophical and social engagements that make radical democracy possible.[3] Note the ways in which the language of "reality" is juxtaposed with the language of "unreality" or "impossibility." When Ishmael speaks of democratic hopefuls such as Steelkilt and Bulkington, the language falls into either the tall-tale or the prayer mode, two ways of expressing a desire in a form that permits plausible denial. "Storytelling" and "realism" each displaces the other. Ishmael and certainly Melville are protected by the *form* of the discourse, insulated so that they themselves will not be understood as conduits of revolutionary agitation.

In its abstract, insulated form, the "democracy prayer" of the "Knights and Squires" chapter, just prior to Ahab's hope-shattering entrance, posits just the sort of man who might have prevented Ahab from sinking the *Pequod*. Though the democracy prayer does not name Steelkilt or his similarly assertive counterpart Bulkington by name, these two mariners best approach the idealized workers of the prayer: "If, then, to meanest mariners, and renegades and castaways, I shall hereafter ascribe high qualities, though dark; weave round them tragic graces; if even the most mournful, perchance the most abased, among them all, shall at times lift himself to the exalted mounts; if I shall touch that workman's arm with some etherial light [. . .]. Bear me out in it, thou great democratic God!" (104–5) The abstraction of this passage marks Ishmael's flight from the actuality wherein his desire will be frustrated into the sublime register in which it can indeed be true that some common man would become the savior of democracy.

The flight from unhappy reality in the democracy prayer is analogous in two ways to Ishmael's telling of Steelkilt's story in "The *Town-Ho*'s Story." On the one hand, the full-blown rhetoric is, in its exaggerated appeal to highest authority, like Ishmael's request to the Dons at the end of "The *Town-Ho*'s Story," for the largest Evangelists available. On the other hand, Ishmael swears that Steelkilt is real, that he has seen him since Radney's death, and so Ishmael's vow parallels the remnant of sincerity in the democracy prayer. Both Ishmael's odd oath and the appeal to God in the democracy prayer signal a displacement from human to divine authority, dramatizing the frustration of earthly possibilities. Though Ahab is not yet on stage, there is a doomed sense to the prayer as Ishmael utters it; the apologetic manner in which Ishmael idealizes the mariners foreshadows the repression of those mariners as political players on Ahab's ship.

The impossible ideal of democratic hope precedes the fall into "reality." Ishmael's God does *not* bear him out, for in the next chapter "Reality outran apprehension; Captain Ahab stood upon the quarter-deck" (109). Ahab's introduction is the reality against which Ishmael's democratic faith appears insubstantial. As Ishmael's impassioned plea is submerged into Ahab's reality, so are the hopes for the *Pequod* represented by a Steelkilt or a Bulkington submerged within *Moby-Dick*.

However, it will not suffice to conclude that the radical democracy theme is merely an undeveloped part of *Moby-Dick*, since the submerged political narrative powerfully influences the course of the novel as a whole. Many critics studying the form of Melville's novel have concluded that the author started one kind of book (an autobiographical narrative reminiscent of *White Jacket*) but finished another. Such readings frequently concede Melville's formal failure so that we may get on with the enjoyment of the novel, but it is premature to conclude that Melville merely lost control of his narrative. It is not enough to notice that *Moby-Dick* is a divided narrative; we should ask *why* Melville veered from one sort of story to another. To approach the novel with this question is to see that "The *Town-Ho*'s Story" contains the remnants of the political novel that *Moby-Dick* might have been.

As I have suggested, some readers argue that misplacement, not displacement, accounts for the strange matter of "The *Town-Ho*'s Story." Revision theories generally see "The *Town-Ho*'s Story" as an early version of *Moby-Dick* that Melville chose to incorporate into his lengthening narrative rather than discard. The revision theorists, those who see "The *Town-Ho*'s Story" as material from the Ur-*Moby-Dick* that Melville just did not want to scrap, see the kinds of parallelism between Steelkilt and Bulkington that I have been describing, but their explanations for Bulkington's bizarre "apotheosis" (98) either beg the question of why Melville revised, or stop short of the kind of inquiry I am recommending. That Bulkington disappears so suddenly and so strangely is an important part of the story, and readers who see this aspect as mere misplacement or revisionary replacement miss the novel's artful pattern of displacement. The juxtapositions of this novel are too well-honed to be mere accidents.

Concerns about the identity crisis within the covers of Melville's book began shortly after the end of World War II. The two-book theories of *Moby-Dick* can be traced back to Charles Olson's categorical statement in *Call Me Ishmael* that "*Moby-Dick* was two books," to Leon Howard's editorial commentaries on the novel's discontinuities, and to Howard P. Vincent's suggestion in *The Trying-Out of Moby Dick* that the original form of the novel was to be something like an expanded version of "The *Town-Ho's* Story." George R. Stewart's 1954 article "The Two Moby-Dicks" develops this approach by looking at the disposition of characters. Stewart bases his argument partly on records of Melville's composition process, such as it can be reconstructed, but the more interesting part has to do with "internal evidence." Stewart mentions Bulkington and Queequeg (two versions of the proletarian George Washington) as characters who were apparently slated for a starring role but were later demoted to walk-on and supporting roles. Stewart in no way discusses the political meanings of the Ur-*Moby-Dick,* but instead suggests that Melville altered his design because of a Shakespearian influence that took hold of him sometime after chapter twenty-five.

James Barbour, perhaps the most astute of the two-book readers, argues that the novel's "discontinuous narrative lines [. . .] are completed in 'The *Town-Ho's* Story,' the digressive Chapter 54 in the novel" (111). His discussion of the completion of the novel's discontinuous elements in "The *Town-Ho's* Story" is excellent, but it does not go on to ask the question, Why did Melville not go on to give Steelkilt's struggle a *novel*? As an account of the composition of *Moby-Dick,* Barbour's account is extremely useful, but he does not consider the narrative irregularities of "The *Town-Ho's* Story" that I have been discussing. Harrison Hayford is one of the most recent revision theorists: "I think Bulkington, in Melville's mind, outgrew his station, 'becoming,' in his heroic role, Ahab. For if Bulkington was a heroic harpooner, at what was his harpoon, in more than a routine whaleman's way, to be pointed? At the White Whale some call Moby Dick?" (156). If we read carefully, there is nothing in *Moby-Dick* to suggest this last possibility, but if Hayford had considered the most striking duplication in the novel, the reappearance of Bulkington in the person of Steelkilt, he might have considered a different harpoon target. All of the two-book theories note narrative inconsistencies and demonstrate that Melville started one sort of book but finished another, but only Charles H. Foster has offered a convincing explanation as to why Melville swerved from one sort of book to another.[4] Of the Melville critics who discuss "The *Town-Ho*'s Story" in relation to the two-book theories, Foster makes the best case, since he is able not only to describe narrative discontinuities, but to explain Melville's odd replacements, omissions, and other aesthetic maneuvers. Foster alone has been sensitive to what Melville *continues to leave out*.

Foster, borrowing a phrase from Allen Tate, comments on Melville's hide-and-seek strategy: "Indeed, 'plotless drama of withdrawal' seems just the phrase for Melville in *Moby-Dick* when we realize the great energy and skill with which he advanced toward a clarifying of the American dilemma in 1850–51 and the almost equal energy and skill with which he covered his tracks, withdrawing into ambiguities and symbols difficult even yet to decipher" (34). Foster goes on to argue that we must replace the "two-book" theory of *Moby-Dick* with a three-book conception: "Understanding that *Moby-Dick* was a three-storied work and that its top story is a fable of democratic protest, we can assign to their proper place in the structure and meaning the radical eruptions such as Father Mapple's sermon, explain the subtle transformation of the White Whale, appreciate why there should be a sharp discrepancy between the disenchanted Ishmael of "The Whiteness of the Whale" and the Ishmael of other chapters expressing passionate conviction" (35). Foster's 1961 article made a powerful case for a political revision of the two-book theories, but, unfortunately, subsequent articles developed the question away from politics.

The repressions in the narrative of *Moby-Dick* are very much a part of that text and are as worthy of our attention as plot, character, style, and genre.[5] Ishmael's six-inch "stoneless grave of Bulkington" may not at first appear to have political or ideological significance, but when we refuse to forget the political consequences of the "unmentionable," the full sentence takes on a different ring: "Wonderfullest things are ever unmentionable; deep memories yield no epitaphs; this six-inch chapter is the stoneless grave of Bulkington" (97). To conclude uncritically that Bulkington just drowns, as more than one thoughtful critic does, is to skip the overarching political dimension of *Moby-Dick*. Bulkington does not merely disappear from the narrative; he is a repressed element in that narrative that returns in "The *Town-Ho*'s Story."

Why "The Town-Ho's Story" Is Submerged

In developing Foster's reading of the novel, my question is not "Why *was* 'The *Town-Ho*'s Story' submerged?" but, rather, "Why *is* it submerged?" The first question has to do with composition and plot choices the author made in constructing the novel; the second brings us to the sublimated form of political dissent in the novel that speaks not only to crises of Melville's day but to conflicts of our own.

The story is one in which violence results from the failure of the political process; that it cannot be told without the use of obscure phrasing, mysterious symbols, and a deus ex machina that goes by the name of Moby Dick suggests an unconscious or at least "unspeakable" dimension not only to the chapter and the novel, but to American political reality as well. Melville offers this suggestion most politely. If the Dons are the image of "owners" that shape the telling of "The *Town-Ho's* Story," they are certainly a far cry from the rude Radney. In fact, these owners come across, in Ishmael's recollection, as pleasant men, and there is no direct suggestion in Ishmael or Melville's narrative that the Spanish Dons of "The *Town-Ho's* Story" are tyrannical.

If we ask History instead of Fiction who the Dons were, we get a less rosy picture. "Many of Peru's problems," the *Columbia Encyclopedia* tells us, "have been inherited from the Spanish Conquest, which might be said never to have finished." That the government who gave little or no voice to creoles and oppressed the Indians was so efficient in its exploitive practices "explains why Peru was the last of the South American colonies to gain independence from Spain" (1523–24). Contrasting the rude Radney with the courteous Dons disguises the general point of Ishmael's story, that oppressive owners will get their comeuppance. One would hardly get the idea from Ishmael's Dons that Peru of the 1840s and 1850s was undergoing a crisis in some ways parallel to the American crisis of approximately the same time. Until slavery was abolished in 1854, there was a total of 25,000 Negro slaves in Peru, a number that was considered an inadequate force for labor on the haciendas. In 1849 Chinese workers were brought into Peru as bonded labor. "These were," writes H. E. Maude, "brought to Peru under appalling conditions in overcrowded ships, often called 'floating hells,' and those who survived the voyage were sold in Callao to the highest bidder" (1). Negro emancipation, the curtailment of Chinese immigration, and a loosening grip on the native American Indian populations led to a crisis in labor, higher prices, and, eventually, the assault on Polynesia by Peruvian slave-ships. Domination over labor seems to have been the foremost problem on the minds of men very much like Ishmael's Dons.

But "The *Town-Ho's* Story" does not *say* that the Dons were oppressors, nor can Ishmael tell the story of revolt without his array of Freudian displacements and narrative containments. This sublimation of revolutionary desire can be accounted for in part by considering the idea that the representation of violence of the oppressed against the oppressor is taboo, and this is the heart of the matter.[6] As James Scully writes in *Line Break*, his argument for class-conscious and politically engaged poetry, "only the violence against the oppressed may be acknowledged. The artist is stuck: confirming and reinforcing victimization, unable to admit to, never mind celebrate, the concrete struggle to destroy the system that produces such stultifying misery" (90). Scully's suspicion that our sense of literature filters out overt conflict is supported when we look at nineteenth-century American literature. When representations of revolutionary violence do occur in canonical fictions, they are contained within either a narrative or a critical framework in such a way as to neutralize the representation. The various representations of liberatory violence in Stowe's *Uncle Tom's Cabin*, Douglass's *Narrative of the Life of an American Slave*, and *Moby-Dick* all confirm Scully's observation.

Harriet Beecher Stowe and Frederick Douglass both represent slaves who physically resist slave-masters, though in slightly different ways. In *Uncle Tom's Cabin* the runaway slave George speaks for the use of violence as a path to freedom: "'I *do* run a risk, but'—he threw open his overcoat, and showed two pistols and a bowie-knife. 'There!' he said; 'I'm ready for 'em! Down the south I never *will* go. No! if it comes to that, I can earn myself at least six feet of free soil'" (125). Even within this highly melodramatic novel, George's will to violent self-defense is presented as an excessive passion; he has a lot of *character*. Though George shoots a man to defend his own freedom, the wounded slave-hunter recuperates as a better person in fairy-tale fashion, and George's violence is ultimately eclipsed by Uncle Tom's martyrdom. George's spirited oration is, in the larger design of the novel, a comic interlude. Robert S. Levine describes the containment and transformation of George's political violence that, I would argue, makes the runaway's inclusion in the narrative possible: "In important ways [. . .] the emphasis on evangelicalism, with its millennial promise, serves to contain the novel's more troubling insurrectionary dimension, particularly as embodied by the rebels George Harris and Cassy. The novel concludes with a series of Christian conversions on the part of the rebels, and with Stowe, through Harris, endorsing African colonization as a possible solution to America's racial problems" (145). The conflict-ridden political theme is ultimately subsumed into God's larger design, as happens in "The *Town-Ho*'s Story" when Steelkilt's murderous desire is refigured as a "a certain wondrous, inverted visitation of one of those so called judgements of God" (208), namely the white whale Moby Dick. In this "visitation," as in the Freudian dream, distortion ennables the problem message to bypass the censor, and so the visitation is "inverted."

Moby-Dick, like most American literary works that have attained "classic" status, sublimates adversarial politics within art. In those stories where the author has adamantly refused to submerge the political theme, the critic may supply the distortion ex post facto. In his *Narrative of the Life of an American Slave*, Frederick Douglass presents a stronger challenge to Scully's argument that violence against the oppressor is taboo than we find in *Moby-Dick*, but prominent critics have critically submerged objectionable material. Douglass does not represent violent self-defense as humorously excessive, nor is the necessity of violence in any way pushed into the margins of his account: "from whence came the spirit I don't know—I resolved to fight; and, suiting my action to the resolution, I seized Covey hard by the throat; and as I did so, I rose. He held on to me, and I to him. My resistance was so entirely unexpected, that Covey seemed taken all aback. He trembled like a leaf" (1913). One might argue that Douglass does not commit violence, that he merely holds Covey (as one reader has suggested to me), but Covey certainly would not recognize his slave's action in such forgiving terms. That the violence is completely unexpected—both by the oppressor and the oppressed—suggests that the sort of ideological muffling described by Scully takes place at various levels. The effect can be found among writers, readers, and even among participant-observer narrators. If the taboo is challenged at one level, the restriction can be maintained at another— but for Douglass the liberatory violence and its subsequent representation without apology are essential in undoing the work of this ideology.

Douglass challenges the taboo against liberatory violence. Criticism has traditionally corrected stubborn authors who fail to conform, and so we may add critical distortion to narrative containment. Either the author disguises taboo material or the work may be distorted in its subsequent reception. Douglass, thus, does not frustrate the proposed model in which the taboo on liberatory violence functions as an ideological censor. He complicates it. According to the model, Douglass's representation of violence should be regarded as non-literature. Douglass's narrative is currently included in *The Norton Anthology of American Literature*, which certainly guarantees its status as "literature" in the American classroom—at which point criticism comes to the rescue. In *The Unusable Past* Russell Reising acknowledges the rise in Douglass's literary stock, but also points out that we must look at the specific ways in which previously excluded materials are belatedly received: "Douglass' place in the American canon has, over the past decade, grown increasingly more secure. Less certain, however, is just *how* Douglass' *Narrative* is to be situated in American literary history" (256). One condition of Douglass's inclusion seems to be a deemphasis of his assertion that physical struggle is necessary to freedom. Reising criticizes a well-known reader of Douglass:

> Houston Baker Jr.'s assertion that "by adapting language as his instrument for extracting meaning from nothingness, being from existence, Douglass becomes a public figure" needs some qualification [. . .]. It is, of course, true that the publication of the *Narrative* launched Douglass's career as a "public" figure. But, while Baker stresses language as Douglass's prime vehicle in becoming public (though he does not adhere to a simple or privatistic notion of language as such), Douglass himself renders language as an abstract medium subordinate to the externalization of that self (partially a linguistic construct) in physical battle. (264)

In Baker's interpretation the utopian realm of language displaces the inherently conflictual realm of political struggle. H. Bruce Franklin has also criticized the academic reception of the *Narrative* in *Prison Literature in America*, noting especially the taboo against liberatory violence. One critic quoted by Franklin finds "irony in the situation in which Douglass must reduce his conflict with slave holders to a question of brute strength and physical violence in order to assert his 'manhood'" (quoted in Scully 90). This reading cannot stand for all criticism, but it does suggest the lengths to which the academic response may go to avoid a taboo. Political action, by definition having to do with conflict,[7] is an embarrassment in literature, and so literary critics often filter out politically charged elements, such as when Baker filters out Douglass's political use of force against an owner.[8]

While some would dismiss Scully's arguments at the outset because he is an engaged Marxist (and is therefore "grinding an axe"), John Fraser, a non-radical critic, reaches conclusions similar to Scully's in his study *Violence in the Arts*. Against the liberal ideology that all violence is unwarranted, Fraser points out that those who hold such views depend on social institutions to obscure the violent defense of their own privileges: "far from being mindless, violence is usually the cutting edge of ideas and ideologies" (162). Fraser also reflects on the political implications of the ideological constraints governing words like "violence": "Politically respectable violence is not considered to be violence at all and the term is reserved for actions that are denied political significance or are felt to possess the wrong kind. [. . .] The military and the police, for example, are not violent organizations" (157). Much of Ishmael's tall-tale humor and melodrama are skillfully manipulated styles that disguise Steelkilt's revolt as "politically respectable" violence, and his violent tale is respectable or at least permissible because the Dons find the story "incredible."

The most respectable violence within *Moby-Dick* (according the socially conservative ideological standards invoked by Fraser) is that of Ahab. Representations of physical violence are rare on board the *Pequod*, mainly because Ahab knows how to use words ("The Quarter-Deck") and cash ("Surmises") as substitutes for force. Still, Ahab is aware that words and cash may not be enough, since, "of all tools used in the shadow of the moon, men are most apt to get out of order" (183). After "The Quarter-Deck," in which Ahab "impulsively, it is probable, and perhaps somewhat prematurely revealed the prime but private purpose of the *Pequod*'s voyage" (184), Ahab knows that he has "laid himself open to the unanswerable charge of usurpation." Ahab's "impulsive" speech is, then, a kind of leak that he must plug, since there is no legal question or uncertainty-of-Hamlet about the situation: "his crew if so disposed, and to that end competent, could refuse all further obedience to him, and even violently wrest from him the command." But Starbuck is highly uncertain, and his uncertainty reflects the ideological taboo concerning violence against authority. The crew can only "violently wrest from him the command" if they can first apply to their own actions the word "violently" and still complete the action. Starbuck shrinks from the word.

Starbuck does not fear politically respectable violence. He is more or less ferocious against whales ("The First Lowering," "The Hyena"), which makes great sense since, as Fraser notes, legally sanctioned violence is given an entirely affirmative name. The label "violent" never hinders Starbuck in his whale hunting because whale hunting is not called violence by whale hunters. The social construction of violence, then, protects Starbuck's vocation as whale hunter, but the same ideological value system leaves him politically powerless when it comes to challenging Ahab's authority. Starbuck would be well within his legal rights in forcefully taking command of the *Pequod*, but he is inhibited in just this attempt by the thought that he should be "violent," as his cry to heaven reveals: "'Is heaven a murderer when its lightning strikes a would-be murderer in his bed, tindering sheets and skin together?—And would I be a murderer, then, if——' and slowly, stealthily, and half sideways looking, he placed the loaded musket's end against the door" (422). Starbuck cannot stand the strain of this legally justifiable violence, and so he puts the musket back in its rack. He is blocked not by a door or a law, but by a concept in his own mind. That "only the violence against the oppressed may be acknowledged" is a truth also well represented by an earlier scene in the novel: "Ahab seized a loaded musket from the rack (forming part of most South-Sea-men's cabin furniture), and pointing it towards Starbuck, exclaimed: 'There is one God that is Lord over the earth, and one Captain that is lord over the *Pequod*.—On deck!'" (394). Clearly, Ahab suffers no inhibition dividing him from his own violent impulses. No sailor is flogged, though all but one die as a result of Ahab's monomania. The struggle between Starbuck and Ahab illustrates the ideological protection offered to "authority" in the United States, and so political novelists in America must begin by considering the "Starbuck problem."

Melville's political activism in *Moby-Dick* is to describe the ideological traps that lay before the political writer, and so we should never confuse Melville with his congenial but politically ineffective narrator. The symbolic equation between Steelkilt and Moby Dick manifests itself in Ishmael's consciousness in a most uncertain way, but the experiences he relates have not at all made him into a political actor of the sort who could challenge an Ahab. He does not appear to have been radicalized by his experiences, and he confesses the limits of his own understanding, in language that foreshadows Freud, in a famous passage:

> What the White Whale was to them, or how to their unconscious understandings, also, in some dim, unsuspected way, he might have seemed the gliding great demon of the seas of life,—all this to explain, would be to dive deeper than Ishmael can go. The subterranean miner that works in us all, how can one tell whither leads his shaft by the ever shifting, muffled sound of his pick? Who does not feel the irresistible arm drag? For one, I gave myself up to the abandonment of the time and the place, but while yet all arush to encounter the whale, could see naught in that brute but the deadliest ill. (162)

Moby-Dick is not a political *Pilgrim's Progress*, and to read it as Ishmael's conversion narrative would be silly. Ishmael's ambiguous and suggestive phrasing suggests that he has been changed in some way by his experience: he saw the whale as malevolent at "that time and the place," but he is not Steelkilt, nor was he meant to be. Ishmael, rather, is the compromised storyteller. Through the creation of Ishmael, Melville ingeniously explores not the costs of but rather the impediments to writing a political novel.

Thus, two stories exist: one a covert political novel and the other an epic vision that is in many ways political but that is as much or more a philosophical quest.[9] The novel as a whole offers a political unconscious for discerning readers, a "submerged political novel" that deals imaginatively with the theme of political rebellion but that ultimately withholds that theme from the main action of the novel. The submerged political novel expresses the anger of a political novel, is structured around a political conflict, or anatomizes society in terms of its political organs, but at the same time its most significant political action is a withdrawal from overt political activity. For reasons that vary from author to author and text to text, the submerged political novel tends toward a conservative form of engagement with the world, even when the submerged themes bespeak the nobility of the most revolutionary sentiments.

Moby-Dick and other submerged political novels like it upset our experience of literature by refiguring art as politics-in-hibernation, and the submerged political novel can be read, in Ellison's words, as "a covert preparation for a more overt action." The risks of writing an overt political novel will be discussed in the next chapter; the greatest risk of writing a covert political novel is that the covert preparations will never result in an overt action, in which case a book's hesitations on the brink must figure into our overall judgment of it. The submerged political novel will avoid many of the inherent risks of overt political fiction, but when we compare it *in political terms* to the overt political novel, the submerged political novel appears to hide behind the motto, "Call me Literature." After writing *Moby-Dick*, Herman Melville boasted by letter to Hawthorne that he had written a wicked book and yet felt spotless as a lamb. By submerging his political passion deep within the text, Melville in a sense kept his hands clean, and if his great novel was unappreciated for more than half a century, it was not because the author was perceived as a political radical.

Notes

1. Foster argues in "Something in Emblems: A Reinterpretation of *Moby-Dick*" that "Discovery of Melville's antislavery theme, of his commitment to radical democracy, furnishes the key not only to the meanings but to the aesthetic properties of the final third of the book" (35). As does Rogin in his 1983 study *Subversive Genealogy*, Foster finds conflicts between Melville's familial loyalties and political positions to explain both the radical democracy theme in *Moby-Dick* and the symbolism obscuring radical themes. Foster attempts to correlate the main

characters of *Moby-Dick* with politicians involved in the crisis of 1850, as does Heimert in "*Moby-Dick* and American Political Symbolism." Heimert quotes heavily from the *Congressional Globe, Appendix* to show that "Ishmael" and "Ahab" were fighting words in the 1840s and 1850s, and that America's imperial "destiny" was often at issue. Duban develops the political identity of Starbuck in "'A Pantomime of Action': Starbuck and American Whig Dissidence." He identifies Starbuck in terms of American political parties in response to the war with Mexico: "Melville's portrait of Starbuck [. . .] comprises a study not merely of one individual's anguished indecision but, allegorically, of what many Americans came to regard as the impotent and valor-ruined response of the Whig Party to President Polk's so-called war of indemnity against Mexico (1846–48)" (433). For an argument relating Melville's radical democracy to the European 1848, see Rogin's chapter in *Subversive Genealogy*. Karcher pays more attention than most critics to the political content of *Moby-Dick*: "The outcome of 'The *Town-Ho*'s Story' thus exhibits the same tensions we have noticed in *Mardi* and *White-Jacket*—once more Melville's strong fellow-feeling for men he equates with slaves vies with his deep-seated reluctance to defy authority" (60). Because Karcher does not always carefully attend to complexities of the narrative framework, she makes a hasty equation between Melville and Ishmael; also, she is at times killing the messenger in her political criticisms of Melville. For an in-depth critique of new historicist readings of Melville that saddle Melville with his narrator's attitudes, see Duban ("Chipping with a Chisel"). Morrison's challenge to American literary criticism, "Unspeakable Things Unspoken: The Afro-American Presence in American Literature," also argues for a political reading of Melville, one in which the novel's primary allegory is of the catastrophic introduction of racist ideology into the American dream. I discuss Morrison's political construction of American literature in chapter 5. See also Spanos's *The Errant Art of Moby-Dick* for a book-length discussion of the relationships between the cold war, the canon of American literature, and Melville's novel.

2. See Kosok, "Ishmael's Audience in 'The *Town-Ho*'s Story.'" Gilmore suggests in *American Romanticism and the Marketplace* an alternative view in which the Dons represent Melville's ideal audience. Surprisingly, Railton has little to say about this chapter in his justly praised *Authorship and Audience: Literary Performance in the American Renaissance*, only mentioning Kosok's article. Railton is skeptical of Melville's "dollars damn me" complaint and generally diagnoses Melville's problematic relationship with his audience as the result of his infantile approach to communication.

3. Jameson criticizes the way formalist readers stop their interpretation at what Marxists call "reification" (a kind of ideologically produced reality-effect) as though it were a brick wall. He objects to "their failure to account for the initial numbness of our perception in the first place, their inability to furnish a sufficiently historical explanation for that ontological deficiency which they can only understand in ethical or aesthetic terms" (*Marxism and Form* 374).

4. Foster: "Melville expressed the democratic revolt agitating him in the spring and summer of 1851 through radical passages and sometimes chapters inserted into the previously written portions of *Moby-Dick*. These interpolations occur too infrequently to color very seriously our reading of the semi-realistic, semi-comic chapters introducing Ishmael and Queequeg. [. . .] Furthermore, the obvious passion with which they were written makes it probable that towards the close of *Moby-Dick* Melville adapted the tragedy of Ahab and the Whale to a more radical meaning than has been suspected" (17).

5. Jameson offers a theory for reading such silences and argues better than most gap-mongers for the necessity of such an inquiry: "the literary structure, far from being completely realized on any one of its levels tilts powerfully into the underside of *impensé* or *non-dit*, in short, into the very political unconscious, of the text, such that the latter's semes—when reconstructed according to this model of ideological closure—themselves then insistently direct us to the informing power of forces or contradictions which the text seeks in vain wholly to control" (*Political Unconscious* 49). Jameson is not, however, discussing the author's conscious intentions, whereas I show that Melville consciously and artistically includes gaps and silences to make readers question the story as it is told.

Jameson's emphasis on the political unconscious's ideological alterity has been criticized by some of his most sympathetic readers. In his critical though mainly affirmative review of Jameson's interpretive method, Jonathan Arac notes that the term "political unconscious" "leads a strangely subdued existence throughout the book" and that Jameson's method of historicizing Conrad's fiction represses more political history than that of Irving Howe (263).

6. For a discussion of ideology and violence in nineteenth-century American literature, see Fisher (*Hard Facts* 22–87). For a new historicist demonstration of how Reagan administration ideological narratives make *state* violence seem acceptable in anti-Communist Latin American countries, see Folena's "Philologists, Witches, and Stalinistas."

7. See the introduction, especially note 6 and the paragraph containing it.

8. It could be argued that what Baker circumnavigates is not politics per se, but physical combat; however, note that only liberatory violence must be apologized for in the academic presentation of the scene.

9. "Thus, two stories exist: one for the public and the other secret, for the initiate" (Sachs 119).

3

How to Read a Revolutionary Novel:
The Iron Heel

During a time when Melville was largely forgotten, London read *Moby-Dick* again and again.
   —Jay Martin

As a reader of Melville, London knew or should have known that you pay a price if you fight city hall. While some novelists try to tell all the truth but tell it slant, others attempt to honor the Quaker demand that we "speak truth to power," and London is of this sort—except that he does not stop with "speaking truth" but insists that it is crucial to act. All aspects of London's life—his literary style, his personal reputation, his fictional personae—are charged with this activism, and it is largely the valence of machismo around so much of what he has written that has disqualified him from the critical attention he deserves within American literature. He does not have the skeptical detachment of more highly praised authors. As a spokesman for "proletarian philosophy," London is anything but indirect, rather more akin to Melville's harpoon-throwing Quakers than to the landlubber variety.[1]

In creating and publishing *The Iron Heel* London knew that he was writing a particularly direct and activist form of political novel and that he was gambling with his reputation to do so. This book presented no apologies to literary critics or others who would resist the mixing of political struggle and literary culture, and for this reason it faced greater critical resistance than other political novels written during the same period: "London spent several months writing *The Iron Heel*, fully aware that no publisher might accept it, that no magazine would dare to serialize it, that it would intensify the attacks upon him in the bourgeois press and seriously impair the sale of his other works" (Foner 95).[2] As Foner notes, London wrote with the knowledge that his political activities would cost him in his career as a writer, and we may say more generally that any writer, radical or conservative, who behaves as a politician between the covers of a novel risks his or her status as a literary artist.[3] From the moment the novel was published, attacks appeared, but these occurred mainly in media outlets committed to the economic status quo.

London could safely assume that the "bourgeois press" would attack him, but what was the response of the radical press, and how did it shape his writing? London was frustrated by the overall reception of his novel-as-political-action, and reviews of this novel were in fact mixed. There was considerable resistance to his socialist message, and London shaped his novel in response to this resistance.

Politics is but one of several dimensions of any given work, though we tend to forget this when reading a revolutionary novel. When we forget that political motivation is one among several, we impair our ability to assess the novel's strengths and weaknesses properly. In "Why I Write" Orwell lists four key motivations, and this four-way division of the political writer's motivations can help us to read *The Iron Heel* in a measured way. Orwell's four categories will structure my discussion of *The Iron Heel* to demonstrate how we may interpret a revolutionary novel without reducing it to a bumper sticker. According to Orwell, a writer puts words on the page, (1) for the sake of pure egotism, (2) out of aesthetic enthusiasm, (3) for a reason Orwell calls "historical purpose," and (4) in pursuit of a political purpose. Orwell's Aristotelian division of the writer's motivation into efficient, formal, material, and final causes can be applied to any writer's work, not just to political fiction, but Orwell's variation on this framework is especially useful to the discussion of the most overt sort of political novel, that which runs the greatest risk of being dismissed or critically misconstrued.

Orwell called his first cause "pure egotism" and gave the infant's primal whine as a possible origin of this motivation. People want to be heard, and it is not always "the principle of the thing" that motivates the language. Rather than discussing any such urge, this section will examine some of the ways in which the supposedly "primal" aspects of the author Jack London are socially constructed (or, at least, reconstructed) in book reviews, advertisements, and various other media. London's macho persona was helpful to him as a political writer, even though for many current readers it is a distinct liability.

Orwell's second category "aesthetic enthusiasm" would for many readers refer to a world apart from politics, but notice the line from Milton that Orwell chooses to illustrate aesthetic delight: "So hee with difficulty and labour hard / Moved on: with difficulty and labour hee" (Orwell 1:2). Is this art for art's sake? Orwell mentions the pure ornament of the extra "e" in "hee," and then there is the repetition and inversion in the pair of lines, but more than anything else there is the genesis of "labour" and, therefore, of class struggle. A discussion of London's aesthetic enthusiasm shall, likewise, demonstrate the ways in which London used supposedly apolitical formal innovations to accentuate his political purposes and also to fend off anticipated critical attacks.

"Historical purpose" is for Orwell basically truth-telling in spite of all the forms of political pressure that warp much of what is written. A political novelist can play the role of political journalist, but with the journalistic role comes the burden of factual credibility. London's novel certainly speaks back to the voices of the bourgeois press that, London knew, would silence him and other radical critics of monopoly capitalism. *The Iron Heel* shows how various political words and phrases were contested in the first decade of this century, and its ways of challenging the everyday language in which Americans had been defining themselves is clearly in line with London's political purpose: to resist increasingly oppressive capitalist government and to aid and abet the yet-unformed proletarian resistance.

Orwell's categories are partitioned for the sake of greater understanding, but the aspects of the work he thus organizes are not segregated in any absolute way. Only by going beyond the banal equation of personal and political experience may we observe nuances in the complex interrelationships between the personal and the political. After deploying Orwell's first three categories to show how political issues have been inextricably linked with biographical, aesthetic, and social dimensions of the text, we will see how London has harnessed all of these aspects of fictional world-making to his political purpose.

A novel does not come with an FDA label listing all its motives, by-products, and secret ingredients. *The Iron Heel* was a novel intended as propaganda in support of the proletarian revolution, but a hostile reader could view it merely as the expression of London's essentially private hatreds or obsessions, since the most efficient way to discredit an overt and activist political novel is to explain the work as an expression of the author's private or even unconscious difficulties.[4] That is, we may take a personal view of the work as a way of avoiding political questions. Without flattening the differences between politics and personal life, we may notice how London's personality, such as he and his publicists put it together, was at once a strength and a liability in his political struggles.

Pure Egotism: Individualism as a Political Tool

Call London Ishmael?[5] When the narrator of *Moby-Dick* says "Call me Ishmael," we know the name has been used as a term of opprobrium to single out those outcasts who despise the group. Ishmael, as the name was used in American newspapers before the Civil War and in other contexts, is the archetypal nay-sayer.[6] Were we to list the "Ishmaelite" authors of American literature, most would not automatically think of London.

However: the reviewer from the *Morning News* (Dallas, 6 Apr. 1908) complained that "That talented Ishmaelite, Jack London, has again turned his attention to those social conditions against which his hand has ever been raised in protest." The review for *The Banner* (Nashville, 29 Feb. 1908) agreed wholeheartedly: "The fact about Jack is that he is more Ishmaelite than Socialist. If he should be born again in the supposed advanced era 419 B.O.M. [Brotherhood Of Man: the utopian future predicted in the novel], he will be against the established order." The novel is doubly reduced: first it is called a tract instead of a novel, and then, regarding it as argument rather than art, the critic resorts to an unsupported ad hominem attack to explain psychologically and thereby neutralize politically the novel's author: London is called an "Ishmaelite" or a neurotic. This critical naming strategy was used against London with only partial success but would in subsequent decades become a regular ploy to discredit overtly political writers.[7]

The romanticized outsider is probably the most typical character in American fiction. Call him Ishmael. Or Invisible Man, or Sula. The tradition of the Adamic individual (the individual conceived in pure opposition to society) is an advantage to the political novelist in that he or she is commonly understood as being *against* the world, but this tradition is a bane to engaged novelists as well since the hero is, by definition, in a weak position to change society. In a partially successful strategy, London capitalized on literary individualism in his own struggle against the iron heel.

London often presented himself and was packaged by his publishers as a tough-guy writer, an atavist and a Nietzschean —a presence leaping and vaulting about on the literary landscape. Rugged, pushy, and macho are the kind of terms most often attached to the name "Jack London" and to the title *The Iron Heel*. Literary history does not remember him for trenchant ambiguity as it does Herman Melville. The Macmillan Company capitalized on London's machismo, publishing a biographical pamphlet entitled "Jack London: His Life and Literary Work."[8] Just after the title page there is a picture of London and his skipper in front of the not-yet-completed Snark, the ship that Jack and Charmian London planned to sail around the world. The first page of text reinforces the image of London as a kind of superman, telling us that "The backing of sturdy ancestral stock enabled young Jack early to prove his mastery over environment," and that "He seems endowed with the force that enables a man not only to prevent being pushed out of his true self by untoward circumstances, but even to shape them to his own ends" ("Jack London" 1910, 5). The sentence about London's "ancestral stock" legitimizes London in literal as well as figurative ways since London was born out of wedlock, and Macmillan's overall presentation of the author was presumably designed to reassure those would-be readers who feared that bookishness marked one as effeminate. Hirsute and vigorous language protects author and reader alike.

Macmillan wanted London's readers to see him as the sort of "real man" who could live out every dream, and London is characterized throughout as a successful competitive individualist. The image of London we receive from these Macmillan publications and similar documents is so pure that, in the age of the spin doctor, we begin to suspect a key rhetorical displacement, as if London the man were the attention-getting alter ego of London the socialist. The pamphlet, which dwells heavily on the Nietzschean-heroic aspect and pretty much ignores the Muckraker persona, quotes London on the joys of masculinity:

> To be a man was to write man in large capitals on my heart. To adventure like a man, and do a man's work (even for a boy's pay)—these were things that reached right in and gripped hold of me as no other thing could. And I looked ahead into long vistas of a hazy and interminable future, in which, playing what I conceived to be a man's game, I should continue to travel with unfailing health, without accidents, and with muscles ever vigorous. As I say, this future was interminable. I could only see myself raging through life without end like one of Nietzsche's blond beasts, lustfully roving and conquering by sheer superiority and strength. (5)

This narcissistic self-appreciation of individualistic virtue is quoted in the Macmillan pamphlet but is clearly repudiated by the note in *The Iron Heel* that refers to Nietzsche as "the mad philosopher of the nineteenth century of the Christian Era" (6). The quotation in the pamphlet becomes even more interesting when we know its origin, London's essay "How I Became a Socialist," wherein London also tells us that, before his "conversion," "my joyous individualism was dominated by the orthodox bourgeois ethics. I read the bourgeois papers, listened to the bourgeois preachers, and shouted at the sonorous platitudes of the bourgeois politicians" (Foner 363). Macmillan not only shielded readers from London's political ideas: the publishers also edited London's already published words so as to leave out the intended irony of London's "macho" self-representation. Thus, literary individualism was, for Macmillan at least, a way of stripping the writer of commitments.

London's persona made good copy. He was celebrated in newspapers across the United States, especially in California, for living the active life in a most public fashion. Macmillan banked on London's reputation for manliness as evidenced by the half-dozen or so "book review" pamphlets they put out that contain mention of *The Iron Heel. The Monthly List of Macmillan Books* of the first months of 1908 briefly mentions social revolution but mainly exploits London's reputation as an adventurer in its advertisement for the book: "Quite apart from its significance as a document or a prophecy, it is perhaps the most exciting story of adventure that Mr. London has ever written—and that is to say much."

The joys of virility are not what they once were.[9] The *Übermensch* persona strikes many of today's readers as unreal or cartoonish, but London has been discredited for many readers also because his rhetorical appeal has been so strongly associated with more specific "fallen" ideologies. Political violence, even terrorism, is sanctioned in *The Iron Heel*, though the violence is ultimately presented as a form of self-defense (since the capitalists have always already used it first), and so readers today are not looking for Mr. Everhard. The figure of the invincible man survives and even flourishes in Hollywood cinema but is much despised everywhere else. "Stalinism" is a universally recognized shorthand term for political brutality in journalistic media. Stalin, meaning "man of steel," was the name taken by a young editor of the newly formed publication *Pravda* in 1913; Stalin and Everhard, the two proletarian strong-men, come into print a half-decade apart. The notion of strong blood coursing through the body of the vigorous man was anything but unique to London (these were the days of Teddy Roosevelt and the Rough Riders), but these images and attitudes as forms of political appeal are tainted in the latter twentieth century. We are bound to associate "conquering by sheer superiority of strength" with Gestapo or KGB agents rather than with those who would resist the iron heel.[10]

In the postwar period the writer who attempts to "push" the reader in any direction is recognized as an ideologue, not an artist. London uses his literary persona to political advantage in *The Iron Heel* and other social writings, but pure egotism alone would hardly count as a strength, and Orwell describes the most personal aspect of the writing most dismissively as "pure egotism" as if to merely get the troublesome matter out of the way. How did London use *art* to defend his message against the sort of attacks he knew it would encounter?

Aesthetic Enthusiasm and Dual Perspective *in* The Iron Heel

Political fictions that exclude all perspectives except for the "party line" sacrifice the element of surprise upon which so much literary response depends. Give the Devil his due: some might argue that both sides of a given controversy should be made equally appealing, lest the artist be liable to charges of having a conflict of interest, of somehow distorting "reality" for the sake of politics. The main problem with a pushy form of discourse such as the revolutionary novel, then, is that it risks being dismissed as a monologic rant, and London's most dedicated defenders[11] assert that *The Iron Heel* errs in this way: "Viewed strictly from the artistic standpoint, *The Iron Heel* is—except for the vivid description of mob violence near the end—a lifeless novel. The hero, haranguing his various audiences with his pretentious ideological pieties, is a relentless boor" (Labor 65). But should we (and could we) look at *The Iron Heel* "strictly from an artistic standpoint"? When we recognize the interrelations between political matters and what seem to be purely aesthetic decisions about literary form, we notice that London achieves variety in *The Iron Heel* through his application of dual perspective.

The Iron Heel employs the "found manuscript" fiction to inaugurate the dual perspective. One perspective, that of Avis Everhard, is the heroic perspective. Avis Everhard reports on her own experiences, but she is mainly concerned to give an account of her husband Ernest Everhard. The other perspective is that of historian Anthony Meredith, written several centuries after Avis's narration of Ernest Everhard's abortive attempt to overthrow the government. Through the corrective lenses of the historian Meredith, we see the shortcomings of Avis Everhard's glorification of her husband. Meredith offers a fuller historical perspective within which to figure the discreet actions of the individual.

The art that makes *The Iron Heel* interesting to contemporary readers develops almost entirely from London's use of the dual perspective. The tension between these perspectives replicates exactly those conflicts an individual would have to endure to resist totalitarian oppression. Whether we speak of resistance to the Nazis in Vichy France or resistance to totalitarian rule in various novels, the success of resistance requires both individual sacrifice and collective action. "Individual sacrifice" presupposes heroism or heroic loss, and yet "collective action" often depends on the suppression of the individual viewpoint. Both approaches are absolutely necessary, and yet these values subvert one another when placed in immediate contact. Given such difficulties, the politician and the writer must bring about an orderly mixture of opposed forces, a *discordia concors*. The political writer must do this even when conjuring apocalyptic accounts of the near future.

Dual perspective allows antagonistic yet interdependent modes of political resistance to coexist in ways that do not impede the reader's pleasure. Readers may at once recognize that the Oligarchy, the group of wealthy men who control the country and persecute the members of the worker-resistance, is not the kind of historical entity that can be dealt with by a lone gunman, yet they may identify with the individual hero's spirit of resistance. Within *The Iron Heel* the same individualist qualities that Macmillan used to improve sales of London's writings were used to popularize radical sentiments. Understanding the organizational fiction of "heroism" in this way, readers need neither underestimate the power of incipient totalitarianism nor fall into despair at the relative powerlessness of individual persons caught within such a system. Since resistance to the Oligarchy must be measured both in terms of generational and individual struggles, and since readers tend to approach novels within the limitations of human life, London uses the dual perspective to find a middle way between disabling extremes and to preempt predictable attacks.

When London's imaginary historian Anthony Meredith writes, in a foreword to Avis Everhard's account, that "events, and the bearings of events, that were confused and veiled to her, are clear to us. She lacked perspective" (1908 ix), London is answering a critic whose words can only be found beyond *The Iron Heel*.[12] A reviewer from the *Wall Street Journal* would in fact later claim that London was too close to events to write about them, and we can find many similar ideological duels within the pages of the novel. The idea that art should be detached, or at least "balanced" to the point of political neutrality, is the interpretive convention that is most often used to discount an activist political novel, and so London devises a way to have it both ways—detached perspective and engaged immediacy—when he fashions a divided perspective in the novel. London's complex response to the problems inherent in writing an overt political novel have been entirely overlooked, largely because readers have taken his reputation as literary macho-man as a given and so have failed to notice the balances he actually built into *The Iron Heel*.[13]

London addressed the hard-nosed, supposedly objective concerns of *realpolitik* through the voice of historian Anthony Meredith while maintaining a more subjective view of class struggle through the voice of Avis Everhard.[14] This division of narrative labor is anything but static: *The Iron Heel* opens with a future historian's certification as to the irrelevance of the document in hand. When historian Anthony Meredith begins his foreword with the sentence "It cannot be said that the Everhard Manuscript is an important historical document," the reader is well aware that this statement is not a direction to discard the hundreds of pages that form *The Iron Heel*. The reader may be supposed, instead, to smile at this incongruity.

Meredith's first footnote appears at the end of Avis Everhard's first paragraph, just after she makes her emotive plea, "That it [the revolt] may not be premature!" The footnote rapidly shifts the reader from Avis's emotionalism into an intellectual and analytic register. In sharp contrast to Avis's immediacy, Meredith glosses over Everhard's plea with the following judicious and distant prose: "The Second Revolt was largely the work of Ernest Everhard, though he cooperated, of course, with the European leaders. The capture and secret execution of Everhard was the great event of the spring of 1932 A.D. Yet so thoroughly had he prepared for the revolt, that his fellow-conspirators were able, with little confusion or delay, to carry out his plans" (1). Any hopes animated by Avis Everhard's worried words are instantly deflated by the information that Ernest was (will be, from the 1908 perspective of the novel's first readers) executed by the Oligarchy in 1932. While the juxtaposition of clashing perspectives adds drama to Avis Everhard's account, the ironic perspective of the foreword and footnotes develops the novel's political philosophy just as it gives texture to the narrative. The reader shuttles between Avis's passion, which is certainly indispensable to any mass movement, and the more dispassionate appraisal of the academic

Meredith. One sort of reader may identify with Avis's passion; those who are wary of or even cynical about group emotions may prefer Meredith's Olympian perspective. The pleasure of Meredith's verbal mode is of course in the sense of superiority it gives to the reader, who is invited to think "I see through the doublethink and sentimentality that character-izes my age." Such a reader is politically "in the know," and this identification is precisely what attracts many activists to a political cause. Meredith's way of knowing can be a source of pride, but there is also something humbling about his perspective for political activists, since Meredith's information qualifies Avis Everhard's "great man" beliefs about social change.

The Iron Heel is, in parts, spoiled by political arrogance. The protago-nist Ernest Everhard is dangerously good and the novel's villains are purely evil. Though Anthony Meredith discounts Avis Everhard's hero worship, Meredith's occasional footnotes qualify our view of Avis Ever-hard only slightly. The rhetoric of individualism is sustained through the story of the Everhard romance, while the collective aspect of the social movement—the part critics will label "rant" or "tract"—is folded into the text in the form of historical footnotes.[15] Through dual perspective Lon-don combines socialist consciousness-raising and the individual expe-rience of persons engaged in the struggle. The resulting novel has its imperfections: the socialist perspective has complexity of a sort, but the "enemy discourse," that of the capitalist owners, has none. London has thumbed the scale in Everhard's favor.

Furthermore, many readers of the novel will get tired of Anthony Meredith's condescension toward Avis Everhard. While the academic framework provided by Meredith's foreward and notes demonstrates that there are limitations to the romantic revolutionary immediacy of Avis's narrative, there is nothing in what Avis tells us that signals the limitations of Meredith's academic detachment. Still, London offers a solution of sorts to this problem, and the solution is again a matter of the novel's dual perspective. By withholding information about the exact demise of Avis and Ernest Everhard, London grounds his dystopian vi-sion in an uncertainty that is an imaginative and suggestive resolution, but the sense of this ending is also politically useful, perhaps even nec-essary. If we had a deterministic theory of history that we believed ab-solutely—if we *knew* what was going to happen—there would be little or no motivation to act, and so skillful activist fiction must steer a course around irrefutable certainty.

In addition to dual perspective, London uses humor to deflect or defuse anticipated charges of political extremity or crankishness. The writer who is aware that he or she will be dismissed as an Ishmaelite, a nay-sayer, a neurotic, or a humorless fanatic may attempt to circumvent the prejudice against political engagement by demonstrating a sense of humor, and this is also a way of demonstrating that one is aware of perspectives other than one's own. London's novel is rich in satire, but this kind of humor is often overlooked when the critic is distracted by prophecy. Would London's first readers have described the novel as prophetic of horrors to come, or would they have recognized it as a representation of their own historical period, albeit artistically refracted? One 1908 reviewer found the "prophecy" and "found manuscript" conventions to be "hackneyed"—and another accused London of plagiarizing from the "Russian revolution"![16] No reviews discussed the particular nature of London's satirical representation of class conflict in America.

The fall of the Chicago Commune at the novel's conclusion is one of the most apocalyptic scenes available to readers of the political novel,[17] but it too contains moments of topical humor, in part as comic relief from the suppression of the revolt. Early in the "Chicago Commune" chapter is a socialist joke on the brutality of industrialized life, recapitulated for the reader in the form of an Anthony Meredith footnote:

> Chicago was the industrial inferno of the nineteenth century A.D. A curious anecdote has come down to us of John Burns, a great English labour leader and one time member of the British Cabinet. In Chicago, while on a visit to the United States, he was asked by a newspaper reporter for his opinion of that city. "Chicago," he answered, "is a pocket edition of hell." Some time later as he was going aboard his steamer to sail to England, he was approached by another reporter, who wanted to know if he had changed his opinion of Chicago. "Yes, I have," was his reply. "My present opinion is that hell is a pocket edition of Chicago."

If the reader smiles, he has been put, if only for a moment, on the side of the proletariat.[18] The John Burns anecdote also uses comic relief to disarm the reader before the utterly serious presentation of the Chicago massacre.

The Burns anecdote, which seems to be a variation on a typical after-dinner speaker's joke, is one instance of how London used traditional humor to direct readers toward some of the less pleasant aspects of contemporary life. We know he was fond of the anecdote since it also appears in his review of Upton Sinclair's *The Jungle* (Foner 517–24). The lengthy footnote from *The Iron Heel* is, in fact, lifted almost verbatim from the beginning of the 1906 review.[19] These correspondences, as well as London's enthusiastic response to *The Jungle*, indicate that London had the Chicago of his own era very much in mind as he was writing *The Iron Heel*. London's comments on Sinclair's novel are "prophetic" of the book he would soon publish: "[Sinclair] selected the greatest industrial city in the country, the one city of the country that is ripest industrially, that is the most perfect specimen of jungle-civilization to be found. One cannot question the wisdom of the author's choice, for Chicago certainly is industrialism incarnate, the storm-center of the conflict between capital and labor, a city of street battles and blood" (Foner 517). The review could have served as a thumbnail sketch of *The Iron Heel*'s Chicago chapters. Certainly London wished to turn his readers' attention to the brutal effects of industrialization *of this century's first decade*, whether he wrote fiction or nonfiction. The humor, often seen as an antidote to the political obsessions that lead one to "rant," is used to return the reader again and again to the political conditions against which the author protests, namely working conditions in Chicago.

Whatever London's contemporary reviewers felt, most of today's readers are disinclined to recognize the muckraker aspect of *The Iron Heel*, which is funny in a way since the muckrakers are so irritating to the oligarchs of the Iron Heel. H. Bruce Franklin's introduction to a 1980 edition of the book credits London with prophetic foresight (1980 i–vi). This edition pictures an iron heel crushing the face of the deposed Chilean socialist Allende on its cover. In Franklin's introduction, the entire book has been marshalled into a political struggle much closer to our own time to demonstrate prophecy and relevance. Prophecy displaces humor. This view, when presented without provisions for artistic modification, can lead us away from, rather than toward, the political actualities London struggled to represent. Here is Franklin on the book's perspicacity: "London foresees: the creation of attractive suburbs for relatively privileged strata of the working class while the central cities are turned into what he calls 'ghettoes' for the masses of unemployed and menial laborers, shoved into the darkest depths of human misery; the deliberate economic subversion of public education in order to spread illiteracy and ignorance; adequate food, health care, and housing priced above the reach of more and more people" (iii). It is true that *The Iron Heel*, as it continues to work as a political novel, brings us to study the consequences of social and political structures on our lives at this very moment, but it should also return us to the world of 1908 and furnish our minds with the elements that made that world seem real to its first readers.

Franklin gestures toward the past when he argues that London was able to create such an impressive story because of his own biographical particulars: "How did London come to such a stunning vision of the future? The answer, I believe, lies in his own contradictory experience within different social classes." While Franklin has very little to say about how this varied experience bears on *The Iron Heel* as a particular work of art, his interpretation of the novel as one written in the prophetic mode occasionally turns in the direction of close reading, and these turns are far and away more valuable to a discussion of the particular book than are the connect-the-dot comparisons between London's 1908 novel and all subsequent injustice in the twentieth century:

> The novel is of course a warning to London's American socialist com-
> rades that their strategy of relying entirely on the ballot box to defeat the
> capitalists is a treacherous illusion. But the Everhard style of roaring
> supermasculine confrontation with the capitalists proves to be equally
> dangerous. As the Iron Heel consolidates its power, the revolutionaries
> are forced to rely on the intricate underground apparatus developed by
> the aptly named Avis ("bird") Everhard, nee Cunningham. (v)

Professor Franklin reminds us that Avis is the Latin word for bird to suggest that vision (that of a bird's-eye-view) and cunning (nee Cunningham) are as important to a revolution as raw strength. London's novel counsels that the revolution will require both stereotypically masculine and feminine talents, however London understood these talents to be divided. There is very little in this interpretation with which one is moved to disagree, except perhaps with the radical earnestness that remains even after Franklin has so aptly drawn our attention to the role of Avis Everhard. The ironies and qualifications have been left out. Even when it describes the fall of the Chicago Commune, London's book is packed with entertaining ironies. Any interpretation should ask why.

Readers in the literary era after James Joyce are pleased more than anything else by a broad philosophical irony, and, as we have said, this kind of irony is something that London's novel does not really aim for. We do not have a cosmological perspective on puny human doings or the view of Hugh Kenner's "colder eye." As the writer of an overt, com-mitted political novel, London does not want to syphon off the book's rhetorical power by convincing readers that all views are in some sense equal. However, he does have both aesthetic and political reasons for complicating the novel's perspectives: dual perspective in *The Iron Heel* teaches activists that they must take *both* the long and short view of political events.

London's use of dual perspective also amuses the reader, such as when he creates comic tensions between Avis Everhard's narrative and Anthony Meredith's historical footnotes to satirize the unreflective attitude that enables everyday language to shape life and behavior in ways that suit one social class more than another. In the chapter "The Philomaths," the proto-oligarch Mr. Wichson sneers at a speech by Ernest on the topic of proletarian nobility and proclaims him a "Utopian." The footnote on this word offers a utopian alternative to Mr. Wichson's "realistic" view:

> The people of that age were phrase slaves. The abjectness of their servitude is incomprehensible to us. There was a magic in words greater than the conjurer's art. So befuddled and chaotic were their minds that the utterance of a single world could negative [*sic*] the generalizations of a lifetime of serious research and thought. Such a word was the adjective *Utopian*. The mere utterance of it could damn any scheme, no matter how sanely conceived, of economic melioration or regeneration. Vast populations grew frenzied over such phrases as "an honest dollar" and "a full dinner pail." The coinage of such phrases was considered strokes of genius. (79–80)

Attacking "newspeak" at about the moment when George Orwell (born Eric Blair) was learning to speak, London created a form of literary satire that was tactically focused to serve his political purposes. As it makes us smile, the footnote satirizes the uncritical attitude in which clichés and other staples of political language are granted the authority of traffic signs: one does not, for example, question the meaning of a sign that says "BRIDGE OUT" if one is racing along a dark road. In challenging this kind of uncritical acceptance, the footnotes remind us that phrases like "an honest dollar" may be truly or deceptively applied. Through the satirical opportunities provided by the dual perspective, London offers the reader a humorous alternative to the unreflective kind of language that authorizes ideological stop signs before words such as "Utopian." Instead of stopping without a thought at the appearance of such a word, London urges that we regard political language with skepticism and with critical attention.

That many political novels have failed artistically because they have preached to the converted is no doubt true, but this does not separate the

genre of the political novel from other kinds of literature: successful artistry always overcomes a number of risks along the way. Still, scholars have
generally seen what I am calling dual perspective as a failure of art. Earle
Labor, the preeminent London scholar and the person who has done more
than anyone to improve London's reputation as a literary artist, makes a
strong complaint against the style that begins the Avis Everhard section
of the novel.[20] *The Iron Heel* is, for Labor, "*1984* as it might have been penned
by Elizabeth Barrett Browning" (*Jack London* 103–4).

But does writing a dystopia in maudlin tones sound like something
Jack London would do carelessly or accidentally? Why, we might ask,
does the Everhard manuscript begin sentimentally with "The soft summer winds" while "Wild-Water ripples sweet cadences over its mossy
stones"? The London who signed many letters "Yours for the Revolution" was not writing only for the intellectuals and activists, and so he
develops narrative techniques that will recruit a wider audience.[21] Avis
Everhard's impressions are framed by those of Anthony Meredith, the
male historian with little or no insight into the importance of her talents.

Like much of the London scholarship, Anthony Meredith's fictional
foreword and footnotes point up the weaknesses of Avis Everhard's
perspective, but we might also ask whether Avis undermines Anthony
Meredith. Meredith speaks the last word, but London presents us, word
for word, with Avis Everhard's view more than that of any other character, and so, at least in terms of emphasis, Avis Everhard's narrative
survives the historian's arrogance. While it is hard to believe that such a
macho narrative works toward feminist goals, *The Iron Heel* is hardly an
advertisement for patriarchy, however masculine its style. As Professor
Franklin reminds us, London, writing before women had the right to
vote, imagined a future in which women would play key roles in resisting the absolutely patriarchal Oligarchy.

We might expect that the historical footnotes would continue to undermine Avis Everhard's narrative throughout the novel, or that her own
voice might somehow "rebel" against Meredith's narrative authority, but
the tension between Avis Everhard and Anthony Meredith does *not* develop. This increasingly static relationship between text and frame is the
book's greatest artistic failure. Perhaps, if we see the commonality between techniques of narrative art and of political rhetoric, it is also a
political problem: London is, midway through his novel, preaching to
the choir. On occasion Anthony Meredith becomes a mere vehicle for
London's ideas, and at other times Meredith, London, and Ernest
Everhard are barely distinguishable sources of Truth. In the chapter en-

titled "The Beginning of the End," Avis Everhard reports one of her husband's prophecies, to which Meredith adds this footnote: "Everhard's social foresight was remarkable. As clearly as in the light of past events, he saw the defection of the favored unions, the rise and the slow decay of the labor castes, and the struggle between the decaying oligarchs and labor castes for control of the great governmental machine" (226). The next footnote merely repeats the sentiment: "We cannot but marvel at Everhard's foresight." When Meredith turns into a puppet, the narrative loses its appeal rapidly. Even supposing London (and, by extension, Meredith and Ernest Everhard) did know the Truth, why bore the reader with such repetition? In later footnotes London attempts to make the historical apparatus less heavy-handed, such as when the footnote glosses a word such as "fake" and "bluff" to suggest that, in the perfect future, such words will fall from the vocabulary of everyday language. Unless we are prepared to imagine London as a socialist Pollyanna, this use of the dual perspective can only be meant to tickle the reader's cynicism. London, no stranger to irony and sarcasm, occasionally cites Ambrose Bierce's *Devil's Dictionary* in Meredith's notes.

Framed so as to combine the certitudes necessary for political action with the uncertainties haunting any political actor, the novel ends in medias res. The narrative of Avis Everhard "concludes" with this unfinished sentence fragment: "The magnitude of the task may be understood when it is taken into" (354). Succeeding this fragment is a footnote to tell us that this "is the end of the Everhard Manuscript" and that Avis Everhard apparently had time to hide it before her capture. By withdrawing certainty about the conclusion of the narrative and about the fate of the Everhards, London's ending improves on what might have been a dramatically deficient narrative. This withdrawal of certainty ironizes the heroic formulas of the popular media to which *The Iron Heel*, up until this point, had conformed. Furthermore, in selecting readers according to their interest in a *specific* political cause rather than a supposedly universal human struggle, the actively engaged political novelist increases the risk to his or her reputation as a serious artist. For this reason the reputations of overt political novelists are, like the fate of Avis Everhard, never quite certain.

Historical Purpose: London vs. the Reviewer's Iron Heel

London's use of dual perspective meant very little to his original reviewers, while his literary machismo counted for a great deal. Fluctuations in London's reputation and in his reception might seem to indicate that Ernest Everhard's days of brotherhood were but a receding phantasm, but it was in London's vision to figure in the tempestuous changes that "common sense" will inevitably undergo with the passage of time. Audiences and their values shift radically from moment to moment, and political writers, who are by definition wed to highly topical material, must devise ways to "broaden their power base"—as we would say of the politician's similar task today. How, if at all, did London accomplish this task?

As we have seen, part of London's solution was to ground his vision of the future in the political and social details of turn-of-the-century Chicago, and the footnotes of Anthony Meredith are a regular way of looking backward to this period. It is a commonplace of futurist fiction that the seemingly stable values of "today" will become questionable tomorrow, and Anthony Meredith's footnotes frequently charm in the way they revise (re-visualize) rarely questioned events of the early twentieth century. Avis Everhard's concern that the socialist revolt may be premature, Meredith's glosses on John Burns and others, London's incorporation of ideas he first published in reference to *The Jungle*—all of these are ways of looking at the present in the mirror of a fictional future. There is a janiformity to this novel; it speaks prophetically to the future and at the same time maintains a satirical dialogue with the present.

By constantly jostling the reader between the "before" and "after" of the socialist revolution, *The Iron Heel* brings that revolution into conceptual existence, page by page. It does this in part by heckling those in the present who think concepts like "Utopia" are foolish illusions. This shouting match often takes place between London and his reviewers, who he knows will dismiss his imagined world as oligarch Wichson dismisses Everhard's Utopia. It is in this dialogue, if we may use so polite a word, that overt political fiction fights its way into existence, taking on first and foremost those double-binds that have been disastrous to the writing and reading of political fiction: the overt, engaged political novel is damned if it is fanciful and damned if it is not.[22] The notion that there is no "play" (meaning both fun and elasticity of meaning) in political novels presents the political novelist with a double-bind: either the fanciful narrative can be dismissed as nonsense for its departures from fact and social science, or a historically precise and theoretically challenging narrative can be attacked for its lack of character development, metaphor, and so forth. These criticisms depend on the conviction that political and aesthetically motivated writing are distinct and even opposed discourses, an assumption that marks many 1908 reviews of *The Iron Heel*.[23] That is to say, London was in a "dialogue" with his world, and that world was not shy about answering back.

   The Iron Heel is certainly fanciful, given London's elaborations on the "found manuscript" trope and the phantasmagoric style of the latter chapters. Reviewers friendly to the book's socialist message found the book to be imaginative, whereas political opponents of the novel suggested that its absurd political extrapolations yielded much unintentional comedy for the snickering reader.[24] In that very few newspaper reviewers assumed London's novel could be ignored, his representations of American politics provided "interest" for readers of various stripes, but for the most part, London was criticized for having foolishly wandered from his proper terrain, literature. The *Brooklyn Daily Eagle* (22 Feb. 1908) complained that the book "affords queer evidence of the medley of notions that have grown up in this author's mind with reference to social problems," but the reviewer complimented London as a craftsman: "So far as the technical construction goes, of course, Mr. London's new book shows the skill of the trained craftsman." Clearly the reviewer and the author had ideological differences: "The primal, the fundamental defect of his work lies in its idea. Humanity, evolution, never turns back on itself—takes no backward steps. The world has passed the stage where the conditions that Mr. London portrays are possible, or even thinkable." London's challenge to ideas of inevitable progress cost him the *Brooklyn Daily Eagle*, at least.

   Nashville was less kind. *The Banner* (29 Feb. 1908) did not water down its complaint against mixing politics and fiction. It is hard to see what, from the reviewer's point of view, London might have done to improve his book: "Jack London's latest book is in the main a Socialist tract, with only enough of narrative and romance to give it the semblance of a novel. [It is listed] appropriately under the head of fiction, but not altogether, because the characters it employs and the scenes it depicts are wholly imagined." A puzzling claim, to say the least. The Duluth *Herald*, the Chicago *Musical Leader*, the Boston *Advertiser*, the Milwaukee *Free Press*, among others, all complained about London's mixing of politics and literature. The Chicago *Inter-Ocean* called it "a socialistic preachment in the guise of fiction" and "an ardent labor of love, since the author is an ardent and radical socialist."

   The socialist newspaper, *The Worker*, however, wrote on 14 March 1908 that "Beyond all question this volume must be considered the high-water mark of Jack London's literary effort." *The Iron Heel* was useful to the socialist cause as political propaganda just as much as it was regarded as a threat by established politicians and mainstream reviewers. When rumors arose that the Socialist Party would nominate Jack London as their candidate for president, Theodore Roosevelt attacked London's skills as a nature writer, calling him a "nature fakir"![25] Quite a few reviews expressed alarm at the book's incendiary potential, which is a bit more understandable since London depicts terrorist resistance to the Oligarchy in a positive manner.

Sherman writes in her overview of the writer's critical reputation that a majority of critics from Beacon Street and Main Street (high-brow and middle-brow) "found *The Iron Heel* unimaginative literature and unconvincing Socialism. It was called a pessimistic bore that would put an anarchist to sleep, or a dangerous tract to be condemned for fomenting social dissension" (xi). In the crude reviews mentioned above, class bias is in no way concealed, but London's more sophisticated ideological antagonists sometimes complimented his craftsmanship, using faint praise as prelude to aesthetic damnation. *The Wall Street Journal* (19 Mar. 1908) contains the most rhetorically effective dismissal of London's novel:

> There can be no doubt that some time a great novel will be written, founded upon the economic struggle which is now in progress in the United States [. . .]. Jack London, however, has not written the great novel of this social revolution through which we are passing. He is an exceedingly clever and interesting writer, and perhaps it is not his fault that he fails in this book to write in a convincing way of the economic significance of the times. He is too close to the events to have the perspective necessary for adequate treatment. Moreover, "the Iron Heel" is, in reality, much less a novel than a presentation of the radical socialist view. It is an argument, rather than a story, although it possesses dramatic interest.

The major formulaic dismissals are all here, especially the assertion that an overtly political novel is somehow not a novel. Also, the writer who chooses to represent political themes is "too close" to events to have the detachment needed for great art.

In 1908, Beacon Street and Main Street reviewers were not London's only readers, even if "ardent socialists" and other kinds of critics have long been the invisible men and women of literary studies. Socialist and other leftist critics have, however, found London to be an important American writer.[26] His novel was published at a time when socialism was growing in the United States, and socialist newspapers gave his book considerable support. As a look through London's scrapbooks will show, London's best reviews were from socialist publications such as *Appeal to Reason* and *Wilshire's Monthly*.[27] When America had a socialist community, *The Iron Heel* had an appreciative audience who valued political fiction and who did not regard politics as an intrusion within imaginative literature.

The novel was reviewed in over 150 newspapers across the United States. Having reviewed the novel's wide initial reception, we know that anti-political critical dogmas were current when London wrote, but these prejudices did not harden into a critical orthodoxy until later. That there was a market and some possibility of a favorable reception in 1908 does not mean that the author of politically dissident fiction met with no resistance in the golden days before the cold war. London was aware of the risks of writing a political novel—especially after *The Iron Heel*. In a letter he wrote to "Comrade Harris" (not Frank Harris) on 26 October 1914, London thanked the good comrade for his appreciation of *The Iron Heel* and complained that it "won me practically nothing but abuse from the opportunistic socialists."[28] Apparently Harris requested a sequel of sorts, as London's continuing complaint hoots at such a notion: "There's no use in suggesting my writing another book of that sort. It was a labor of love, and a dead failure as a book. The book-buying public would have nothing to do with it, and I got nothing but knocks from the socialists." The letter to Comrade Harris (first name unknown) tells us more about London's anxieties as a commercial artist than it does about his reception among socialists, however. It is true that the Macmillan Company did not emphasize *The Iron Heel* in the 1910 version of "Jack London: His Life and Writings," but the novel received mixed reviews in American newspapers and magazines; it has gone through a good number of editions in many languages, and it is in print to this day. Be that as it may, London's most overt political novel was not received nearly as kindly as was his nature writing. The practicing novelist knows or ought to know that he or she risks just this sort of criticism by writing an overtly political novel. The writer who gains a reputation as a political novelist endures diminished hopes that other gifts will be recognized.

Political Purpose: The Political Novel as a Pushy Genre

In "Why I Write" Orwell defined "political purpose" as a "Desire to push the world in a certain direction, to alter other people's idea of the kind of society that they should strive after." Overt political fiction will seem aggressive and intrusive to those who insist on the mythical methods of modernism, a literary ethos that is predisposed against literature that is "pushy."[29] Postwar criticism has tended to praise Auden, who wrote that "poetry makes nothing happen" (50) rather than Orwell, who wrote that "The opinion that art should have nothing to do with politics is itself a political attitude" (4:2). "Pushiness" of the sort characterizing overtly political literature has, in American literary studies, been frowned into a corner. We have been taught to prefer books that say "Call me literature" to those that make political claims upon us.

As Joan R. Sherman pointedly asserts, Henry James and Jack London both died in 1916, and "American literature" mourned the former but not the latter: "as our literary history makes clear, there are two 'American literatures,' and only one would genuinely feel London's loss" (xiii). Challenges to "American literature" as a hegemonic, exclusionary, genteel concept abound in contemporary criticism, resulting in two main camps. There is the American literature that has cherished Melville, Hawthorne, Dickinson, James, and so forth, and there is the "other" American literature. The other American literature includes previously ignored literature by women and people of color, immigrant writing, and also politically radical texts that have been marginalized, the argument goes, by literary standards in service of elitist ideologies.

London is probably more a counter-hegemonic author than a hegemonic one,[30] and among counter-hegemonists he is less bashful than most. Those novelists who construe American political structures as entirely unsalvageable will very likely envision, in the present or in the future, a political emergency in which the political system will undergo the desired changes, and London is one of the very few widely known American novelists to "plot" with approval the overthrow of the current system of American government. The overt political novel pushes the reader toward such eventual changes by linking them directly to political conflicts of the day. In an imaginary way, this sort of book "sends the reader to the barricades," meaning that it inspires political resistance against whichever corrupt systems of power it has named.

A book that pushes the reader toward social action instead of toward an enriching aesthetic experience will, predictably, be found to be artistically unsuccessful, and Rideout makes just this point in *The Radical Novel* when he claims that such activist aims are an alien presence in the world of literary fiction: "A novel does not send its reader to the barricades or the altar, but rather enlarges his experience, makes him realize more fully the possibilities of the human being. The novel, whatever its formal ideology, is essentially a humanizing force" (289). Rideout's idea that even a radical novel does not send its readers to the barricades reproduces the baseline assumptions of those literary ideologies that are conservative or even reactionary in regard to political change.[31] His position that we must make working distinctions between literature, politics (the barricades), and religion (the altar) is perfectly sensible; but we should also recognize that insistence on *absolute* differences between political and artistic uses of language puts handcuffs on the critic examining political fiction. According to such lights, political stories are always *reductions* of real, lived experience. Such a view is guaranteed to obscure the ways in which political fiction can do exactly what the best literature is supposed to do: surprise us with a new way of seeing the world. Even future historian Meredith, writing from within the time of the Brotherhood of Man, has overlooked this moral of the manuscript he edits and presents: Avis Everhard is someone whose experience was *enlarged* because she was drawn into a political struggle, and readers who follow her story, which leads through the trenches of early twentieth-century class struggle, can only come away with a seasoned sense of American literary and political history.[32]

A novel like *The Iron Heel* is a challenging text primarily because it flouts the sort of conventional notions that have often framed our sense of literature. The unsaid either/or formulation in which a book *either* sends us to the barricades *or* enlarges our experience has interfered with the ability of even the most subtle and sympathetic readers to appreciate American political fiction as it is actually written. Avis Everhard's manuscript is, in a sense, still waiting to be found.

How to read a revolutionary political novel? The problem of how we should read political fiction in fact reaches far beyond Jack London's *Iron Heel*, since the Americanist critical evasion of political fiction is in part an expression of a more widespread American impatience with the nature of political work.[33] Americans, after all, have become a people who love to hate politics. The solution to this problem is not, I believe, in any revolutionary modes of literary interpretation, but rather in what might be called "radical republicanism." E. J. Dionne Jr., in his trenchant study *Why Americans Hate Politics*, argues that what America most needs, though the idea will sound utopian to some, is to return to a notion of politics that does not damn the whole enterprise from the start:

> The American political tradition contains such an idea, an idea that reaches back to the noblest traditions of Western culture. The idea is what

the Founding Fathers called republicanism, before there was a political
party bearing that name. At the heart of republicanism is the belief that
self-government is not a drab necessity but a joy to be treasured. It is the
view that politics is not simply a grubby confrontation of competing interests but an arena in which citizens can learn from each other and discover an "enlightened self-interest" in common. (354)

The disdain with which many Americans have come to regard the political process has led some readers to despise any kind of political activity within the domain of literature, and it has led as many or more
to envision the essentially privatized politics that I have discussed in
chapter 1 as "tropological activism." Dionne's republicanism (an idea
London's Everhard cynically dismissed and utterly despised, by the way)
is the best starting point of any Americanist criticism that would cheat
neither politics nor culture. A "republican criticism"—no reference to
Rush Limbaugh where none intended—is one that attacks at its root the
notion that politics is "Other" to the concerns of culture.

Notes

1. London incorporated sections of his own political speeches into the arguments of his heroic socialist, Ernest Everhard. Thanks to Erica Briscoe for pointing this out in her unpublished essay "The Meaning of Dualism in *The Iron Heel*."

2. Compare Rideout's phrasing with Siebers's discussion of Arendt in the introduction, note 6.

3. The notion that politics and literature are antithetical discourses invariably
came into play in hostile reviews of *The Iron Heel*. One possible counter-argument
to my position that political writers jeopardize their status as writers when they
mingle political and artistic concerns would be to say that only some writers—
the bad ones—are punished with poor sales. Good writers, the argument would
go, do not suffer this lot: Upton Sinclair's *The Jungle* (1906) was initially successful and has always had strong standing as a work of "American literature." As I
argued in chapter 1, critics have frequently defined their way around the problem of the "good" political novel, such as when Joseph Blotner defined *The Jungle*
as a "sociological novel." Recent cultural histories have begun to recover overtly
political fictions that were vastly popular in their day but, having been defined
as either sub-literary or nonpolitical, fell through the cracks. See for example
Conn's *The Divided Mind* for discussions of several such forgotten books.

4. Such, such were the interpretations when Anthony West claimed Orwell
devised the hellish punishments of *Nineteen Eighty-Four* in order to get back at
English society for having put him through the boyhood humiliations described
in Orwell's essay "Such, Such Were the Joys." See West, 150–59.

5. Jay Martin, drawing on Richard O'Conner's *Jack London: A Biography*, notes that "During a time when Melville was largely forgotten, London read *Moby-Dick* again and again" (234).

6. On "Ishmaelite," see chapter 2, note 1.

7. Political writers, it is true, are sometimes justly accused of "preaching to the choir." Alfred Kazin wrote to Josephine Herbst on 4 February 1966 that "It's hard writing about the thirties, for the curious reason that it *was* an age of faith." Herbst, however, addresses the dismissal of political activism as neurosis in a return letter to Alfred Kazin: "I don't know for whom I am doing this piece; perhaps for the young people who protest at California Univ. and elsewhere, or for those who go to Selma and Mississippi. The sane can even call them neurotics for all I care; it's what the big athletic lugs at the Univ. of Cal. in my day called me, throwing an arm affectionately around my shoulders and saying, 'Now Jo, don't get neurotic.' And I thought, if this is being neurotic, then let me go where there are other neurotics" (Herbst Collection, Beinecke Library). Herbst's "piece" was a review for *The Nation* of Vincent Brome's study of the International Brigades.

8. These pamphlets (and the largest collection of London's papers and books) are in the Huntington Library's Jack London Collection; see items 262252, 434989, and 435917. The pamphlet was published first in 1905, revised in 1910, and republished again as recently as 1972.

9. In her introduction to Theweleit's *Male Fantasies*, a theory of fascism that examines the journals of the Freikorps who roamed Germany after World War I, Barbara Ehrenreich warns specifically that we must not confuse these particular men with all men—but this does very little to undo the work of the title, which suggests a matter-of-fact link between masculinity and fascism.

10. Orwell remarks that the taint of cruelty surrounding London is no mere error of literary history. In a review of London's stories, Orwell claims that London wrote well about political oppression because of his own capacity for cruelty: "London could foresee Fascism because he had a Fascist streak in himself: or at any rate a marked strain of brutality and an almost unconquerable preference for the strong man as against the weak man" (4:25). Orwell acknowledges these aspects of London not out of approval, but out of a sense that these particular aspects of London's make-up in part account for his abilities as a political writer. We might call this the "it takes one to know one" theory of political novelists, the consequences of which are quite troublesome. If it takes a "flawed" person to recognize and communicate the nature of a flawed political regime, then one may reject the political writer either because of the personal flaw, or by arguing that the "innocent" writer is, in fact, too pure to comprehend the political situation. Orwell's solution was to accept the necessary impurities of the political writer.

11. I must qualify "most dedicated defenders," even if it means entering into a civil war. There are and always have been London defenders (and Jack Lon-

don attracts defenders like no other writer) who champion the political work and who strongly resist the formalist division of politics and aesthetics. Jay Williams, editor of the *Jack London Journal*, argues that for earlier readers "London's socialism can enter the frame of critical analysis only via biography, not aesthetic production" and is prepared to argue that London "was revitalized in the 1960s on the condition that we forget he was a socialist" (personal communication, 24 Mar. 1997).

12. Unless otherwise noted, all references are to the first edition.

13. "At his best, in his books London entertained imaginatively the imperatives of life for the individual and for society, and the clashes between them. Unfortunately for his reputation London's work has been misrepresented" (Martin 235).

14. To use the term popularized by Deborah Tannen, the two primary narrative perspectives of the novel are organized by "genderlect." For Tannen, the male genderlect is characterized by an urge to establish dominance, the female genderlect by the desire to create community. London's novel, then, speaks in both the masculine and feminine genderlects and thus reaches a wider audience.

15. For a more satisfied interpretation of London's dialogical balances, see Christopher Gair's "Looking Forward/Looking Backward: Romance and Utopia in *The Iron Heel*." Gair and I agree that London uses dual perspective to advantage, but his essay does not find fault with the static nature of the Anthony Meredith/Avis Everhard narrative tension in the middle sections of the novel.

16. See the Nashville *Banner* on "hackneyed." For charges of plagiarism, see the Chicago *Post* (4 Apr. 1908): "Nominally a novel, 'The Iron Heel' is really a pamphlet for socialism [in which] the details of the Russian revolution are reproduced with much of Mr. London's plagiaristic ability." Hostile reviewers often accused London of plagiarism, though some recognized that London was developing rather than "stealing" a literary idea. See the San Francisco *Chronicle* review from March 1908: "Jack London has developed his Socialist ideas and gratified his hatred of the capitalist class in his new story, 'The Iron Heel,' which is brought out by The Macmillan Company. London refers in this book in very complimentary terms to H. G. Wells, and the framework of his story owes much to several of Well's [sic] romances of the future, notably 'When the Sleeper Wakes.'"

17. The fall of the novel's commune also initiates the twentieth-century tradition of apocalyptic fiction, as Joseph Blotner has argued (1966). While London drew heavily upon nineteenth-century dystopias such as Ignatius Donnelly's *Caesar's Column*, he had little or no patience with the rosy future of Edward Bellamy's *Looking Backward*. Many critics describe Bellamy as an influence on *The Iron Heel* without acknowledging that London's own novel, like Donnelly's *Caesar's Column*, offers a critical revision of Bellamy's optimistic future. There is no copy of *Looking Backward* (1888) in London's book collection at the Huntington Library. For an overview of London's political and literary influences, see Johnston (120 and 140 n.50).

18. Or, Erica Briscoe reminds me, on the side of the Englishman against the Yank.

19. Another link between *The Jungle* and *The Iron Heel:* London also uses the same epigraph, the Tennyson quatrain that begins "At first, this Earth," for both the book review and his own novel. In neither place does London attribute the lines to Tennyson, though he does in the manuscript of the review (HEH collection).

20. Labor finds *The Iron Heel* to be, politically, London's bravest book, but he is not convinced that London's use of dual perspective rescues the book from its narrative quandary: "a major flaw lies in the telling—in London's unfortunate choice of narrator. Even Professor Meredith's dry, pseudo-scholarly footnotes cannot relieve the cloying sentimentality of Avis Everhard's prose" (*Jack London* 103). In the 1994 revision of *Jack London,* Labor and coauthor Reesman substituted "a Harlequin romance writer" for the "Elizabeth Barrett Browning" reference.

21. On "Yours for the revolution": Martin writes that London "was the first important American writer to close his letters with the Socialist formula. He was also, perhaps, the last to do so meaningfully. His career spans the years of the socialist hope for utopia. His letter of resignation from the Socialists he pointedly signed 'Yours for the Revolution, / Jack London'" (238).

22. Assumptions excluding imagination from political theory have also been a problem, as Wolin complains in *Politics and Vision:* "fanciful statements are not of the same status as propositions that seek to prove or disprove. Fancy neither proves nor disproves; it seeks, instead, to illuminate, to help us become wiser about political things" (19).

23. London hired a newspaper clipping service to collect all reviews of his books, which were then pasted into his scrapbooks, probably by Charmian London. These scrapbooks are in the Huntington Library in San Marino, California. My quotations and summaries of reviews and advertisements are drawn from the Huntington's microfilm copy of these scrapbooks (JL 917). The names of the newspapers and the dates are sometimes legible, sometimes not, but all 150 or so reviews of *The Iron Heel* were published between early February and early May of 1908.

24. This comment from the *Advertiser,* Boston, Mass., 5 March 1908, is typical: "This latest effort of Jack London is bally nonsense. Why a talented writer of fiction persists in writing silly misinterpretations of socialism is one of the things [. . .] no man can understand." The key assumption in this review and almost all hostile reviews of the novel is that politics and fiction do not belong together.

25. See Lutts for a comprehensive discussion of this controversy.

26. Sherman wittily notes that "A writer can no more choose the critical establishment of his time than he can choose his family, and London seems to have had bad luck with both" (x). She points out that London has fared better during the political upheavals of the 1960s and also in the Soviet Union: "In Russia, where London remains the most popular foreign fiction-writer, 9 separate *Collected Works* (in 8 to 30 volumes each, totaling 164 volumes) plus over 130 single-volume anthologies and editions of his work were published in 1910–1961" (viii).

27. There seems to have been something of a bidding war over who would distribute London's sacred socialist text, one seller dropping the price from $1.50 to $1.20, and then finally to $1.08. The penny-wise socialist could get *The Iron Heel* and Sinclair's *The Metropolis*—postage paid—"for a two-dollar bill."

28. A carbon copy of this unpublished letter is included in London's personal copy of *The Iron Heel* at the Huntington Library. On London's disenchantment with American Socialism, see Earle Labor and Robert C. Leitz III's "Jack London on Alexander Berkman: An Unpublished Introduction." Also see Foner and Johnston on London's political vicissitudes.

29. Some have argued that London's work is heavily discounted because it is unrepentantly transitive: modernists have dismissed *The Iron Heel* for expressing the idea that literature should *do* something (Labor 104). Recall again Virginia Woolf's contempt for the book that could cause a reader to write a check, or Beckett's praise for Joyce's writing that was not about something but was that thing itself.

30. London is against the order of things—depending largely on whether one constructs "hegemony" in terms of class or gender. A feminist critic might not see him as counter-hegemonic.

31. That "literature" is an ideologically effective category has been argued most forcefully by Bennett and Eagleton. Bennett writes that "there is no such 'thing' as *literature*, no body of written texts that self-evidently bear on their surface some immediately perceivable and indisputable literary essence which can be invoked as the arbiter of the relative merits of competing traditions of literary criticism" (9). Bennett adds that we must examine how different concepts of literature function. In *Literary Theory* Eagleton speaks for many when he argues that the function of literature (in the standard sense) has been politically reactionary: "I shall end with an allegory. We know that the lion is stronger than the lion-tamer, and so does the lion-tamer. The problem is that the lion does not know it. It is not out of the question that the death of literature may help the lion to awaken" (217). Note that Eagleton mentions the political relevance of literary theorizing but must all but qualify that relevance out of existence. While it "is not out of the question" that a rejection of literature as a category might help exploited people to realize their power, it is more likely that the intentional confusion of politics and literature will only distract us from struggles in the world.

32. As Martin has recognized: "Like the utopian novels of Bellamy and Howells, London's novel has as its basic theme the transformation and regeneration of its narrator, in this case Avis Everhard, who moves from self- to social-concern. Her metamorphosis anticipates and symbolizes the eventual rejuvenation in her society" (236). Martin distinguishes the transformations of *The Iron Heel* from the rosier visions of change of Howells and Bellamy.

33. Perhaps Americans have no patience for politics because they have less and less patience for public life. Dionne and Siebers have been mentioned; on the decline of public intellectuals, also see Jacoby's *The Last Intellectuals*.

PART 3

Individualism and Political Power
in Contemporary America

4

Adamic Purity as Double-Agent
in *Harlot's Ghost*

"There is no emotion on earth more powerful than anti-Americanism. To the rest of the world, America is the Garden of Eden. Unmitigated envy, the ugliest emotion of them all."
"Yessir."
—Norman Mailer

Few living writers in America have identified themselves with political movements and have taken political history as their subject to the degree that Norman Mailer has, and yet he is a rather politically *outré* writer. Perhaps, as some would have it, the center will not hold: notions of American identity or of an American literary canon have depended upon ideologies that have lost their hegemonic power. If this is so, we may now observe the ruins of identity, with or without romantic attachment . . . but go on we must. According to the once-ruling concept, Americans are innocent, new, and exceptional. Poised against this center is an emergent, "marginal" conception in which innocence and newness are disguises supplied after-the-fact: the origin is never freedom but rather domination.[1] In any event, these narratives and counter-narratives continue to work with the same vocabulary to designate the existence of an American identity, called by R. W. B. Lewis "the matter of Adam." This matter has persevered in the decades after Watergate, Vietnam, and the civil rights movement, and it continues to influence the composition and reception of American political fiction. Mailer has, in his end-of-the-century fictions, approached this evolving mythology with impressive artistry and political passion.[2]

David Van Leer suggests that "perhaps the best summary of the whole tradition of postwar individualism was the career of Norman Mailer" (493)—notice the use of "was"—but this most individualistic of writers has been anything but asocial or apolitical, having pursued political ideas across decades. There at first appears to be a contradiction in Mailer's dual aptitude for representing and resisting American mythologies, but Van Leer notes also that Mailer scrutinizes the political potential of individualism in his writing: "Mailer finally acknowledged the limitations of radical individualism in his masterpiece, *Armies of the Night* (1968). Here, combining the techniques of nonfiction and the novel, he satirized his own persona as existential hero to suggest that although true political activism might arise in conjunction with individual rebellion, it could never result from it" (493). As Van Leer's comment suggests, Mailer's career is as much a warning about literary individualism as it is a celebration of its possibilities. His work clearly participates in and contributes to the fiction of an American national identity predicated upon individual freedom, but there is at once a counter-thrust in Mailer's work that finds not a simple, authoritative voice naming the world, but an imbroglio of voices including those expressing what Mailer has called "the mind of the State."

Postwar Literature and the Problem of Adam

The events of postwar political history, including the excesses of the cold war and consequent debacles such as the Watergate affair and the American involvement in Vietnam have caused many writers and large segments of American intellectual culture to have a more dubious view of American identity. *Nocere*, root of innocence, means "to harm": blacklisting in the 1950s, a journalist's photograph of a young girl branded by napalm, the decades of mistrust Americans have felt for official government since President Nixon was forced by threat of impeachment to resign—these have all contributed to feelings of national guilt casually referred to as "the Vietnam Syndrome" by President Bush and others. In reaction against this feeling of national hesitation, political leaders such as Presidents Reagan and Bush told America that it was innocent as often as they could. Many novelists have railed against this discourse of innocence, such as when Robert Coover presented political leaders such as President Nixon in scabrous situations in *The Public Burning*, but the notion of the American innocent is a highly popular concept for Americans, and it has survived the attacks of the most able novelists.[3]

Adam was born, in a sense, in the midst of the cold war. Lewis's 1955 study, *The American Adam*, explored a variety of nineteenth-century American writings to show that "the American dialogue" has largely been about notions of American innocence, about whether the American self is Adamically new, fallen into the corruption of history, or fortunately fallen. This projected historical self-concept could be figured as a self-creation specific to postwar American needs. American identity can be blamed for the specifically American refusal to examine class conflict that is sometimes called "American Exceptionalism."[4] The American self-concept, the argument goes, masks class conflict, since "the simple genuine self against the whole world" is by definition a being without class affiliation. Critics of Lewis (and of similar theorists of American culture and identity) have insisted that mythologies of American innocence function to narrow the American horizon of expectation, specifically to exclude political conflict, such as when Russell Reising accuses Lewis of segregating politics from literature in *The Unusable Past: Theory and the Study of American Literature* (115, 119).

Lewis is faulted for being "ahistorical" since his study of the American dialogue pays no attention to such nineteenth-century controversies as the slavery debates.[5] Whether or not we would agree that Lewis is guilty as charged, the literary criticism his seminal work fostered certainly acquired a sharply ahistorical tendency within one generation. In *Radical Innocence*, Ihab Hassan discusses some versions of the American Adam as he is reincarnated in an existentialist, alienated, A-bomb afflicted postwar world. Refiguring the opposition between Emerson's "Plain old Adam, the simple genuine self" and "the whole world" against which the opposing self was defined, Hassan sees the oppositional nature of the American protagonist as essentially "radical": "His innocence [. . .] is a property of the mythic American self, perhaps of every anarchic Self. It is the innocence of a Self that refuses to accept the immitigable rule of reality, including death, an aboriginal Self the radical imperatives of whose freedom cannot be stifled" (6). This radicalism has nothing to do with political radicalism, however. The word radical in Hassan's usage means something like "profound," and the imperatives driving Hassan's neo-innocent are rooted entirely in psychological rather than social or political self-definition. An "aboriginal Self" suggests an identity prior to present modes of law, politics, and history. Hassan's free radical transcends all obligations, political and otherwise.

The radically innocent Adamic character, remaking him- or herself on a daily basis in a proper existential fashion, *can* be interpreted as a self from which to develop a political intelligence, since the American Adam as a social outsider has not been corrupted by "the system." One's status beyond the pale qualifies one to comprehend the society within.[6] Thus, Adam is an anarchic self not governed by party affiliation or any other sense of communal debt, but at the same time this Adam is most definitely on the outside looking in, an apparently ideal cultural critic, at least from the individualist/existentialist point of view that became so popular in the late 1950s and 1960s. For Hassan radical innocence is an indispensable political credential precisely because it offers and justifies the transcendence of traditional styles of political engagement—those styles that became an embarrassment during the cold war, it so happens.

More recently Lewis's "noble but illusory myth" has come to be regarded primarily as a false consciousness from which the literary critic can deliver us. The image of the American Outsider has in recent years lost authority for those who charge that the tendency to "transcend" quotidian history is "one of the major political effects that the work of American ideology as a whole helps to reinforce" (Kavanagh 313). Such recent criticisms have almost invariably come in the form of the blanket statement, yet we recall that Leo Marx begins *The Machine in the Garden* with criticisms of American ideologies such as that of the American Adam, and he cites Richard Hofstadter and Henry Nash Smith to demonstrate ways in which "this ideal has appeared with increasing frequency in the service of a reactionary or false ideology, thereby helping to mask the real problems of an industrial civilization" (7). The pastoral fantasy has of course been a common mode of escape from the pressures of the real world, and Marx goes on to point out how American Renaissance writers employed the mode as a way to dodge social and political conflicts that endangered their sense of artistic detachment: "Our writers, instead of being concerned with social verisimilitude, with manners and customs, have fashioned their own kind of melodramatic, Manichean, all-questioning fable, romance, or idyll, in which they carry us, in a bold leap, beyond everyday social experience into an abstract realm of morality and metaphysics" (343). American literary mythology, in sum, has often been used as an escape from the clash of the world. It directs our attention to the problems of the individual rather than toward the obligations of the individual to the community, and Hassan's shift from Lewis's Adamic self to an "Anarchic self" certainly suggests the pattern of increasing entitlement that American literary mythology can be made to serve.

With these charges in mind, it may be a surprise to remember that Lewis called for a kind of Adamic resistance to cold war containment: "Ours is an age of containment; we huddle together and shore up defenses; both our literature and our public conduct suggest that exposure to experience is certain to be fatal" (196). Lewis's epilogue, "Adam in the

Age of Containment," is an explicit consideration of the relationship between American literary mythology and political culture. While it is certainly true that some writers "light out for the territory" to escape political conflict in their work, there is also a political strain within the Adamic tradition.

Postwar critics and novelists alike have celebrated individual freedom over group affiliation. Unlike the Popular Front writers of the 1930s, postwar writers who have used fiction as a mode of political resistance have tended to fashion "parties of one," and Norman Mailer's Left Conservatism of the mid-1960s, like Henry Adams's earlier "Conservative Christian Anarchism," can hardly be said to have broken the "one man, one party" rule.[7] No postwar fiction was more committed to a group political action than Mailer's *Armies of the Night*—even though that book expends half of its energy distancing its author from the social movement with which he is inextricably linked! Mailer's career exemplifies the ways in which the postwar American Adam is very much a divided self.

Mailer's Ghosts

We can see the conjunction of mythic identity and political consequence in the first paragraph of *The Executioner's Song* (1979), a book most notable for the way it challenges the border between history and fiction. The book mainly concerns Gary Gilmore, a man who was executed for killing two people in Salt Lake City, Utah. Mailer opens this book, "a true life novel," by retelling the story of the Fall with Gilmore in the Adamic role: "Brenda was six when she fell out of the apple tree. She climbed to the top and the limb with the good apples broke off. Gary caught her as the branch came scraping down. They were scared. The apple trees were their grandmother's best crop and it was forbidden to climb in the orchard. She helped him drag away the tree limb and they hoped no one would notice. That was Brenda's earliest recollection of Gary" (17). Without Brenda's memory of Gary before the Fall, it is hard to imagine why we should care about this murderer. In presenting Gary Gilmore's twisted life story as a novel with an Adamic origin, Mailer encloses Gilmore within the ultimately forgiving myths of American literature.

Archetypal fall from forbidden tree as prologue to fear and memory: Mailer stirs this theme into his "true-life novel" *The Executioner's Song* just as he does into his other novels. It is his favorite way of fusing the motifs of American literature with the developing phenomena of American history, and he uses this mythical method each time he reincarnates revered

American literary characters into highly political contexts. Gary and Brenda are resonant of Quentin and Caddy Compson, and Gary catching his cousin refigures Holden Caulfield catching his little sister Phoebe—but, in Mailer's retelling, the larger context happens to be a nationwide political struggle concerning the propriety of state executions.

Freedom from the burdens of history is another typical motif of literary Adamicism. To express the individual's alienation from history, Mailer has begun three novels with amnesiac narrators (*Barbary Shore, Ancient Evenings,* and *Tough Guys Don't Dance*). However cut off from experience, Mailer's protagonists begin but never finish with the kind of Adamic purity that we tend to associate with Ishmael's pantheistic acceptance. In book after book, Mailer's younger man relates to an older man in a way that bestows upon the younger man a temporary, relative innocence, which is for Mailer the only kind of innocence that makes sense in a world in which we may be put into death camps. Absolute innocence is politically useless; none of Mailer's characters has ever wanted to be a "catcher in the rye." Innocence is, for Mailer, a point of departure rather than a destination.

Like *Barbary Shore* (1951), *The Deer Park* (1955), *An American Dream* (1965), *Why Are We in Vietnam?* (1967), and *Armies of the Night* (1968), Mailer's 1979 book mixes the transcendental theme of the American Adam with the historical specifics of American political struggle. Hemingway and Fitzgerald, the ghosts of a literary golden moment (within orthodox versions of American literary history), haunt much of Mailer's work, but they are particularly manifest in the McCarthy-haunted situations of *The Deer Park*. Stephen Richards Rojack, a postmodern Christopher Newman, finds himself on a double-date with John F. Kennedy in the first sentence of *An American Dream*, Mailer's most surreal novel. Ike McCaslin, reborn as the Texan youth D.J., encounters radical innocence on his way to Vietnam, and the self-mocking jeremiad of Henry Adams, echoing in the Hay-Adams Hotel, is heard throughout *Armies of the Night* (see Taylor, "Of Adams and Aquarius").

If political utility is one strike against pure innocence, history is another. Mailer's most important metaphor for history in the latter part of his career has been the persistence of ghosts, and this is fitting as the American self-concept in recent decades has been haunted. Since the country began the swing to the Right that has been called the Age of Reagan, an age that might be thought of as a flight from the ghosts of history, Mailer has told three stories of major importance, each of which is profoundly political—and each of which is a ghost story. *The Executioner's Song* (1979) concerns the value and values of a man who was executed for murder. *Ancient Evenings* (1983) presents the stories of two ghosts entombed in ancient Egypt some centuries after the empire has crumbled, stories that intersect at all points with the life-cycle of the Egyptian empire. *Harlot's Ghost* (1991) is a ghost story in many senses; through its corridors run the ghosts of American political history, of the cold war, and of John F. Kennedy in particular. The narrator may or may not be a ghost.

It would be hard to imagine three more various novels by the same author, and his versatility and innovation in matters of literary genre reflect Mailer's refusal to simplify his part in what Lewis called "the American dialogue." Mailer's novels resist being excluded from any level of the American conversation. From the language of headlines and case-studies in *The Executioner's Song*, to his sounding of a cultural and political unconscious for the Western world in *Ancient Evenings*, to the investigation of America's political superego the Central Intelligence Agency in *Harlot's Ghost*, Mailer has taken roads less traveled. No other writer of political fiction in America has demonstrated his Odyssean range. Each of these works is in the Adamic tradition, and in particular *Harlot's Ghost* uses the mythology of the American Adam to create a fictional history of the secretive Central Intelligence Agency, thereby politicizing the American mythology of innocence.

Mailer resituates his Adamic hero in each book to undermine the moral certainties that Adamic mythology is often used to sustain.[8] By the end of *Ancient Evenings*, the narrator Menenhetet II says "I do not know if I will labor in greed forever among the demonic or serve some noble purpose I cannot name" (709), and Harry Hubbard is in a similar position within the pyramidal bureaucratic structure of the CIA. Instead of having his heroes name the world unconditionally, every interpretive act is a dialogic venture that occurs within a maddeningly uncertain context, and Mailer foists this same uncertainty upon his readers increasingly with each book, often by mixing the noble with the trashy and by expressing notions of questionable taste in exquisite sentences. By positing moral and aesthetic qualities that are not publically digestible to American society but that would appear to be secretly necessarily, Mailer challenges the assumptions that ground "bad taste." In *Armies of the Night* he defends obscenity and other kinds of low humor for the salutary political effects of a language that is at once obscene and distinguished: "In the Army he discovered that the humor was probably in the veins and the roots of the local history of every state and county in America—the truth of the way it really felt over the years passed on a river of obscenity from small-town storyteller to storyteller there down below the bankers and the books and the educators and the legislators—so Mailer never felt more like an American than when he was naturally obscene" (58). The complaint that Mailer is nothing more than a literary self-publicist, a seeker of shock-value for its own sake, conveniently ignores the confluent political and aesthetic aims of his obscenity: the four-letter words that some publishing houses and journals have found unspeakable are, for Mailer, the life-blood of American identity.

Mailer's Egypt novel is truly shocking. In *Ancient Evenings* the indigestible phallus of Osiris, an odd metaphor that first arises in Mailer's study of Henry Miller, *Genius and Lust* (1976), expresses the painful but necessary aspects of existence that must be honestly confronted if we are to achieve personal and political integration. Menenhetet tells his life story, warts and all, on the "Night of the Pig" in the hopes of achieving such an integration, but he is thwarted by Khem-Usha, the High Priest who ultimately divides the power of the pharaoh to the detriment of the kingdom. In the final pages of *Ancient Evenings*, Menenhetet II, who is both grandson and protégé of the experienced man, endures the old man's bitter knowledge. The scene is exquisitely grotesque, but, even if we conclude that it is merely "bad taste," it is beyond belief that Mailer does not know exactly what he is doing. The art of the gambit is to give a piece away with the design of winning back greater value in the long run, and Mailer gambles with bad taste throughout *Ancient Evenings*:

> Then all of him came forth, and in great bitterness. His seed was like a purge, foul and bitter, and I would have liked to vomit but could not. I had to take into me the misery he felt. [. . .]
> So, with the phallus still in my mouth, I knew the shame of Menenhetet. [. . .]
> I also knew his exhaustion. It came down upon me like a cataract. In none of his four lives had he found what he desired. That much I knew, and then I swallowed, and all the venom of his Khaibit that would now be my knowledge of the past.
> I would live by the guidance of his shadow. (689)

Of the seven souls, the Khaibit is known as the shadow and is most strongly associated with memory, but memory does not come without a price. We often discuss "memory" and "history" as if these were unquestionably good things, something we should always choose instead of something we must earn.

In *Ancient Evenings* Mailer imagines a time before innocence. In imag-
ining a world view before the rise of monotheism, before Adam became
the first man, Mailer struggles to connect readers with the history of what
came before their own time, and, in so doing, he critically apprehends
the motivations behind Adamic innocence: we wish to imagine ourselves
as innocent primarily because we do not wish to swim the Duad of historical awareness. The lesson for Americans is clear but hardly attractive.
Accepting the burden of history is not merely a matter of dispensing with
the ahistorical mythologies that give our culture a form; we must *endure*
history to know it.

Ancient Evenings circumscribes the limitations of the Adamic mythology by crossing it with Egyptian mythology. We are told by the historian
of Egyptian antiquity James Henry Breasted that Egyptian society was
rigidly hierarchical, and that only the pharaoh had access to the gods
through prayer. Mailer imagines an individual who disrupts this orderly
chain of command, and in so doing he also resists the temptation to ex-
aggerate the degree to which his individual is an outsider. The two ghosts
in the center of an Egyptian pyramid are from the center of Egyptian
society. Menenhetet I, having attempted to become the chief political
officer of Egypt, the vizier, has been very close to power: he at times may
pity himself for failing to attain all he wanted, but he can never regard
himself as "a simple genuine self against the whole world."

Though Adamic Americans are stereotypically supposed to be unin-
terested in power, Mailer refuses, and this refusal opens up other avenues
in his work besides the matter of American character. American power
structures in relation to American character has been his chief theme:
massive architecture gives us the feeling that we are in the presence of
great power. As the pyramid is a widely recognized symbol of central-
ized Egyptian power, the Pentagon serves a similar function in American iconography. In *Armies of the Night* Mailer ponders the Pentagon and
finds it comparable to Egyptian architecture:

> He had made the grand connection between Egyptian architecture and
> the Pentagon. Yes. The Egyptian forms, slab-like, excremental, thick walls,
> secret caverns, had come from the mud of the Nile, mud was the medium
> out of which the Egyptians built their civilization, abstract ubiquitous
> mud equaled in modern times only by abstract ubiquitous money, filthy
> lucre (thoughts of Norman O. Brown). And American Civilization had
> moved from the existential sanction of the frontier to the abstract ubiq-
> uitous sanction of the dollar bill. (178)

This paragraph and others like it in *Armies of the Night* form the secret passageways connecting Mailer's Egypt novel and his novel of the CIA. As in all of Mailer's novels, the effective resistance to totalitarianism is not contempt but comprehension. *Ancient Evenings* argues that the effort is worth even the while of forgotten ghosts in a crumbling tomb.

The American Adam in the CIA: Harry's Story

It is a commonplace of Mailer criticism to note that he follows in the Adamic tradition as defined by Lewis.[9] Readers of Mailer's work have noted his tendency to regenerate typically American voices in each individual book, but so far there has not been a satisfactory theory to explain what this tendency means when regarded as an overall design.[10] If we note that Mailer consistently takes ahistorical American selves and transfers them to explicitly political situations, we recognize that there is a method not only to his revisions of the American character, but also to his stylistic derangements.

In *Harlot's Ghost* Mailer reworks the supposedly apolitical Adamic mythology to reveal the inner workings of the CIA. Adamic ideology, it has been argued, stands between American novelists and political fiction of the first rank. Whether it is referred to as Adamic ideology, American individualism, or pastoralism, the argument is that the American insistence on the primacy of the individual experience and the measurement of that experience in terms of "innocence" will inhibit or thwart the creation of political novels.[11]

The American narrative in its cruder forms has often expressed the belief that we Americans are somehow not to blame for the fallenness and impurity of history. There is always a time, further back, when there was entitlement without condition and when one could name the world with assurance.[12] It is currently fashionable to condemn authors who work within this tradition, and in a 1912 essay Donald Pease has accused Mailer of presenting "official American history" in his novels rather than something subversive like new historicism. This is a fairly odd claim, since in Mailer's writings there is never a clear line between the fictions and myths with which we construct our national identity and the political ideologies that struggle for prevalence in our society. Actually, Mailer does what Richard Slotkin has said the literary critic must do: "We can only demystify our history by historicizing our myths—that is, by treating them as human creations, produced in a specific historical time and place, in response to the contingencies of social and personal life" (80).

Although Harry Hubbard does begin his career as a spy from a position of naiveté, it would be a mistake simply to read him as Adam before the Fall, and the CIA as the fallen world, strewn with apple cores. At the beginning of "Alpha," Hubbard knows little or nothing about the inner workings of the CIA, and in this sense he is Adamic, but this phase is very brief. When he quickly gets caught in an internecine bureaucratic struggle, his patron Harlot gets him out of trouble by changing his code-name so rapidly that Harry's antagonized superior officer will never know who to blame. Harry Hubbard's introduction to CIA life is, then, an inversion of the simple, referential language of Adam before the apple. Agency life trains Hubbard to suspect every memo, every individual word, of falsehood or indirection. In complicating his Adamic protagonist's innocence, Mailer has moved beyond the fictions of pure opposition, of narcissistic antipathy toward the fallen world of political reality.

In placing his American Adam within "the Company," Mailer reveals the ideological similarities between the myth of the American Adam and that of the American Century: both are organized groups of ideas that entitle and empower *American* activity. Both sets of ideas necessarily conceal the self-interest behind this ideological empowerment, instead creating the belief that an "unfallen" motive underlies the endeavor. On the individual level, the self-concept of Adamic innocence promotes individualistic activity by freeing the simple genuine individual from the consequences of social corruption: the individual is an exception to social rules. On the national level a similar idea is at work: the American nation is capable of its greatest political follies when it believes itself to be the simple genuine democracy against the whole world.[13] As Noam Chomsky and other radical critics of American foreign policy have pointed out repeatedly, the American media will always depict American invasions of other countries (Nicaragua and Grenada are recent examples) as a *defense* of an American value rather than an offensive attack (Chomsky 59–82). The cameras will focus on a simple American self (a medical student who has been studying in Grenada, a lone soldier drinking coffee), rather than the enemy dead. Adamic ideology is typically used to portray agents of American power as underdogs, and Mailer is short-circuiting just such an ideological construction when he makes his American Adam a CIA agent.

During the cold war, it had sometimes seemed that the American Adam was a double-agent in the garden. The degree to which a protagonist has individual freedom determines how much "agency" that character has, and thus how much a character may represent a general resistance to institutions or social trends that threaten individual freedom. In the individual, political agency takes its most decentralized form. At the same time, the containment of dissent within the Adamic individual insures that no *collective* resistance to institutions such as the CIA may form. In attempting to comprehend the harlot in the garden, Mailer's fictional interpretation of American intelligence work does more than any other work of literature to help readers gain access to "the imagination of the state."[14]

The imagination of the state in *Harlot's Ghost* is, through and through, a cold war imagination, and so the inversion and frustration of Adamic simplicity begins with the title and runs through the novel. First of all, who or what is "Harlot"? In an earlier period Mailer might have claimed to know, but the act of naming has become much more complicated in his recent work. "Harlot's ghost" can refer to the ghost of Hugh Tremont Montague, the high-level CIA officer whom Mailer based on the historical James Jesus Angleton. Like Angleton, Hugh, code-named Harlot, is a literary man, an obsessed counter-spy, and probably a tragic failure. The title *Harlot's Ghost* refers, in part, to the long shadow Hugh casts, even after he has lost a central position within the agency.

The name also refers to the narrator Harry Hubbard. He is a ghost-writer in the employ of the CIA, where he produces ideologically sound detective fiction, but he used to have a more dashing role in that organization. He is doubly a ghostwriter in that he becomes an assistant to Hugh in the years after Watergate. Hugh asks Harry to help him investigate the possibility that the CIA as a whole is on the verge of becoming an essentially private organization, one that is entirely self-funded and thus in no way dependent upon or answerable to American political processes at any level.[15] While acting as Harlot's ghostwriter, Harry Hubbard also writes the Alpha and Omega manuscripts.

Not only is it an open question to which individual the title phrase "harlot's ghost" refers—the very concept of individualism is taken apart in *Harlot's Ghost*. The structural relationship between Harry's Alpha and Omega manuscripts reflects the psychological thesis his wife Kittredge has pursued as a CIA analyst, and this bicameral approach to the human personality is an adroit way for Mailer to explore parallels between individual and national identity.[16] In order to explain theoretically the inner workings of the double-agent, Kittredge develops the notion that each person is not an individual but is instead inhabited by *two* personalities, the alpha and omega selves. Large sections of *Harlot's Ghost* are made up of a correspondence between Harry and Kittredge: Harry's apprenticeship years in the CIA test Kittredge's theories. Large-scale political formations (such as the cold war divisions between the United States and the USSR) organize the communal identities of both sides and of smaller groups, and this encounter forms an overall identity that has important consequences. Nuclear war only becomes an option when this overall "person" feels despair; so long as one superpower has hope, it will not back the other into a corner. This dialectical approach to identity runs through the novel at all levels until we are left wondering if international divisions follow from the bicameral personality, or if the divisions in the self follow from the political polarization of human experience within contexts such as the cold war.[17]

In that each is the product of a dialectical interaction, personal and political identities are homologous in Mailer's cold war world. Just as the two superpowers shape each other's identity, Harry and Kittredge are similarly interdependent. When they meet, Kittredge is about to be married to Harry's mentor Hugh, but after many years their epistolary (and, therefore, "innocent") love affair turns carnal when Harry, intuitively sensing that Kittredge will commit suicide, saves her life. From that moment on, Kittredge structures Harry's life, just as her ideas about alpha and omega determine the form of his literary memoirs.

Mailer also creates structural parallels to develop his conception of the divided self and comment on sexual politics. The pattern of the book (and thus of Harry's life) forms an implicit critique of the sexist division of good and evil expressed in the Fall from innocence in the book of Genesis. In the biblical story Eve is the temptress who pulls Adam down, and in Milton's retelling it is worse for women—noble Adam cannot abandon his domestic partner. In the Omega manuscript, the one hundred page thriller that precedes the encyclopedic Alpha, we are presented with a cold war revision of the Adamic narrative. Upon the death of Harlot (if he has died), Kittredge runs off with the devil-figure Dix Butler, and Harry Hubbard (like Ishmael, Huck Finn, Dick Diver, and Jake Barnes) takes flight from American civilization. Kittredge has, by this time in her marriage to Harry, been running all kinds of operations under her husband's nose, and the Omega manuscript ends with revelation upon revelation of corruption. What came before Harry's flight seems, relatively and retrospectively, like innocence. But Kittredge has not become merely a scapegoat by the end of the lengthy manuscript, as Harry makes clear when he begins to read it to himself. She is, for Harry, at once the Eve of his paradise lost and the heavenly muse that may reconnect him to that distant world:

> *Even as we and the Soviets had spent years jamming each other's radio broad-*
> *casts, so would I recite the manuscript of Alpha whenever Kittredge became too*
> *alive. Such observances did not always work, but when they did, I could turn*
> *the corner. The ghosts of long-gone deeds would not appear, and I could live with*
> *Kittredge. Alpha was all I had of her now. I began, therefore, to recite my first*
> *sentences aloud, slowly, quietly, intoning the words; the sounds themselves came*
> *forward as forces in the unseen war of all those silences in myself that rode to*
> *war when I slept.* (107)

Instead of the prior Adamic entitlements of pure individualism and referential language, Harry's postwar world is an interdependent multi-
verse. Narrative alone holds these painfully impermanent perspectives
in place: Harry names the CIA, but no name is certain. He gives it a history in a prayerful observance of its ghosts, but his prayers are meant to
protect him from the ghosts of history. This form of communication is
quite a jump from the confident language of Adam described by Lewis.
Though Harry claims that the Alpha manuscript is something he writes/
recites to quiet the ghost of his failed marriage, for readers it will certainly
be something more than that, since the story also gives narrative embodi-
ment to the ghosts of American political history.

From Innocence to Irony: Mailer's Tale of Hoffman

Harlot's Ghost is composed of two tandem "manuscripts": the Omega
manuscript, which covers Harry Hubbard's experiences from 1983 to
1984, and the much longer Alpha manuscript, which focuses on his CIA
career from 1955 to the Kennedy assassination. These manuscripts are
also stylistically distinct, and Mailer uses style to orchestrate the larger
movements of his obsessively dualistic novel. This formal division also
works to fend off anticipated critical attacks, since Mailer gives the
shorter manuscript the psychological intensity and narrative discipline
that he knows critics will find wanting in the longer manuscript.[18] The
Omega manuscript has a gothic urgency that accelerates until the man-
sion burns down in romantic fashion.

 The narrative that ends up in the land of Poe begins rather more
Edenically: "Even guidebooks for tourists seek to describe this virtue:
'The island of Mount Desert, fifteen miles in diameter, rises like a fabled
city from the sea. The natives call it Acadia, beautiful and awesome'" (4).
Harry parodies the language of guidebooks in this tongue-in-cheek description to demonstrate his own complex attitude: America is at once a
land where great purity can be seen and experienced, but it is also a cul-

tural landscape that sustains almost invincible dreams of innocence in spite of great evidence to the contrary. It is a land where almost any wrong can be, if not forgotten, aestheticized. The island under Hubbard's Keep is haunted by the memory of the Abnaki Indians of the Algonquin tribe, reminders in the first pages of *Harlot's Ghost* that Adamic mythology can be a cloak of innocence to hide a more sinister history: "The ghosts of these Indians may no longer pass through our woods, but something of their old sorrows and pleasures join the air. Mount Desert is more luminous than the rest of Maine" (4). The opening pages of the novel, so reminiscent of the travel guide's tone of innocent enjoyment, are troubled by ghosts, specifically ghosts that precede Adam, be he American or Hebrew. To indicate the historicity of the myth, *Harlot's Ghost*, like *Ancient Evenings*, travels back to a time before Adam.

Just when it seems that Mailer's narrator is going to see the CIA through Acadia-shaded glasses, the chapter ends with an italicized passage in which Harry Hubbard, in March of 1984, is fleeing from the United States to Moscow, where he hopes to find a still-living Harlot: *"Due for arrival in London in another few hours, I felt obliged to read the rest of Omega, all of one hundred and sixty-six pages of typescript, after which I would tear up the sheets and flush away as many of them as the limited means of the British Airways crapper on this aircraft would be able to gulp into itself"* (11). The stylistic shift (reminiscent of the shift from the well-cured style of the first book of *Ancient Evenings* to the obscene gravy of the second book) conditions our reading of any Adamic or otherwise idealized perceptions in the Omega manuscript and the Alpha manuscript to follow.

By carefully separating earlier and later perspectives in this way, Mailer's CIA novel introduces the Adamic self into cold war America, adapting the Adamic myth to the realities of CIA life. "'Oh, darling, I love giving people names. At least, people I care about. That's the only way we're allowed to be promiscuous. Give each other hordes of names'" (21). Kittredge, Harry Hubbard's wife, comments on the penchant for nicknames, acronyms, and code-names in agency life. Naming is, for Kittredge, a compensation for the sexual power she has given up to obtain her position in society and in the CIA. This sublimation of sex into language is one of many reflections of the Protestant ethos that shapes life in the agency.

The Adamic power to name is the privilege of American "agents" in general, but higher ranking namers approach the biblical power of the original Adam: "It was Allen Dulles who first christened him thus" (21). In naming each other, Mailer's characters are partial manifestations of the complete, Adamic entitlement that was lost in the Garden of Eden. They are people who presume they have political power: "Did people in Intelligence shift names about the way others move furniture around a room?" (22).

Lewis described the Parties of Hope, Despair, and Irony as the choices available to the American writer who wished to take a position in the American dialogue, but Adamic entitlement in the CIA is a more slippery affair. When Harry Hubbard, who has just spun out on an icy road, calls home to his wife Kittredge, she says "'Are you really all right? Your voice sounds as if you just shaved off your Adam's apple'" (24). Unbeknownst to Kittredge, Harry has just betrayed her sexually and is returning from a visit to his mistress. Just after his car slides into a spin and then mysteriously rights itself, Harry quotes *Paradise Lost* to himself, as if to say Adamic entitlement and paradise lost exist side by side in the CIA. In Harry's personal life, as in his political activity, the ideology of American innocence is inseparable from transgression.

The coexistence and interdependence of good and evil run through Mailer's work but receive supreme expression in *Harlot's Ghost*. Mailer begins this theme with the name of the novel, as we note from "Harlot." The word apparently has nothing to do with the "innocence" that we usually associate with American Adamicism, but if we track it to its root, we see that Mailer's Harlot and Lewis's American Adam have some rough similarities. The word harlot descends from the Middle English *herlot*, meaning "rogue" or "vagabond." In this sense, the harlot has a freedom from ethical, economic, or other kinds of historical constraints, and in this freedom the harlot resembles the adventurous Adam whose absence Lewis laments in the final pages of *The American Adam*. Mailer's ghostly American self is Lewis's American Adam in between incarnations.[19]

The coexistence of Adam before the Fall and Adam Fallen is a puzzling theme in Mailer's work, since to understand it we must fuse Adamic linguistic confidence with existential dread. Mailer insists that our moral action is predicated on a Kierkegaardian uncertainty, and his novels develop this moral insight in a variety of ways.[20] As uncertainty is the defining condition of the individual, Mailer shows it to be the formative condition of the CIA; it is certainly at the heart of *Harlot's Ghost*, a thirteen-hundred page novel that ends with the words "TO BE CONTINUED." This is a shocking way to end the novel. The reader confronts a formal uncertainty, since we do not know if the narrative is over, if Mailer is pulling our collective leg, if he is in fact continuing and planning to finish the trilogy he began with *Ancient Evenings*, or if he will simply write a sequel to *Harlot's Ghost* that will take us from the Kennedy assassination, through Watergate, and up to the Iran/Contra scandal and beyond. The formal uncertainty reverberates throughout the novel, since, at the novel's inconclusive conclusion, Harry wonders from inside his Moscow hotel room if he will find Harlot alive or not. Has Harry Hubbard defected? Ending, after thirteen hundred pages, with the scandalous "TO BE CONTINUED," the novel denies us all the assurance provided by the insider formulas and neat conclusions of spy thrillers. Mailer maintains this uncertainty from the moment Harry becomes a fully initiated member of the organization, which is the only way Harry can still be a "simple genuine self against the whole world" after having been an integral part of attempts to assassinate a foreign head of state.

Uncertainty is one way to keep the idea of innocence alive; the problems inherent in writing and interpretation offer another. That is, Harry can fashion an innocent self even though that self is clearly guilty of crimes against civil liberty if he becomes a writer, since on the written page he can deploy selves at will. He can begin in youth, as he does in the Alpha manuscript, and approach the complex world of the CIA as a beginner. Despite prohibitions, Harry has written about the CIA. In fact, the prohibition against writing about the CIA becomes another source of innocence, since it pits Harry, a simple genuine self compared to the men he works for, against the CIA, which is Harry's whole world:

> I had navigated my way across half of a large space (my past) and if I put it in that fashion, it is because I did not see how I could publish the manuscript, this Alpha manuscript as I called it—working title: *The Game*. Of course, it did not matter how it was christened. By the pledge I had taken on entering the Agency, it was simply not publishable. The legal office of the Agency would never permit this work to find a public audience. Nonetheless, I wished *The Game* to shine in a bookstore window. I had simple literary desires. (35)

Simple literary desires. The simple, genuine writer against the legal office does not even claim power to name (christen) the manuscript. He resigns himself to the fact that he must be a secret writer, that is, one whose discourse can be neatly divided into public and private. Writing is the perfect expression of Harry's double consciousness, since the individualistic and defiant act of writing gives him claim to innocence even as he writes the story of his own complicity in matters such as political assassination. Mailer at once engages in and subverts Adamic ideology.

What are we, then, to make of what is perhaps the strangest moment in *Harlot's Ghost*, that moment when Hugh, Kittredge, and Harry go to a nightclub and accidentally confront the cultural revolution to come, incarnated in the body of Lenny Bruce? The evening is profoundly disturbing to the three CIA agents and is analogous to that moment in *Ancient Evenings* when Menenhetet I, advocate of a polytheistic world and psychology, makes known his awareness and complete disapproval of the upstart monotheist Akhenaton. Lenny Bruce's freedom of speech and cultural politics are completely intolerable to the prim troika, and Kittredge announces she will go home and have a stiff drink even though she is pregnant. What is really surprising about this scene is the degree to which Mailer has imaginatively entered his characters and sympathetically rendered their complaints. We have to remind ourselves when reading this scene that Mailer for decades did not publish in *The New Yorker* because the editors would not let him write "fuck."[21] To this day Mailer points out the significance, in terms of his own development, of his most Bruce-like *Advertisements for Myself*: this, Mailer says, is the book in which he found his own voice. Are we to conclude from the emphasis of *Harlot's Ghost*, a book in which the cultural revolution of the 1960s is reduced almost to a footnote, that Mailer is no longer a literary Lenny Bruce? Lenny Bruce, in trying to defend his brand of obscenity as free speech protected by the First Amendment, became a kind of cultural hero, a raunchy but straight-talking, genuine self against the conformity of his times: a home-grown mythological creature. A generation later this spirit of free speech would be reincarnated once again, this time in the body of one Abbie Hoffman, the clown-activist who bedeviled the "Establishment" in similar ways. Mailer's writing on Hoffman provides clues about the evanescent appearance of Lenny Bruce in *Harlot's Ghost*.[22]

Mailer has reflected on the relationships between literary irony and politics in his writings on Abbie Hoffman. When he wrote an introduction to Hoffman's collection of essays *Soon to Be a Major Motion Picture*, the novelist praised the activist's lack of irony, but he revised this sentiment in a foreword to *The Best of Abbie Hoffman*, collected after Hoffman's suicide. In the latter appraisal Mailer confesses that he had previously regarded Abbie Hoffman as a clown, which, in retrospect, he decided was an unfair assessment: Mailer came to believe Abbie was sincere. Even so, through the spectacles of hindsight, Mailer finds fault with Hoffman's lack of literary irony. We can only wonder if, in this capsule biography, Mailer is gazing at a possible fate that could have been his own:

Abbie was serious. His thousand jokes were to conceal how serious he was. It makes us uneasy. Under his satire beat a somewhat hysterical heart. It could not be otherwise. Given his life, given his immersion in a profound lack of security, in a set of identity crises that would splat most of us like cantaloupes thrown off a truck, it is prodigious how long he resisted madness and death. He had to have a monumental will. Yet it is part of the civilized trap of literature that an incredible life is not enough. The survivor must rise to heights of irony as well. This was not Abbie's forte. His heart beat too fiercely. He cared too much. He loved himself too much. All the same, we need not quibble. We have here a document of a remarkable man. In an age of contracting horizons, we do well to count our blessings. How odd that now, Abbie is one of them. Our own holy ghost of the Left. Salud! ("Foreword" viii–ix)

Lenny Bruce, Abbie's ghost, the long-gone Mailer who once wrote "the shits are killing us"—the fantasy of the simple, genuine (and often obscene) self against the prim, conformist world of Eisenhower's America has died, but in American literature we see its karmic return. Mailer's affection for the outrageously free voice of Abbie Hoffman shows a lingering attachment, but there is also a feeling of sadness and resignation: a man profoundly serious, but cursed with a reputation for clowning. A monumental will that, in vain, defends a hysterical heart. Exactly these oppositions are put to the test by Mailer's writings, just as they were by Hoffman's life. In acknowledging the demands of "the civilized trap of literature," Mailer avoids the problematic position of "naive" Adamicism: he does not, in his later writings, sentimentally condemn civilization and align himself completely with civilization's discontents as he did in an earlier stage of his career.

The Age of Reagan was not *in* the wake of the New Left so much as it *was* the Wake of the Left, and so the hope of the Left is apparently a dead thing—a coat upon a stick—but in Mailer's cosmology death is a fine beginning. The spent life, even that of a failure, may continue as a ghost or even be reincarnated. Though wrinkled and sweaty from its last owner, the garment of hope may be cleaned and ironized. Abbie Hoffman's suicide provided an appropriate body for this wake, for if we conceive of his death in relation to the Age of Reagan, we immediately confront the divide between cynicism and paranoia. Did he kill himself because he was worn down by years of resistance to fascist tendencies in America? In the paranoid version of his death, Abbie Hoffman is a latter-day Walter Benjamin. More cynical attendees at the wake will prefer to think that the whole New Left enterprise was built on the neurotic grandiosity of counter-cultural figures such as Abbie Hoffman and General Marijuana, a.k.a. Norman Mailer. Mailer, the archetypal survivor, counsels that we steer a course between cynicism and paranoia (as does Harlot in his "High Thursday" lectures at the CIA).

The ghost of Hoffman, in reminding us of the fate Mailer avoids, provides a key to Mailer's progression as a writer through *Harlot's Ghost*. He seems to have determined, somewhere between the novels he wrote in the 1960s and those he wrote in the 1980s, that the "radical innocence" he was attempting to fashion in novels such as *An American Dream* was not the most skillful response to the political and cultural events of postwar America. While the absurd has always been forbidden for Mailer, he does come to argue consistently that our political resolve, our hope, must be tempered with a profound sense of irony if it is to survive the disappointments that are the promise of history. In *Ancient Evenings* the metaphorically resonant "balance of Maat," Maat being a god whose tendency is to bring all forces in the universe to balance, debunks many an affectation. It would be hard to say exactly when Mailer's tolerance for irony shifted, but "Miller and Hemingway," a pivotal essay that demonstrates how Mailer approaches political ethics through an essentially literary vocabulary, divides our philosophical relation to postmodernity into two basic choices: there is the "grace under pressure" response of Hemingway, and there is the "swim across the river of shit" alternative of Henry Miller. Mailer contrasts Hemingway and Miller's styles as responses to a culture increasingly characterized by waste, interruption, and disorder. However heroic Hemingway's invention of the Jake Barnes persona may have been, it is not a posture, Mailer came to believe, that sustains life in this world (see Mailer's "Miller and Hemingway," *Pieces* 86–93). Miller's laughter in the face of all that is obscene and humiliating is a greater source of strength. Mailer can never laugh away the social consequences of a man's life with the assurance of a Henry Miller, but in *Ancient Evenings* and *Harlot's Ghost* we see that a higher tolerance for the *verboten* absurd has tempered Mailer's world.

Mailer is not alone in seeing an antithesis between ironic and politically engaged world views. Hayden White states this position most succinctly in his study *Metahistory*: "As the basis of a world view, irony tends to dissolve all belief in the possibility of positive political actions. In its apprehension of the essential folly or absurdity of the human condition, it tends to engender belief in the 'madness' of civilization itself and to inspire a Mandarin-like disdain for those seeking to grasp the nature of social reality" (38). White is careful to say that irony can be used "tactically" by politically engaged persons, but as a world view it is incompatible with political engagement. In *Harlot's Ghost* Mailer takes tactical irony to its limit, but, as ever, he refuses the flight from responsibility that he takes the philosophy and aesthetic of the absurd to be.[23]

Political Cynicism and Adamic Affirmation

The thoroughly cynical political novel offers an imaginary stairway to transcendence, since the novelist's *reductio ad absurdum* invariably elevates private irony above and beyond the humiliations of public life. However, it results in a morally crude vision of history so frequently that Robert Alter has dismissed the cynical tendency of postwar American political fiction: "If the conventional political novel tends to assume that, despite troubling agitations of the surface, all's well with the Republic, what the adversary political novel of the past two decades has generally assumed is that the Republic is rotten to the core" (*Motives* 39). But Alter's judgment in this case brings us to overlook key features of postwar American writing. If one *knew* that a government were "rotten to the core," why detain oneself with the messy details of history or the delicacies of art? Alter's formulation suggests a new meaning to Adorno's notion that poetry after the Holocaust is barbaric. We can understand the comment aesthetically rather than ethically if we believe that history has revealed its apocalyptic face through the emergence of death camps and totalitarian organization in modern societies. If we *know* the meaning of history in an absolute sense, fine distinctions, formerly the poet's province, have become outdated. The only appropriate poetry in this barbaric age will be "barbaric" poetry.

In the days of "apocalypse now," the argument continues, artistic subtlety is a form of nostalgia. In the days of Moloch, poets must howl. Mailer evoked Nazi genocide to justify the excesses of the hipster in the first sentence of "The White Negro" and howled against cold war conformity throughout the rest of *Advertisements for Myself*. These essays, short stories, semi-poetry, and less classifiable texts form a "Howl" in prose. Like Ginsberg in his more outraged verse, Mailer in the 1950s adopted the attitude of the outraged outsider. There is one problem with this poetic rationale, however. It can be considered true that the writer's barbaric yelp from the rooftops is the sweet and fitting response to the age if and only if the historical backgrounds of which we speak can properly be called "apocalyptic." But in postwar America, where we have economic slumps, periodic foreign wars, and above-average scores in terms of old age, sickness, and death, we see writers oddly scrambling for personal affliction. We all know that "writers need to suffer," and this notion follows directly from the entitlement granted to the storyteller who has suffered. We pause to hear the story of the car accident or the dramatic fall. Catastrophe confers authority.

In the postwar period the apocalyptic mood has received its greatest support from the revelations of Auschwitz. Against such horrors, what can a writer *not* say? Totalitarianism has, in the same paradoxical manner, been the source of *power* for many cold war era political novelists.[24] Willie Stark, ominously, has a forelock in *All the King's Men*. General Cummings predicts an Americanized version of fascism in *The Naked and the Dead*, and Lieutenant Hearn is proved to be short-sighted in his belief that liberals will band together to form an adequate response. William Burroughs's anti-heroes are chased across the galaxy by fascist divisionists and innumerable other political forces dedicated to exterminating whatever is eccentric or individual. Billy Pilgrim finds a "world elsewhere" on Trafalmador. American versions of the Holocaust and of totalitarian oppression have been adapted to American themes, particularly to the myth of the American Adam. We see this especially in "The White Negro," an essay that (unconvincingly) justifies the murder of an innocent man by contextualizing the violence as an act against corrupt society. The binary logic operating in the essay and many postwar fictions recreates innocence in opposition to corrupt society: the corruption of the world empowers "Adam" to act, and an insane world entitles the opposing self *completely*. Thus, Adamic individualism is, in many 1960s texts, an inverted form of America's Faustian hunger for power.

This kind of postwar Adamic entitlement does not sit well with Alter, however. He expresses irritation with American political fiction in the days after Vietnam and Watergate not because the literary form is a spring of protest, but rather because it became a mode of protest that too often settled for nothing less than pure opposition: by casting the republic in an absolutely diabolical light (Alter argues that Coover does this in *The Public Burning*), the novelist forsakes the moral variegations of history. The aesthetic result is often somewhat melodramatic, a chiaroscuro of good and evil in which the authorial voice is conveniently identified with the forces of good.[25] Almost never, complains Alter, does the writer have to measure politically offensive policies or practices against more palatable ones. The writer is most content, and most empowered, on the outside, but to judge politics from the outside, to judge without ever taking a positive stand that can itself be subject to criticism, is cynical. If we keep in mind Alter's demand that political writers be historically responsible, we avoid being charmed by the sirens of cynicism.

Mailer tends to pick up American politics by the "affirmative" handle, though the nature of this affirmation becomes increasingly qualified throughout his work. In strictly political terms, his novels can be shown to profess a belief in the "balance of powers" that is perhaps the most intellectually defensible tenet of American civil religion. His books hardly suggest that all is right with the republic. Mailer agrees that everything has two handles, one good and one evil, but for Mailer there is no Emersonian confidence about our ability to choose properly between them.[26] Mailer's novels put into play the most unlikely scenarios—he can find gods battling in the sexual act as well as in a grain of sand—but it is important to realize that the greatest failure of human life is not to enlist on the "wrong side" of the vast moral battle, but rather to refuse to face the uncertainties that are the painful foundation of human existence.

Harlot's Ghost does *not* ask "Which side are you on?" in the manner of a political song, and in this characteristic the novel takes a different road from that of, say, *Barbary Shore*, which was a radical novel in Rideout's sense of the term. *Ancient Evenings* brings us into the major and minor struggles that determine the fate of an empire, and this is an alternative to writing a book for or against imperialism. Each novel Mailer writes is noticeably less activist than its predecessor, and yet Mailer is not less of a political novelist than when he wrote *Why Are We in Vietnam?* or *Barbary Shore*. What, we should then ask, does he *do* as a political novelist? Because Americans have become increasingly cynical about politics and politicians, Mailer has chosen to affirm, in *Ancient Evenings* and *Harlot's Ghost*, the intellectual validity of political thinking. The effort of the late work has been to encourage readers to imagine themselves in dialogue with political powers-that-be, and this imaginary engagement is essential to any more specific form of political struggle.

Mailer has attempted to communicate with political powers directly, and his imaginary personae have petitioned God, gods, pharaohs, and presidents. Thrones, powers, dominions: the Satanic machinery of *Paradise Lost* also has a necessary place in this essentially mysterious world. The puritan division of good from evil is a condition that Mailer has worked through, and his late novels are built on the interdependence of heaven and slime. We see this interdependence in that moment in the Omega manuscript where Harry Hubbard almost dies—or may have died. Having almost driven over a cliff—he is not certain that he is still alive—on the way home from his earthy mistress' trailer, Harry Hubbard realizes in great fright that "'*Millions of creatures,*' I said aloud to the empty car—actually said it aloud!—'*walk the earth unseen, both when we wake and when we sleep,*' after which, trundling along at thirty miles an hour, too weak and exhilarated to stop, I added in salute to the lines just recited, 'Milton, *Paradise Lost,*' and thought of how Chloe and I had gotten up from bed in her trailer on the outskirts of Bath a couple of hours ago and had gone for a farewell drink to a cocktail lounge with holes in the stuffing of the red leatherette booths" (22). Millions of creatures . . . Manichean battles. Intolerable to Mailer is the overly clear separation of gods and devils, of the high and the low, of the heavenly from the red leatherette—and thus of the political from everything else in American life. He is one of the few authors who does not tell us that we are better than politics, and his whole career has been a struggle to discover the meeting place of God and the Devil, to get Ishmael and Ahab to sit at the same table, to get readers to talk back to the "electronic malignity" of the television set. Each one of these conflicts could serve as a metaphor for the others in Mailer's work. His work declares the futility of any search for "a virgin land" or "a world elsewhere" beyond political consequences.

Notes

1. I place the word marginal in quotation marks since much American fiction continues to offer the reader an Innocent with whom to identify. This aspect of American literary tradition, which was at its pinnacle in the two decades after World War II, has fallen into critical disrepute.

2. I am calling recent that fiction that has emerged just before, during, and since the Age of Reagan. Said's essay, Adamic in its freedom to name the world, names the 1980s "the Age of Reagan": "Opponents, Audiences, Constituencies and Community."

3. Given the success of recent movies such as *Forrest Gump,* a film in which an absolutely simple and genuine self is the subject who endures American history yet is untainted, one could conclude that the Adamic mythos still has the power to name American social realities.

4. Jameson presents a thumbnail review of American Exceptionalism in one of his essays: "One of the most persistent leitmotivs in liberalism's ideological arsenal [. . .] is the notion of the disappearance of class [. . .]. We are told that the existence of the frontier [. . .] prevented the formation of the older, strictly European class antagonisms, while the absence from the United States of a classical aristocracy of the European type is said to account for the failure of a classical

bourgeoisie to develop in this country—a bourgeoisie which would then, following the continental model, have generated a classical proletariat over against itself. This is what we may call the American mythic explanation, and it seems to flourish primarily in those American Studies programs which have a vested interest in preserving the boundaries of their discipline" (*Signatures* 35).

5. In *The Unusable Past* Reising discusses Lewis as one of the "founding fathers" of American literary studies who excludes social and political reality from canonical American literature (107–22).

6. In Porter's formulation, Emerson initiates a mode of *detached* pragmatism: "when Emerson becomes a 'transparent eyeball,' joyfully announcing 'I am nothing; I see all,' he articulates the position of both the transcendent visionary poet (to whose role he himself aspires) and the neutral scientific observer (whose role he wishes to counteract). That is, the detached observer, like the visionary seer, appears to himself to occupy a position outside the world he confronts" (xii).

7. In *Criticism and Social Change*, Lentricchia makes the generalization that in America "parties of one" have flourished (6). Reising uses the same phrase to name his sub-section on Lewis: "Parties of One: R. W. B. Lewis" (107–23).

8. However much Mailer admires the philosophical mission of Protestant America, and he has admired it increasingly since writing *Of a Fire on the Moon* (1970), his writings always resist the morally corrupting certainties that he has repeatedly named "Faustian."

9. See especially Adams's *Existential Battles: The Growth of Norman Mailer* and Wenke's *Mailer's America*. William V. Spanos also lists Mailer as a "post-Adamic" author.

10. Leeds, *The Structured Vision of Norman Mailer*; Cowan, "The Americanness of Norman Mailer" in Braudy; and Taylor, "Of Adams and Aquarius" mark Mailer as Adamic. Adams counters in *Existential Battles* that Mailer is not part of the American tradition as defined by Lewis (13).

11. On the common ground of critics such as Lewis, Marx, Fussell, and Fiedler, see Graff, "American Criticism Left and Right" in Bercovitch and Jehlen, eds., *Ideology and Classic American Literature:* "In one way or another, all these theories tend to see American literature in terms of some form of escape from social categories [. . .]. These theories of the American element in literature actually make many of the same points in different vocabularies. (Roughly, Adamic innocence equals pastoral equals frontier equals evasion of heterosexual love, over and against which are the machine, coextensive with genteel society, coextensive with women and domestic love, etc. The collision results in tragedy, symbolism, etc.)" (106–7).

12. American writing, as distinguished from the songs of this continent before the first contact with Europe, begins with and is characterized by Adamic entitlement. The power to name and political dominion are each assumed by the same poetic flourish: Columbus renamed the rivers without concern that the native peoples called them by different names. See Bartolomé de Las Casas's "Journal of the First Voyage to America."

13. Ronald Steel criticizes American idealism divorced from political realism in *Pax Americana:* "Because the cold war, like the Second World War, was conceived as a moral crusade, it inflated an involvement that was essentially pragmatic into a moral mission. Since we were accustomed to victory in battle and were stronger than any nation had ever been in history, we believed that the world's problems could be resolved if only we willed hard enough and applied enough power. Convinced of the righteousness of our cause, we became intoxicated with our newly discovered responsibilities and saw them as a mandate to bring about the better world we so ardently desired. American military power, consecrated by the victory of the Second World War and reconfirmed by the development of the atomic bomb, joined forces with the power of American idealism to inaugurate a policy of global interventionism" (5).

14. "The imagination of the state" is Mailer's main concern in *Harlot's Ghost.* It is the title of narrator Harry Hubbard's unfinished work within the fictional world of the novel, and it was also the subject of an international conference organized by Mailer during his term as PEN president. While writers such as Donald Barthelme responded positively to the topic, saying that the imagination of the state and that of the writer "are in radical conflict all over the world," the South African novelist Nadine Gordimer objected that the state had no imagination since imagination is "private and individual." But if the writer is alienated from the state precisely because the state is certain "it is always right," as Gordimer also claimed, then the state is in some sense an entity with an imagination. For details on the conference and its various controversies, see Rollyson (338–49).

15. Mailer spells out this thesis in his nonfictional "Of a Harlot High and Low" (*Pieces* 159–208).

16. The personal intermingles with the political: it is intimated that Kittredge's unfinished work *The Dual Soul* follows from a life-long effort to comprehend her first husband, Hugh.

As for the word "bicameral," made famous by Jaynes's far-reaching theories on the origin of human consciousness, Mailer has denied that Jaynes holds the keys to his castle. "After paying due respect to Julian Jaynes," Mailer notes that his ideas seemed "awfully fancy" (personal communication). Clearly Mailer has considered Jaynes's argument that our bicameral attitude toward state and self-government follows from a biological development, but this idea is too far removed from human agency for Mailer to find it useful. Mailer's foundational prejudice against such bio-behavioral solutions is found in "The Psychology of Machines," a section from *Of a Fire on the Moon:* "psychology assumes free will. A human being totally determined is a machine. Psychology is then a study of the style of choice provided there is freedom to choose" (147).

17. Mailer has used the word "bicameral" on several occasions. His use of the term in the preface to *Pieces and Pontifications* is proleptic of the interrelationships between literature, psychology, and politics in *Harlot's Ghost:* "I would say to the

reader that you hold in your hand the work of a divided man. Not schizophrenic—divided. His personality is bicameral and built on two points of reference. (Perhaps this is why his body, whenever he eats too much, is shaped like an ellipse.) The reader, however, need feel no vast superiority. Metaphorically, all too many of us are, these days, kin to pregnant women, and feed not one person within us but two. Here, then, are two sides of myself as I survived the Seventies—my literary ghost looking for that little refinement of one's art which becomes essential as one grows older, and the cry of the street debater, front and center, who always speaks in the loudest voice" (x).

18. *Harlot's Ghost* was excoriated in *The Los Angeles Times Book Review* by Jonathan Franzen (29 Sept. 1991), in *The New York Review of Books* by Wilfrid Sheed (5 Dec. 1991), by Louis Menand in *The New Yorker* (4 Nov. 1991), and by Paul Gray in *Time Magazine* (30 Sept. 1991). The funniest excoriation is John Leonard's in *The Nation* (18 Nov. 1991). Like all reviews of Mailer books since *The Executioner's Song*, each of these reviews begins by acknowledging Mailer's brilliance, promise, or achievements—before giving the just-published book the back of the hand.

For a discussion of Jack London's similar use of aesthetic self-defense, see chapter 3, the section titled "Aesthetic Enthusiasm and Dual Perspective in *The Iron Heel.*"

19. Mailer uses reincarnation as a structural principle in *Ancient Evenings*, but he has spoken in numerous interviews of his personal belief in reincarnation as a way of understanding continuity and difference within identities (see various comments on reincarnation in Lennon's collection of interviews). Clearly he is as playful about the idea as he is serious: "if we're reborn, everything that was good and bad about us goes into the reincarnation. And God—I suspect and hope, if God isn't too tired—is exceptionally witty. So when you come up for that judgment, the post you're given for the next time out may not be exactly to your heart's desire" ("His Punch" 69–70). Mailer's conception, serious or playful, departs significantly from the Buddhist view, in which, precisely because there is no savior or judge, one's actions are determined by "your heart's desire."

20. Schrader has a much more disparaging view of Mailer's Kierkegaardian aspect. His essay "Norman Mailer and the Despair of Defiance" (Braudy 82–95) is highly critical of Mailer's existentialism, but I would argue that Schrader's essay describes the early Mailer. First published in 1961, it renders the philosophical corollaries to Mailer's immature Adamicism: "He identifies with the hipster both because the White Negro is in full-scale rebellion against civilization (defiant) and unleashes the life-giving force of primitive emotion. The very notion of the White Negro symbolizes the opposition between civilization (White) and instinctual passion (Negro). It is not only a dialectical but a *contradictory* idea in that rage and rebellion derive their force and meaning from civilized passion and can by no act of violence gain reentry into the innocence of immediacy. Mailer refuses to accept original sin as a fact of human life and would undo the Fall of mankind. He will, if need be, carry the human race back to the Garden of Eden

on his own shoulders—even if he must tread upon all the edifices of civilization to do it. The courage he wants is heroic, epic, Promethean, but, also, futile." In later work such as *Ancient Evenings* and *Harlot's Ghost*, Mailer becomes increasingly aware of the insufficiency of the absolute Adamic separation of individual and society, but this realization does not lead him to abandon the Adamic metaphors through which the specifics of American identity have been constructed.

21. Times and editors change, and Mailer has published the following political poem, titled "Homage to Faulkner," in the 11 December 1995 issue of *The New Yorker*: "Newt Gingrich looks for angry votes; / Ergo, he hammers welfare folks. / There lie his Presidential hopes: / Apotheosis of the Snopes" (42). This poem illustrates perfectly my thesis that American writers deploy apolitical literary narratives within manifestly political contexts.

22. Mailer may have learned the "disappearing hero" trick from Melville, though he has credited E. M. Forster for this technique in interviews when he discussed the sudden disappearance of Lt. Hearn from *The Naked and the Dead*.

23. Horsley's *Political Fiction and the Historical Imagination* takes issue with the notion that irony must be equated with escapism in political fiction. While, Horsley argues, "Irony is sometimes charged with being a form of acquiescence," upon examination we see that "the critical realism of the ironist constitutes one of the most tenacious forms of resistance to irrational belief, ideological certitude, and unthinking assimilation into irresponsible forms of political life" (255).

24. For a discussion of totalitarianism as the theoretical anchor of cold war discourse, see William Pietz's "The 'Post-Colonialism' of Cold War Discourse."

25. Novelists (e.g., Doctorow 85–86) have answered Alter's criticism, noting his intolerance of political criticism or dissent *when it comes from American authors*.

26. During the coffee gathering after one of Mailer's readings at Brown University in 1984, my wife Helena asked him, "What do you say to people who don't believe in 'evil'?" Mailer, throwing up his hands, said "I throw up my hands!"

5

Invisible Prophet: Sula Peace, 1965

At his best he does not ask for scapegoats, but for the hero as witness.
—Ralph Ellison

We like the individual witness. We have a feeling that to the extent politics or political passion or social or religious passion gets into a novel, that it's an impurity.
—E. L. Doctorow

This chapter describes some political uses of the scapegoat in three African-American novels: *Invisible Man, A Different Drummer,* and *Sula.* Though my readings of the first two largely prepare the way for the third, it should perhaps be conceded outright that there are many works to serve the cause of a public rally better than Morrison's *Sula.* It is a work of fiction that seems to shun political engagement, and yet it is the sort of novel that has been much discussed in terms of its politics in the decades after the 1960s. Novels exploring the social worlds of those who are most powerless, those who have, in Ellison's words, been cut off from the "instrumentalities of power," are political novels of a sort, but clearly not the same sort as *The Iron Heel.* In this chapter I examine three novels by African-American authors to present an evolutionary history of sorts: Ellison's *Invisible Man,* as a "covert preparation for an overt action," presents itself as a kind of submerged call to political action; Kelley's *A Different Drummer,* in spite of a superficial reticence, clearly presents a strategy for overt political action; and Morrison's *Sula,* taking a third path, upends the distinction between the personal and the political. The politics-of-identity novel can be seen as an imaginary bridge between powerlessness and the instrumentalities of power.

But, first, what of the American "mythical innocence" that supposedly hampers political expression in literature of the United States? American mythical innocence is either a joke or a nightmare in the context of African-American life, and so many would argue that African-American writers engaged in political struggles have not been hampered by demands for Adamic transcendence in the same ways as white Americans. In fact, pretensions to Adamic innocence in African-American literature are often the greatest sin, since admissions of such innocence are tantamount to a denial that the African-American holocaust ever occurred. Authors like Ellison who have insisted on their prerogative to write as *American* writers—to create characters who speak as simple, genuine selves to (primarily white) readers—have been charged with Uncle Tomism. Instead, in the African-American context political engagement and the subordination of art to politics are more likely to be proof of "innocence." While white authors are damned for mixing politics and literature, black authors are damned if they do and damned if they do not. In one sense it is easier for African-American authors to write political fiction in America, but in another sense it is even more difficult. White and black authors are invited to choose between being a poet and a politician, but the black author is, with some condescension, given more encouragement to go into politics.

There are real differences between the African-American and American literary traditions (leading many to speak of "literatures of the United States" rather than any single tradition), and yet there are continuities as well. African-American culture develops within American culture, and so the moral, ethical, and political vocabulary that Lewis designated "the matter of Adam" continues to operate within African-American writing, albeit in a very different way. The dialogue of innocence and experience abides in African-American stories, since African Americans have strong reason to regard themselves as victims of the blindness upon which American idealism is predicated. This victim position has had great power in generating what might be called "relative innocence," since the victim of society is innocent in relation to that society as a whole (which is figured mainly or entirely in its oppressive capacities), even when that character does something awful. Sethe of Morrison's *Beloved* could be described as innocent compared to those men protected by the rule of law who have crossed state lines to repossess her and her children. The gambit of relative innocence is hardly new within American literature, and so we recall that Huck Finn, Jake Barnes, and others who confess directly to American readers are, at best, relatively innocent.

African-American literature is now undergoing a creative and critical renaissance, and this may in part follow from the unavoidably social nature of its subject matter: readers after New Criticism and poststructuralism yearn for the touch of the world. Why, then, do we find African-

American authors of the first rank *denying* political activism in and discouraging political interpretations of their works? It may at first seem surprising that an African-American writer would feel the need to sublimate a political message, and yet Ralph Ellison, William Melvin Kelley, and Toni Morrison each have discounted political interpretations of their work. I believe this resistance to political interpretation is expressive of the special dilemma facing every American political novelist, namely the idea that one must choose between politics and literature. The pressures are greater for the African-American writer, however, since he or she may be faulted as much for *not* writing politically as for writing an overtly political novel.

The Politics of African-American Identity

The politics-of-identity novel often begins with an "invisible" subject matter. Ethnic minorities have historically been excluded from Ellison's "instrumentalities of power," and so the political expression of such groups, as it might appear in literature, is ignored (*Going* 62). When this situation continues unchallenged, literature and politics work hand in hand in a cycle of exclusion. In this sense any novel by a nonwhite author could be regarded as political—whatever its contents—especially when its achievements or failures are attributed a racial cause or significance. As we shall see, this well-intentioned critical presumption has become a source of resentment among some African-American authors. All of the authors discussed in this chapter rebel at being boxed into political engagement in this way, but when we look beyond these particular denials of politics we see that Ellison's *Invisible Man*, Kelley's *A Different Drummer*, and Morrison's *Sula* all deal obsessively with community organization and change—with the instrumentalities of power in America. All three novels dramatize the ways in which the scapegoat becomes a powerful agent of community organization, but each novel also counters the risks inherent in conceiving of the victim as a source of power.

The denial of political intent takes on special significance for minority writers, since the ascription of political intent to any writer solely on the basis of ethnic heritage is a perfect example of what Ellison meant by invisibility: it is a potentially racist refusal to see a person in all of her or his particularity. The author of a comprehensive history of postwar American fiction cautiously notes that much African-American fiction can be regarded de facto as political: "It would be possible to see the fictions of several black novelists as political in nature, their entire experience as political. Even when they focus on individual lives, the state as agencies, local power groups, the police, the community is authoritarian and totalitarian for them" (Karl 254). In looking at *Invisible Man*, *A Different Drummer*, and *Sula* together, I wish to show how the external pressures of political identity bear on literary form, but I never assume that a novel is political merely by virtue of the fact that its author is African American. Ellison challenged this demeaning notion when he wrote, regarding protest in *Invisible Man*, that "The protest is there, not because I was helpless before my racial condition, but because I *put* it there" (*Shadow* 142).

When we consider Ellison's specific objection about the way his particular protest was being interpreted, other confusing instances in which African-American writers deny the validity of political protest become clear. Ellison protests against the "protest" label because it is frequently a way of pigeonholing African-American talent, and James Baldwin made his famous anti-protest protest on the grounds that protest fiction was so often a predictably reductive mode of literature: "The failure of the protest novel lies in its rejection of life, the human being, the denial of his beauty, dread, power, in its insistence that it is his categorization alone which is real and which cannot be transcended" (quoted in Albert Murray, 114). None of the authors discussed in this chapter are unconcerned about the realities of race and politics, and yet all are troubled by the implications of "protest fiction." The protest novel, like the African-American protagonist of *Invisible Man*, is at once "highly visible," and yet it is invisible: more than any other book, it will be judged by its cover.

We find the protest-against-protest in the literature and nonfiction of authors such as Ellison, Kelley, Morrison, and also James Baldwin. I will look at Morrison's *Sula* in depth for the light it sheds on problems of African-American literary protest. While Robert Grant is persuasive when he writes that "Morrison's *Sula* focuses less on conventionally defined 'protest' than on a depiction of the black experience" (91), this statement still leaves room for us to understand *Sula* as an *un*conventional protest novel. As Grant points out, part of what makes *Sula* "unpredictable" as a literary-political statement of protest is its very insubordination in the face of the demands of a literary form known for strictness: "*Sula's* rebellion both derives from and coheres with the author's own rebellion from certain black novelistic traditions that decree, and enforce upon readers the expectation, that all black texts must be politically determinate, amenable to some ideological translation be it 'black protest' or 'radical feminist'" (93). Though Morrison, like Ellison, is wary of any response that indiscrimi-

nately imposes a politics on her imagined world, thus restricting its freedom and denying its individuality, *Sula* nonetheless covertly supports the
marches it only apparently disdains. Whether its representation of political struggle is more overt or covert, the political novel-of-identity nonetheless organizes our sympathies and our hatreds in a way that encourages political activity geared toward social change. Morrison's writing is
especially interesting in this regard since she has consistently expressed a
dim view of political processes and even political change in interviews,
longer critical writing, and in her novels.

If *Sula* is to be recognized as an innovative sort of political novel, it
must be admitted at the outset that it is political in the most complicated
and qualified sort of way. Politics is a demon that Morrison will not leave
out of her world, but she will not let it in except on her own terms. To
understand these terms we will have to discuss the issues that complicate the status of politics in her world. The integration/separation dilemma faced by black intellectuals (the arguments of Ellison and Murray
for artistic integration on the one hand; the Black Aesthetic insistence on
separation on the other) and the feminist implications of the slogan "the
personal is the political" are very much in the foreground when we read
Morrison's fiction and attempt to understand fully her political vision.

The slogan "the personal is the political" has been used to open up
readings of political literature, but it can also function to overwhelm distinctions and trivialize politics if it is not deployed responsibly. The personal and the political are interrelated significantly in the poem that appears as the dedication to Alice Walker's *In Search of Our Mothers' Gardens*,
a poem that leads gently into the sometimes vexing matter of identity
politics:

> To my daughter Rebecca
> Who saw in me
> what I considered
> a scar
> And redefined it
> as
> a world.

The incident alluded to in the poem is taken up again in the final essay
of the collection, where we learn that the author's brother "accidentally"
blinded her in one eye when he shot her with a BB-gun and told her not
to tell anyone.[1] Scarred as she was, she would not pick her head up, she
was less attractive to her parents, and, while her self-esteem plummeted,

her family insisted nonetheless that she behaved no differently after the accident. Only when her daughter saw the wandering eye (wandering "I") as a world could the wound really heal. The poem and the essay bracket essays about Martin Luther King Jr. and the achievement of the civil rights movement, Coretta Scott King and the place of women in that movement, and one about Langston Hughes's revolutionary ideas and limitations called "Good Morning, Revolution." The personal brackets the political in this collection, but in Alice Walker's writing it also explains the political to a large degree. The personal detail is never presented without the sort of contexualization that meaningfully relates it to larger social struggles.

The title of the book, the framing of the ideas, and the intellectual content of the collection argue for an undoing of the either/or logic that has made many readers habitually hostile to the appearance of politics in art. In Walker's "world" racial and sexual difference, the political vision that she shares with readers, and even the search for Zora Neale Hurston's unmarked grave are all political. Literary politics (making a place for Hurston, Margaret Walker, and others in the mainstream literary imagination), personal politics (the problems of relating to her brother, her husband, or a friend who insists all women are lesbians), and politics as conventionally understood (public marches, disillusion, the flawed nature of a political leader) all exist side by side in her essays and in her fiction. The personal would not resonate so strongly were the public side of her writing absent.

The public side of political action has been for the most part dispensable for academic critics, some of whom even call having a political program "trivial" (Lentricchia, "American Writer" 241). If having a program is trivial, what can it mean to say a writer is "political"? Dittmar argues in "Will the Circle Be Unbroken?: The Politics of Form in *The Bluest Eye*" that "the formal operations of [Morrison's] work function ideologically" (138). There is a very common sort of confusion at work here: the distinction between "ideological" and "political" is suppressed, allowing for a conflation of these kinds of meaning, which then allows for the direct substitution of personal or aesthetic choices for political ones. It is the substitution that is objected to here, not the interrelation of the personal and the political. Dittmar's essay happens to be an excellent discussion of the relationship between pervasive racism and Morrison's uses of literary form to call attention to the ideological effects of uncritical identification, but there is no discussion of politics as the word is commonly used off campus. Such a use of the word "political" divests it of the associations with larger social groups and/or governmental policy without which political programs truly are trivial.

In contrast, Richard Kostelanetz maintains the worldly sense of politics in *Politics in the African-American Novel:*

> A political choice is one that implies *change through group action,* even though the choice may at first affect only the chooser.... Going underground, as the narrators in fiction by both Richard Wright and Ralph Ellison do, is to intentionally change one's relationship with the above-ground world, symbolically as well as physically; and if many Afro-Americans expatriated themselves underground they would have pursued a collective political decision—engineered a change in their situation as a people to a larger society. So, any individual action in a novel that implies a group action can be interpreted as embodying a political meaning. (3)

Novelists tend to deal with individuals rather than sociological sectors, yet the standard for "political" that Kostelanetz offers—individual action as expression of group desire or group action—is well grounded. Like much of the criticism that supplants "politics" with "ideology," Dittmar's article becomes quite general when it is time to discuss the political consequences of literary form, such as when she quotes two prior Morrison critics to establish the terms of Morrison's political engagement: "The issues of difference which McDowell identifies as operating in *Sula* are political, not just literary or personal. 'Difference,' it turns out, is a site of struggle which involves the material as well as theoretical consequences of ideology" (137). The highly abstract "site of struggle" and the Derridean reference maroon this struggle in groundlessness. In place of any recognition of the group affiliation or actions that constitute politics proper is the celebration of "difference" and cultural inflections. The kinds of resistance Dittmar describes in her discussion of *The Bluest Eye* are real and are connected to politics somewhere down the line, but they are somewhat detached from the kinds of public engagement for which many political novelists have drawn fire.

Ellison's Two-Front War

Not everyone loves the idea of the politics-of-identity novel. When Ellison's Invisible Man says "I am not complaining, nor am I protesting"(7), he is of course both complaining and protesting, but his protest is rhetorically complicated because of the particular problems inherent in American ethnic identity. In "The Little Man at Chehaw Station," the lead essay in his collection *Going for the Territory,* Ellison argues that "ethnicity" is an honorific code word for "rites of symbolic sacrifice in which cabalistic code words are used to designate victims consumed with an Aztec voracity for scapegoats" (*Going* 16). From the vantage point of the carnival atmosphere of the 1960s (of which he did not, in Bakhtinian fashion, approve), Ellison looked back to a prior time before the fall into ethnicity: "During the nineteenth century an attempt was made to impose a loose conceptual order upon the chaos of American society by viewing it as a melting pot. Today that metaphor is noisily rejected, vehemently disavowed. In fact, it has come under attack in the name of the newly fashionable code word 'ethnicity,' reminding us that in this country code words are linguistic agencies for the designation of sacrificial victims" (*Going* 21). Ellison does not trust ethnicity, and so he argues in his fiction and nonfiction for American identity as a whole, though he readily admits that this identity is formed through "ceaseless contention," "a war of words" and "a clash of styles" (16).

Like Kenneth Burke, Ellison has shown a fondness for martial imagery, as we see when we examine his military metaphors in relation to the political debates surrounding his art. The term "two-front war," then, could well be used to describe his work and also that of other African-American writers. On one front the writer who is equally serious about politics and fiction is criticized for being too political, and on the other there will be charges of Uncle Tomism, of not being political enough—especially for writers who do not turn their backs completely on "white" literary tradition. The pressures on the political writer continue in a sense from the general bias against political fiction, but the burden on African-American novelists who consider political themes is greater because of the presuppositions we bring to texts by African-American authors. African-American novelists, damned if they do and damned if they do not make politics the first priority, write from within a two-front war that situates the African-American political novel within a slightly different literary tradition than that occupied by other American political novels.

One response to this dilemma is to shift the status of the hyphen, to approach double-consciousness as central rather than marginal to the American experience. Ellison became the chief spokesman for this view. One consequence of this strategy is that universalizing double-consciousness can seem to be a withdrawal from politics, but this is a hasty conclusion to make. When he was asked, after giving a talk at West Point, whether *Invisible Man* was a protest novel, his response was largely that of a modernist artist who would fly by the nets of society, politics, religion, and so forth for the sake of great art—but not entirely. There is also an insistence on political agency in Ellison's response:

> Q: Would you call it a protest novel?
> A: I would think that implicitly the novel protests. It protests the agonies of growing up. It protests the problem of trying to find a way into a complex, intricately structured society in a way which would allow this particular man to behave in a manly way and which would allow him to seize some instrumentalities of political power. That is where the protest is on one level. On another level, the protest lies in my trying to make a story out of these elements without falling into the clichés which have marked and marred most fiction about American Negroes, that is, to write literature instead of political protest. Beyond this, I would say very simply that in the very act of trying to create something, there is implicit a protest against the way things are—a protest against man's vulnerability before the larger forces of society and the universe. (62)

That Ellison chose to write literature *instead of* political protest indicates that his artistic and political choices have clearly been shaped by a belief that politics and literature are different and even exclusive kinds of discourse, and it is this belief more than any other that explains the rhetorical denials of politics in a novel about the central political issues of postwar black America. In interviews and in criticism of the novel, we find many claims that Ellison's fiction is not a narrowly partisan rant but rather a protest against "the universe," one offering a resistance that is only vaguely political. The novel's symbolic action as described by Ellison and his critical champions is so general that it does not take sides on a particular issue in a way that would violate modernist standards of detachment. For Ellison it is necessary, ultimately, to affirm American ideals, and to affirm these ideals and the sense of identity they construct demands that one attempt to be universal rather than partisan (in the sense that a "protest novel" is a partisan statement).[2] From Ellison's modernist/universalist rhetoric we might conclude that he did not write about the narrow and temporal struggles for power that constitute the political, but even a casual reading of *Invisible Man* qualifies these claims of universality. Clearly he *has* written a protest against racist pseudo-philanthropists, against those who exploit African Americans for political gain, and against the demagoguery of some black leaders. His novel arouses resistance to these forces among individuals and communities alike, and Ellison's fictional and nonfictional appeals extend also to questions of American identity at the national level. In Ellison we see a writer who, in public statements, speaks as though he has been forced to choose between politics and art. His novel's protagonist, however, has been understood equally well as an African-American political leader and as a fledgling artist.[3]

Ellison's sometimes contradictory public statements on the relationship between art and politics earned him some praise and much blame. He repudiates "protest" in the above-quoted question and answer session from the late 1960s, during the historical moment when Black Power was becoming an increasingly visible option for African Americans. Perhaps his repudiation of "protest" is more a criticism of the most radical strain in black America's long postwar protest than a rejection of political protest per se.[4] Ellison has been attacked by promoters of the Black Aesthetic for abandoning black America in his quest for modernist assimilation.[5] He comments in *Shadow and Act* and *Going to the Territory* on the way in which one is accused of "being white," and we see the way he is lumped in with the enemy in Ernest Kaiser's reference to him from *William Styron's Nat Turner: Ten Black Writers Respond:*

> Styron has lived through twelve years of the Negro social revolution and struggle in the U.S., but this upheaval has not touched him as a novelist. He wrote *The Confessions* just as he would have written it in 1948. His writing is impervious to Negro social change and struggle and to the facts of Negro history. His book is a throwback to the racist writing of the 1930's and 1940's. The decline in the writing of Styron, Ellison and many other American novelists is directly traceable to this tragic American separation of art and politics. (65)

In the literary-political debates centered on the question of assimilation versus separation, Ellison has been solidly on the assimilation side, and, as Alan Nadel has pointed out so well in *Invisible Criticism,* he has in both fiction and nonfiction championed nineteenth-century American literature because it was more able to assimilate the racial and political range of American culture than American writing of the twentieth century. But engaging in a political struggle, even a literary-political struggle, has its price, and attacks on Ellison have been the price of his willingness to defend the assimilationist position. The Invisible Man's "covert preparation for an overt action" has been linked by many critics to the overt actions of the civil rights movement, but Ellison was extremely cautious about linking artistic assimilation (the desegregation of black and white literary traditions) to the legal and political struggles for equal rights and social integration. He insisted that artistic and political questions must be kept separate, however much he mixed them in his own writing.

When he did express his political views, Ellison's sympathies were indisputably assimilationist. In a rarely commented upon essay "The Myth of the Flawed White Southerner," Ellison addresses the political struggle for civil rights more directly than he does anywhere else. He begins by recounting his response (unqualified endorsement) to President Johnson's 1965 comment "Art is not a political weapon" and then objects to the tendency of northern liberals to see Johnson in aesthetic rather than political ways: "I must dismiss any temptation to see President Johnson, or any living President, strictly in terms of his possibilities as a fictional character—which, I believe, is the impulse of many literary intellectuals when confronting a presidential role" (*Going* 82). For Ellison, Johnson was in many ways unattractive, but politically he did a lot of good for African Americans. Ellison concludes with a strong affirmation of Johnson as the president who signed the Civil Rights Act of 1965: "When all the returns are in, perhaps President Johnson will have to settle for being recognized as the greatest American President for the poor and for the Negroes, but that, as I see it, is a very great honor indeed" (87). His belief that we should not confuse literary and political judgment was in no way a refusal to make political judgments.

Ellison is extremely cautious about mixing politics and art because, as a reading of *Invisible Man* suggests, Ellison tended to agree with Henry Adams that politics is the organization of hatreds. The Invisible Man expresses such doubts about politics when he asks "And could politics ever be an expression of love?" (391). He learns the answer when he attempts to organize the hatred of African Americans around the death of Tod Clifton. Just before Clifton is shot by a fascistical[6] police officer, he has been selling Sambo dolls to a crowd. Nadel argues in the chapter of *Invisible Criticism* devoted to Tod Clifton that he is a "Christ figure," but the Invisible Man, in defending the funeral he had arranged for the man whom the Brotherhood insisted was a traitor, answers that the funeral served the cause "by organizing their anger" (402). Cyclopean Brother Jack is not on principle opposed to politics as the organization of hatred. We know this because he tells Invisible Man, whom he speaks to in a most condescending, mocking, and coercive manner, "And do you know what discipline is, Brother Personal Responsibility? It's sacrifice, *sacrifice*, SACRIFICE" (410). The Invisible Man discovers that these sacrifices will be made by the Negro but not necessarily *for* the Negro, and it is partly in reaction to just this sort of betrayal within causes supposedly for the advancement of African Americans that Ellison has charged the novelist with a responsibility to the community as a whole. Ellison's political writing is tempered by his knowledge of political struggle, and so he writes that "At his best [the novelist . . .] does not ask for scapegoats, but for the hero as witness" (*Going* 14). Ellison's celebration of the writer as a maker of witnesses rather than the maker of scapegoats is partly an urge to transcend politics, to keep his hands clean of the hatred. But Ellison's statements are also partly rhetorical defenses, *claims* of transcendence that bolster the Invisible Man and give him credibility so that he will be, politically, a more effective witness of American society. Perhaps because of this form of "Engaged Transcendentalism," Invisible Man, the transparent eyeball of Ellison's novel, has been the most effective witness in postwar American writing.

Kelley's Non-Universal African

Some novelists deny protest in order to protest, and some critics, in defending a novel, may downplay its political activism in order to defend it from those who would condemn its "stridency." Davis does just this in "W. M. Kelley and H. D. Thoreau: The Music Within" when he begins his article in this way: "That one of William Melvin Kelley's primary concerns in his first novel, *A Different Drummer*, is race relations is obvious even to the most casual reader; but to insist too strongly, as most readers have done, upon that single theme's centrality leads to both the diminution and the misinterpretation of an important, but generally overlooked work" (2). I will quickly agree that the book has been forgotten and that it is worth more attention, but I believe the reasons for this have a great deal to do with the book's overt engagement with the motives, aims, and techniques of the civil rights movement. Put as simply as possible, Kelley's first novel fails to be politically unpredictable.

In response to the pigeonholing that followed the novel's publication and fame (it received an award from the National Institute of Arts and Letters), Kelley distanced himself from political protest: "An American writer who happens to have brown skin faces this unique problem: Solutions and answers to the Negro Problem are very often read into his work" (Davis 2). Certainly a writer who has taken up politics in a book does not want every subsequent word he or she writes to be fashioned into a manifesto or a sociological argument by a waiting critic, but the political interpretation is certainly fair game for any reader of *A Different Drummer*. More important, to say the novel is also interesting as a collage of styles, as a study of interfamilial dynamics, or as an expression of Thoreauvian individualism (Davis's preferred reading) is not necessarily to exclude a political interpretation. The either/or reflex that would have us choose between art and politics is utterly devastating to the aims and achievements of political writers in general, and it can only have a numbing effect on readers of a novel such as *A Different Drummer.* For an even more capacious sense of the novel's meanings, we can combine Davis's philosophical quest with the overt activism of the work (which its author discounted publicly).

Kelley avoids charges of reductiveness by making his novel into a political-epistemological mystery in which the very failure of the southern whites to understand Tucker Caliban explains (as well as anything else) why he chooses to sow salt into his fields, burn his house and shoot his animals, and leave the novel's imaginary southern state—only to be followed by every other African American in that state. Kelley gives the modernist use of fragmentary perspective a thoroughly political function[7] when he juxtaposes the anatomy-by-perspective of Tucker Caliban's exodus to the prior objectification of his ancestor the African by the slave-owner General Dewey Willson: "Folks said he just looked like he was pricing something—looking at the African from head to toe and adding totals: so much for the head and the brain; so much for the build and the muscles; so much for the eyes—making notes on a piece of paper with a crayon" (11). General Willson dividing the African Prince into parts in order to assess his worth in dollars is analogous to the inability of Tucker Caliban's white contemporaries to recognize the present-day "African" for what he or she is.[8] Various chapters of *A Different Drummer* dramatize the ways in which white citizens misconstrue Tucker Caliban, the latter-day African of the novel. In *Playing in the Dark* Morrison urges that we examine the effects of racism not just on African Americans, but also on Euro-Americans, and Kelley does just this when he shows General Willson, in a stupor from chasing the African without respite, mumbling to himself "But I am. I'm worth a thousand too! I am!" (15). That General Dewitt Wilson has become an African-American "wannabe" is subtly indicated in the excerpt from "THE THUMB-NAIL ALMANAC, 1961" that forms the novel's first chapter: "*On April 5, 1889, having just returned from the dedication of a ten-foot bronze likeness of himself which the towns-people of Sutton had erected in the Square, he was stricken and died*" (1–2). Bronze in color, ten feet tall—it is as though Dewitt Wilson lived as long as he did just to fulfill his desire to become "the African."

The novel begins shortly before the exodus of all blacks from an unnamed state in the deep south. As they try to comprehend the mass movement, a group of men on the Thomason Grocer Company porch chew straw and figure "the South'll get along fine without them." Mr. Harper, the sage who sat down in his wheelchair thirty years before because life had no more to offer, tells the story of "The African," the direct ancestor of the Tucker Caliban leading the present-day exodus, to account for the movement. The African is an *Übermensch* who, when his slave-ship landed in New Marseilles, pulled chains out of the ship's side, killed everyone who got in his way, and marched into the swamps. From there he began a series of Nat Turner-style raids on slave plantations, liberating slaves and fighting a guerrilla war against the white planters. In this mythically compressed parable, he is betrayed by a Judas figure, a half-white helper who fled with him initially but who betrays him for money alone because, he says, "I am an American; I'm no savage. And besides, a man's got to follow where his pocket takes him" (17). Note the organization of hatreds here: Africans have manly strength and loyalty; Americans have profit motive, racism, and feminine decline. Kelley plays at once to a Black Nationalist (and thus supposedly non-American) readership who will be gratified by such distinctions, but at the same time he positions his narration solidly within American literary tradition, alluding to Thoreau in his title and imitating the stylistic melange of Faulkner's *The Sound and the Fury* as well.

In the swamp the African is trapped but will never surrender and so prepares to die. Accepting death before slavery, he prepares to be shot—but then remembers he must kill his child first so that his son is not brought up as a slave.[9] General Willson, who has been tracking the African obsessively, blows the African's head off in a final shot before the child can be killed, after which the slave-owner raises the child, naming him "Caliban." Each succeeding generation in the African's line is physically smaller. Tucker Caliban is quite a small man, but he is, it turns out, a condensed reincarnation of the African's indomitable spirit. The African is, in Kelley's imagined state, the Black Adam whose words are untainted by all the compromises of history. Insofar as he differs from "Americans," he is a non-universal character in American literature; insofar as he is an original man—a simple, genuine self opposed to a corrupt world—to that degree he is a new version of Emerson's old Adam.

The mythical power of Africanism and the inherent machismo attributed to it align Kelley's novel with some of the more ardently masculine polemics of the Black Aesthetic, and in this alignment Africa is masculine and positive, whereas Europe is in feminine decline. This gendered view of racial differences comes through most clearly when the men on the porch object to Mr. Harper's interpretation of events. Through the elucidation of context, the novel historicizes the ahistorical mythos of the black superman, but, still, the men on the porch cannot believe that an ancestral "African" accounts for the carpetbags, families in line, and exodus-by-bus that they are witnessing. Mr. Harper is, like many men on the porch, portrayed as a lesser man: his long hair and protruding belly, not to mention his refusal to walk, mark him as a weakling and as a partial woman. Other men on the porch are marked as feminine as well; Mr. Thomason wears an apron. Mr. Harper's legends of African machismo on the rise is incomprehensible to his auditors on Mr. Thomason's porch.[10]

The novel is, for the reader if not for the men on the porch, a modernist quest for unity among fragmentation. The remaining chapters give us various perspectives in various styles and in this way portray Tucker Caliban, our latter-day African, from a child's perspective, a liberal white man's, and that of a white housewife. We also learn that the one white character with pro-Negro liberal leanings has been forced underground politically because he was a Communist at one time and now fears anti-Communist persecution: race, gender, and class are discovered to interrelate in mysterious ways. The white liberal is rejuvenated by Tucker's action, and this rejuvenation saves his marriage. Marriages that suffered from tensions *apparently* unrelated to race suddenly begin to improve in conjunction with Tucker's political realignment of the unnamed southern state. In *A Different Drummer* all roads lead to race, and racial separation is, for the moment at least, the road to peace.

The men on the porch are at first bemused by the exodus, then they are more anxious to know its causes, and by the novel's conclusion they smolder with hatred. It is at this inopportune moment that the novel's scapegoat appears on the scene. Rev. Bradshaw, a black religious-political leader, arrives on his own quest for meaning. The only African-American male described as effeminate (60), he appears to be wealthy and preaches that Jesus was black. His large car, his chauffeur, and his membership in the National Society for Colored Affairs (read "NAACP") signify that he is a corrupt assimilationist. Unfortunately for him, he arrives in town to investigate the new black leader (whom he recognizes as a political competitor) just as the whites begin to question the departing blacks in a more threatening way. He is associated in the minds of the men on the porch with a political movement in which he has had no organizing role. In the novel's conclusion he is lynched by the furious whites. This murder is an echo of the catastrophic history of the African-American struggle for freedom and rights, but it is also a symbolic punishment of Bradshaw the collaborator.

The ideal of African leadership is pure and undivided in the original African Adam, the man who chose death over slavery. By splitting the later incarnations of the African leader into the pure leader (Tucker Caliban) and the corrupt leader (Rev. Bradshaw), the novel sidesteps the dirty hands problem in which political activity—involving as it does broken promises and compromises—is inherently corrupting. Bradshaw is prosperous and is tainted by the power and wealth granted him by white America, whereas Tucker Caliban is so ascetic that he slaughters his animals and destroys his land rather than let the sale of either benefit the whites. Whereas the whites who remain in the state focus increasingly on Bradshaw, the African Americans who leave the mythical southern state pay no heed to the corrupt leader. The exodus has been purified of "politics as usual."

Critics have attacked Kelley's closing the novel with Bradshaw's murder on the grounds that it is "tacked on," "ideological," or a deviation from Kelley's true story, but this reading is amiss.[11] This interpretation fails to take measure of the novel's homage to the totemistic aspects of African religion in the text. The novel is itself a symbolic action, a kind of spell against demons, perhaps even a literary precedent for Ishmael Reed's literary Hoodoo. Kelley's African mumbles over a pile of rocks at several points, and though the whites cannot fathom the meaning of this ceremony, General Willson (the African's shadow) envies his would-be slave and fears that no one would pay a thousand dollars for him. When he finally kills the African, he takes the top stone from the pile honored by the African and keeps it, in respect for its power. The novel itself has totemic power, and the most important symbolic action Kelley performs with this power is to purify black leadership in African terms. Tucker Caliban and Rev. Bradshaw represent the African and American poles of the inherently divided African-American identity, and Kelley's solution to the problem of divided consciousness is, symbolically, to kill off the leader tainted by assimilation. To consider the totemic motives behind the fiction is to see Bradshaw as the scapegoat whose death allows Tucker Caliban to march out of the state unhindered.

The ending is well-anticipated and in keeping with the symbolic action of the novel as a whole. Before the white men kill Bradshaw, they make him sing a song called "Curly-Headed Pickaninny Boy" (178–79). In singing this song, Bradshaw plays a role similar to that of Tod Clifton in Ellison's *Invisible Man*, that of the sacrificial victim around whom the community is organized, but Ellison's and Kelley's novels register sharply differing attitudes about the social benefits of the sacrificial scapegoat. The Invisible Man is deeply troubled not only by the waste of Tod Clifton's life, but also by Clifton's dissociation from political struggle at the end of his life when he mocked his prior convictions by selling Sambo dolls to people on the street. This dissociation ultimately leads Ellison's hero to revolt against the Brotherhood's opportunistic willingness to exploit black suffering for the sake of party ends. Bradshaw's final humiliation is not an expression of his own doubts but only of his weakness: he is far from the mythical African who chose death before humiliation. Subsequent events in each of these novels lead us to sympathize more with Tod Clifton but less with Rev. Bradshaw. Politics as the organization of hatreds is presented in an acceptable light in *A Different Drummer*, but it is rejected in *Invisible Man*.

The mythical African, nameless and unyielding, is sometimes a character out of the tall tale as Brück has argued, and he is very much a romantic creation as Davis has argued. As a heroic presence, he is also the descendant of Melville's Bulkington and London's Ernest Everhard (though the strong-man solution to political evil has, in recent years, become an "invisible man" in American literature). Kelley spared himself from most, though not all, of the cultural-nationalist attacks met by Ellison, and yet Kelley's novel is not even mentioned in the latest literary histories.[12] Ellison's protagonist promises that his hibernation has been "a covert preparation for a more overt action" (16), but, even though *Invisible Man* is a profound meditation on American racial politics, Ellison clearly did not urge readers to take sides in an extant political controversy to the degree that Kelley did. There should be room in American literature both for those who make the invisible visible and those who march to the different drummer of more overt political engagement.

Morrison's Denial of Politics

After Ellison's American modernist and Kelley's Black Aesthetic/ Africanist modes, Morrison yokes Ellison's ideology of independence (from social movements) to Kelley's Black Aesthetic when she devises a feminist reorientation of the Black Aesthetic. Like Ellison and Kelley, Morrison denies political engagement in her work, but we must approach Morrison's denial of politics with as much skepticism as we do that of Ellison and Kelley.

Morrison has said in an interview with Tom LeClair that "If I tried to write a universal novel, it would be water" (257), and in attacking the terminology of literary assimilation she apparently allies herself with the

Black Aesthetic critics of the 1970s.[13] The hostility she voices against "universal" literature stems from the belief that so-called universality functions to keep American literature white: "Behind this question is the suggestion that to write for black people is somehow to diminish the writing. From my perspective, there are only black people" (257). This statement clearly denies that the writer must write for America as a whole. And yet, even while Morrison has this common ground with the Black Aesthetic writers, there are also important differences. She refuses all prescriptive political statements or the notion that aesthetic decisions must march in lock-step with group action.[14]

While Ellison, in his effort to (re)integrate the American canon, self-consciously exploited the literary resources of Adamic naiveté, he also imagined a nameless character whose day-to-day efforts to impose meaning on his world invariably meet with frustration. Morrison, however, refuses the traditional novelistic entitlements of innocence, largely because the general identification of "American" with "innocent" is a symbolic license that has been denied in black communities. The denial of origins, of innocence, and of the power to name are marks of social exclusion and, in Morrison's fiction, are directly related to political powerlessness. In Morrison's *Song of Solomon* a street is called "Doctor Street" by its inhabitants because the city's only colored doctor lived and died there. When the post office returns mail stamped "no doctor street," the people who live on that street begin to call it "Not Doctor Street." In the · most literal sense this anecdote on naming is political, since "Some of the city legislators, whose concern for appropriate names and the maintenance of the city's landmarks was the principal part of their political life, saw to it that 'Doctor Street' was never used in any official capacity" (4). Residents of Not Doctor Street cannot name their world in the way that white civic leaders can. This denial of Adamic privilege is at the crossroads of politics and literature in Morrison's writing, and yet the black community monumentalizes the white prohibition of the black power to name when they ultimately cause the street to be officially named Not Doctor Street. Whereas the Euro-American versions of the Adamic mythos can indulge in the illusion that naming marks history's origin, the black American Adam always exists within a historically specific struggle with white namers.

Though her stories have strongly confronted the mythologies of American culture in relation to the facts of American political history, Morrison has in interviews disowned political process as "white" and "male." The idea that change is antithetical to the black experience is strongly expressed, without any apparent qualification, in *Sula*. Shortly

after Sula, "accompanied by a plague of robins" (89), returns to her home-
town Medallion, the narrator firmly puts the need for change in its place:

> What was taken by outsiders to be slackness, slovenliness or even gen-
> erosity was in fact a full recognition of the legitimacy of forces other than
> good ones. They did not believe doctors could heal—for them, none ever
> had done so. They did not believe death was accidental—life might be,
> but death was deliberate. They did not believe Nature was ever askew—
> only inconvenient. Plague and drought were as "natural" as springtime.
> If milk could curdle, God knows robins could fall. The purpose of evil
> was to survive it and they determined (without ever knowing they had
> made up their minds to do it) to survive floods, white people, tubercu-
> losis, famine and ignorance. They knew anger well but not despair, and
> they didn't stone sinners for the same reason they didn't commit sui-
> cide—it was beneath them. (90)

Morrison finds the nobility of African-American experience in the values of everyday life and in a communal refusal to flatter itself with any
mythical purity or power—the Bottom reveres no mythically masculine
African chief. Power, at least initially, has a different face in Morrison's
fictional worlds. The faceless politicians of Chicago in Song of Solomon's
opening pages will not allow African Americans to name their immediate locale in terms of the community's pride, and many such fictional
scenes in Morrison's work identify the "politician" with the dominant
classes of American society.

Politics is the domain not only of the upper classes but, by Morrison's
lights, of the white and male members of these groups. In an interview
with Claudia Tate, Morrison further attributes the desire for change itself to whiteness and maleness: "Men always want to change things, and
women probably don't. I don't think it has much to do with women's
powerlessness. Change could be death. You don't have to change everything. Some things should be just the way they are. Change in itself is
not so important. But men see it as important. [. . .] Women don't tend
to do this. [. . .] Black people have a way of allowing things to go on the
way they're going" (123). Morrison's female revision of the Black Aesthetic accepts the primacy of the African-American reader and the priority of African-American experiences, idioms, and even cosmologies in
the creation of literature.[15] At the same time, by identifying the "fix-it"
mentality with whiteness and maleness, Morrison rejects a main tenet
of the Black Aesthetic.[16]

However much Morrison separates herself from aspects of the Black
Aesthetic, she consistently conceives of her own work in opposition to

mainstream America, such as when she deconstructs the American Dream in her study, *Playing in the Dark: Whiteness and the Literary Imagination*: "Young America distinguished itself by, and understood itself to be, pressing toward a future of freedom, a kind of human dignity believed unprecedented in the world. A whole tradition of 'universal' yearnings collapsed into that well-fondled phrase, 'the American Dream'" (33). The quotation marks around "universal" will not themselves be controversial. Morrison's analysis proceeds, along the lines of current critical theory, to reverse the binaries at the heart of a system of thought: "One could move from discipline and punishment to disciplining and punishing; from social ostracism to social rank. One could be released from a useless, binding, repulsive past into a kind of history-lessness, a blank page waiting to be inscribed. Much was to be written there: noble impulses were made into law and appropriated for a national tradition; base ones, learned and elaborated in the rejected and rejecting homeland, were also made into law and appropriated for tradition" (35). The vocabulary of Foucault (excepting, perhaps, the partial admission of nobility) will not shock academic readers, but the argument that the American Dream is *not* a quest, however flawed, for the kind of universal freedom that we might associate with phrases such as "all men are created equal" is shocking. When King argued in his famous "I Have a Dream" speech that America had written African Americans "a check" for freedom and equality that had bounced, he was demanding that America make good on the check (871). Morrison, alternatively, is saying that there is a fundamental error in the American Dream. Her revision of the American Dream in *Playing in the Dark* describes a zero-sum approach to freedom in which one person gains "freedom" by taking it from someone else.[17] The "one person" and the other are hardly arbitrary, as Morrison comes to the provocative conclusion that, in American literature, "one" is always white, and the Other of American literature is invariably an Africanist presence: "Certainly no American text of the sort I am discussing was ever written *for* black people—no more than *Uncle Tom's Cabin* was written for Uncle Tom to read or be persuaded by. As a writer reading, I came to realize the obvious: the subject of the dream is the dreamer. The fabrication of an Africanist persona is reflexive; an extraordinary meditation on the self; a powerful exploration of the fears and desires that reside in the writerly conscious" (17). That is, the Africanist presence that Morrison proposes to examine in white American literature (Cather and Hemingway are two authors she discusses) is the projected expression of the American literary unconscious.

As in many African-American novels (and in much of postwar American culture), the American Dream in Morrison's writing becomes nightmare—but what is the consequence of Morrison's understanding of the American Dream upon political engagement? The American evasion of racial reality produced "a master narrative that spoke *for* Africans and their descendants, or *of* them. The legislator's narrative could not coexist with a response from the Africanist persona" (50). In identifying the white "master narrative" (which excludes black voices and audiences) with the "legislator's narrative," Morrison is collapsing all the variegations of history into the simplicity of either/or. The pleasure of this kind of text is that it allows for the rhetorical entitlements of political activity without the attendant frustrations of fighting city hall. And by speaking in the quasi-Lacanian mode that has become popular with some academics, the critic easily evades the problem of gradations of meaning and the necessary small compromises that are part and parcel of genuine political activity. Morrison, in *Playing in the Dark,* depreciates political activism: "I intend to outline an attractive, fruitful, and provocative critical project, unencumbered by dreams of subversion or rallying at fortress walls" (3). While "dreams of subversion" and rallying gestures are figured as encumbrances in her opening argument, Morrison is highly critical of American literary criticism when it is "unencumbered" with politics: "When matters of race are located and called attention to in American literature, critical response has tended to be on the order of a humanistic nostrum—or a dismissal mandated by the label 'political.'" The prejudice against overt political content in American literary studies leads to a fear of dismissal, and this is the condition that accounts for the "underground" nature of so much of our political literature. If the consequence for literary art is the development of subterranean modes of political statement, Morrison finds the consequence of this prejudice upon literary criticism to be mindlessness: "Excising the political from the life of the mind is a sacrifice that has proven costly. I think of this erasure as a kind of trembling hypochondria always curing itself with unnecessary surgery. A criticism that needs to insist that literature is not only 'universal' but also 'race-free' risks lobotomizing that literature, and diminishes both the art and the artist" (12). Matters of race, especially within the American context, are inherently political, but matters political have been played down consistently in American literary contexts.

In criticizing the critic, is Morrison herself engaging political struggle in all its complexity? While her own critical project can certainly be said to challenge the oppressively reductive standards implied by "universal" artistic values, her subsequent invocation of a political enemy suggests that her program is, like much contemporary criticism, largely a matter of gesture:

> Like thousands of avid but nonacademic readers, some powerful literary critics in the United States have never read, and are proud to say so, *any* African-American text. [. . .] I suspect, with much evidence to support the suspicion, that they will continue to flourish without any knowledge whatsoever of African-American literature. [. . .] It is interesting, not surprising, that the arbiters of critical power in American literature seem to take pleasure in, indeed relish, their ignorance of African-American texts. (13)

Who are these "arbiters of critical power"? When Morrison names a name to support her charges, it is in reference to an article published in 1936, even then not written by one of the shapers of American literature. This kind of McCarthyite generalization shows either a lack of awareness or a willful obliviousness about progressive achievements in the American academy she means to criticize.[18] If Morrison were merely another author disparaging political engagement, the simplistic views expressed in *Playing in the Dark* would not call for lengthy treatment. What is interesting about Morrison's expressed denials of political engagement is that, in both her fiction and her nonfiction, the denial disguises a measured though unrelenting engagement with just those "fortress walls" that she disdains in the opening pages of *Playing in the Dark.*

Sula's Prophecy

If Morrison's *Playing in the Dark* indulges in a certain amount of politically correct shadow-boxing, her fiction is a much more reliable guide to the intra-communal politics organizing African-American communities and American society as a whole. Her claim that her second novel "bears witness and suggests who the outlaws were, who survived under what circumstances and why, what was legal in the community as opposed to what was legal outside it" ("Interview" 253) leads us to exactly those themes and issues in which *Sula* confronts political realities every bit as concretely as did *A Different Drummer* and *Invisible Man* before it. Morrison's politics-of-identity novel combines the strategies of Ellison and Kelley, in that it holds the politics of scapegoating up for scrutiny, as does *Invisible Man;* and yet it contests assimilationist ideology, as does *A Different Drummer.* To demonstrate the centrality of political organization throughout *Sula,* I will discuss the novel in five "acts": (1) From Timelessness into History, (2) Identity and Aggression, (3) The

Politics of the Pariah and Sula's Prophecy, (4) The Loss of the Scapegoat, and (5) Sula's Apotheosis. Once we recognize these five moments in the novel, it is not as politically "unpredictable" as Grant has suggested.

From Timelessness into History

Montgomery has written about the tension between Africanist cyclical time and Western linear time in *Sula*, and to her suggestive reading of the structural and thematic interconnections of the novel I wish to add the tension between the unstoppable movement from timelessness into history and the countervailing ability to recover timelessness in memory, an ability that is contingent upon historical (and, it turns out, political) conditions. We know the first section is "timeless" because the Bottom, the black community that Morrison evokes in the brief opening chapter, has already been destroyed—and yet it has not *yet* been destroyed in the sentences that introduce the Bottom to readers. We understand literally that the neighborhood that once existed in the Ohio hills has been obliterated by a golf course, and yet "they tore the nightshade" exists side by side with "A steel ball *will* knock to dust Irene's Palace of Cosmetology" (3, my emphasis). A few characters are mentioned, their meaning is questioned, and the puzzling question about this place—"was it heaven?"—is carefully introduced.

From timeless heaven to the accumulated wrongs of history: the "nigger joke" about the white farmer who tricked the black people into choosing the hilly land over the valley, since the mountains were the "bottom" of heaven, introduces us to a complex tone. We are challenged to recognize the "adult pain" that underwrites this joke, or, rather, what separates it from Stepin Fetchit, blackface, and Sambo humor. This evocation of adult pain is the "knell" that will chime throughout the novel, until Nel finally hears it in 1965. The Civil Rights Act of 1965 is not explicitly mentioned but nonetheless is, I will show, the revolution that moves Nel from timelessness to time. Until she hears the music of time, she is trapped in a kind of timeless nostalgia. She has, in a sense, plunged out of history like Tod Clifton, except Nel has become a goody-two-shoes visitor of the ill instead of a hawker of Sambo dolls. Is this not strange, to measure the changes of 1965 through the consciousness of a never-very-oppressed, church-going, hospital-visiting woman? The challenge of *Sula* as a politics-of-identity novel is to combine a recognition of large-scale historical change with an equal or greater recognition of persons routinely deemed insignificant to the movement of History.

Morrison has claimed that historical change is unimportant to many of the people she writes about, and yet *Sula* resonates with all the great conflicts of this century. She does not begin the narration with Nel and Sula, but with a young man named Shadrack who finds himself amidst the surreal horrors of World War I. The hostilities of war and the difficult return from war are racially inflected in Shadrack's imagination: "The day was cold enough to make his breath visible, and he wondered for a moment at the purity and whiteness of his own breath among the dirty, gray explosions surrounding him" (8). In this sentence white is good while less-white is dangerous; it is historically resonant that Shadrack entertains this perception in the cold-white world of Europe. When Paul Fussell wrote about the formative significance of World War I on post–World War II American writers in *The Great War and Modern Memory,* he could have discussed this sentence from *Sula:* "stubbornly, taking no direction from the brain, the body of the headless soldier ran on, with energy and grace, ignoring altogether the drip and slide of brain tissue down its back" (8). Shadrack's perception of war's mindlessness costs him his own mind. He is shattered and wrecked by battle, and his return to America contributes to the general shock of an American society that must deal with all of the war memory and trauma returning home at that moment. Will America assimilate the trauma? In the overwhelming present, Shadrack's trauma is unspeakable, but in time the headless soldier, his shattered perception of his own body, and the racist consequences on the traumatized nation become part of the American story.

As the wreck of the pathetic individual before huge historical forces, Shadrack is emblematic of the larger historical and political currents of America. When Shadrack awakens in a VA hospital, the reader learns what the bewildered Shadrack will not understand: that segregation and institutionalized racism were part of a complex social history; they were in part a national response to the trauma of the "Great War." The chapter entitled "1919" contains racial segregation in two distinct forms, both of which link race-trauma to war-trauma. These two responses can be called black racism and white racism, the first being the need for racial separation felt by a shell-shocked member of the black community, the second being the cruel reassertion of racial hierarchy by whites. Shadrack's separatism comes first in the text:

> Shadrack stared at the soft colors that filled these triangles: the lumpy whiteness of rice, the quivering blood tomatoes, the grayish-brown meat. All their repugnance was contained in the neat balance of the triangles—a balance that soothed him, transferred some of this equilibrium to him. Thus reassured that the white, the red and the brown would stay where they were—would not explode or burst forth from their restricted zones—he suddenly felt hungry and looked around for his hands. (8)

This ordering of basic elements (the white, red, and brown representing European, native, and African roots of American identity) is a symbolic or "artistic" segregation of the races that eases Shadrack's mind after the trauma of war. To understand this need for symbolic segregation without sympathy would be cruel, since it is clear that Shadrack is a victim of circumstances. He is relatively innocent when seen against the background of the Great War. Shadrack's psychological response to huge historical forces that have overrun him arouses pathos, but racism as the word is understood in civil society (a racially motivated or focused expression of ignorance, fear, or cruelty) can be seen in the attitude of the white orderly:

> His hair was parted low on the right side so that some twenty or thirty yellow hairs could discreetly cover the nakedness of his head.
> "Come on. Pick up that spoon. Pick it up, Private. Nobody is going to feed you forever." (9)

The absurd vanity of combing a few strands of blond hair over a bald spot is a racial marker, and this information conditions our interpretations of the white orderly's insensitivity to the pain of Shadrack, who, in undergoing a baffling rediscovery of his own body, is in a sense reborn in the gaze of the impatient white man. As *A Different Drummer* offers a ritual purification of the black leader, *Sula* offers a purification of racism. Shadrack's paramedic response to trauma is forgivable—whereas the orderly seems merely insensitive.

Shadrack's refusal of integration symbolizes Morrison's revision of the Black Aesthetic, and it is also a subtle trail marker that tells us we have passed Ellison's exposition of invisibility and Kelley's overt expression of withdrawal. Morrison's leg of the journey involves turning from the white mirror altogether.

Shadrack's rebirth/return is a parable of the genesis of African-American identity that parallels Jacques Lacan's oft-mentioned "mirror stage." As the infantile self is tormented by a fragmented awareness of its own body parts, so is Shadrack horrified by the sight of his own hands, which loom monstrously in his vision. Lacan claims that the (illusion of a) unified self is produced sometime between six and eighteen months, when the infant discovers him- or herself in the mirror. The "mirror" is the metaphoric expression of the eye of the other, and, in literary and philosophical elaborations of Lacan, its meaning has been generalized so that we may regard culture as a mirror in which to form a socially recognizable identity—from which the emerging self then feels alienated.

An important part of the political impetus in African-American literature and literary criticism has been to demonstrate the social effects of
the mirror of American literature, especially when that mirror reflects
only white America. Shadrack's mirror is, shockingly, a toilet: "There in
the toilet water he saw a grave black face. A black so definite, so un-
equivocal, it astonished him. He had been harboring a skittish apprehension that he was not real—that he didn't exist at all. But when the blackness greeted him with its indisputable presence, he wanted nothing
more" (13). Shadrack has become "visible" to himself, but his mirror is
the lowest thing in the world, "the bottom." This detail is an ingenious
recurrence of the "nigger joke" of the Bottom that begins the novel. In
Shadrack's rebirth and in the community's origin, white cruelty has a
direct formative role on black self-consciousness, even when the mirror
is "black." The indisputable presence of a self-image is a momentary god
in Shadrack's universe of maleficent forces, and he is grateful for the
protection of a "self."[19] His choices for a mirror are so limited that he must
gaze into the toilet, into the bottom of the white universe. Shadrack's
mirror displays an even less flattering image than does that of Stephen
Dedalus's "cracked looking glass of the servant" in James Joyce's *Ulysses*.
Like Joyce, Morrison pursues the imaginary connections that link villages
and nations into a recognizable world and shows how these connections
are anything but politically neutral.

Identity and Aggression: Nel and Sula

Shadrack's mirror is a parable about the danger of self-hatred, and *Sula*
as a whole may be read as a study in the economy of self-hatred. Most
characters in the novel focus their hatred specifically on one other person so that a free-floating hatred does not contaminate all social life, and
some characters survive through the ritual expression of self-hatred.
Individual behavior expresses communal options. The reformation
through which the once-confident young Shadrack turns into the
community's first inside-outsider recapitulates in individual form the
organization of the Bottom as a political community; the forms are alike
because the communal and the individual self are shaped in the same
mirror. The "nigger joke" and the dark toilet water are the origins of
African-American self-hatred that will, as the novel develops, be consoli-
dated into the hatred of the pariah Sula. In a sly inversion of the logic by
which politics is the organization of hatred, Sula, following Shadrack, will
become something of a "community organizer." By hating Sula, the
Medallion community creates its own scapegoat, a source of social power.

The hatred of Sula lends itself to a communal assertion of what the people of Medallion claim they are not, but since Sula is very much a part of the community, scapegoating is a risky strategy. Sula, like the other elements in the catalog of lost idiosyncrasies that begin the novel, is part of what makes the community different from the rest of the world, and her death is the first sign that the community as a whole will vanish.

By despising Sula the community gains self-assertion but may, vicariously and unknowingly, express self-hatred. Before Sula became the community scapegoat, Shadrack provided a means for the community to deflect or at least channel the energies of self-criticism and despair. Shadrack's National Suicide Day is a comic institutionalization of self-hatred and despair, and his bizarre march through town is a kind of safety valve through which self-hatred receives carnivalesque expression. If Shadrack at first seems an eccentric, we must notice that this community is made up mainly of similarly unusual people. Eva's lost leg, indicating self-mutilation to many in the community, is another dire expression of this internalized hatred (though Eva's tall tales about the leg just walking away are hardly tragic). All we know is that Eva came back with one leg less and ten-thousand dollars more. Self-mutilation as a form of self-empowerment may at first seem quixotic, such as when Sula cuts herself with a knife to frighten off the Irish boys who threaten her and Nel,[20] but we can understand all of these strange behaviors as attempts to take in the hatred of the outer world so that one may control it and thus survive it. Sula does not cut her own fingertip off because she dislikes herself in any direct way, but in reflecting the Irish boys' low opinion of herself back at them, she scares them off. In this scene Sula lives with her head in the lion's mouth.

Sula's passive acceptance of her status as pariah seems less quixotic when we see her choices alongside those of Nel. In this manner the novel is a lengthy comparison-and-contrast essay, with early paragraphs on the mothers and grandmothers of the two girls. The Eva-Hannah-Sula line is a study in aggression: Eva loses her leg, postpones anger for several years, and, when she one day has the leisure to know her feelings, shakes off the urge to commit suicide. She can do all this because she does not disown aggression. When the husband who abandoned her (leaving her to the mercy of winter) shows up with a girlfriend on a sunny day, the girlfriend's ugly laugh precipitates Eva's self-discovery:

> Knowing that she would hate him long and well filled her with pleasant anticipation, like when you know you are going to fall in love with

someone and you wait for the happy signs. Hating BoyBoy, she could get on with it, and have the safety, the thrill, the consistency of that hatred as long as she wanted or needed it to define and strengthen her or protect her from routine vulnerabilities. (Once when Hannah accused her of hating colored people, Eva said she only hated one, Hannah's father BoyBoy, and it was hating him that kept her alive and happy.) (36–37)

Like many writers, Morrison routinely denies anger as a literary motive, but in this passage she proves herself to be among the supreme poets of hatred in all of American literature.

Nel's mother Helene Wright, on the other hand, substitutes conformity to communal law for aggression. When communal values do not protect her, such as when she takes Nel on a train ride to New Orleans and is humiliated by the conductor when she accidently enters the "whites only" car, Helene responds to the taunts of the conductor with a puppy-like smile and with obedience. Nel witnesses her mother's compliance and is disturbed by the implications of it: "if *she* were really custard, then there was a chance that Nel was too" (22), but Nel also learns on this trip that she has a self of her own, and that she can be different from her mother: "'I'm me,' she whispered. 'Me'" (28). Nel's realization, after the trip to New Orleans, is the promise of life unbounded by too-restrictive communal definitions of self, and it is the many dangers of individuation associated with the trip—the train episode, the problem of Creole language and identity, and the abandonment of sexual mores represented by Nel's prostitute grandmother—that awaken this sense of a new, individual self in Nel. Sula, however, lives out this dream, and Nel loses this possibility of an authentic self (as opposed to a "custard" self) when she breaks with Sula. She returns to "I'm me" again only when she finally grieves for Sula in 1965.

The Politics of the Pariah and Sula's Prophecy

Sula and Nel break apart after Sula sleeps with Nel's husband Jude. To discuss the formation of identity and the course of friendships of this sort as a "political response" risks trivializing the risks of overt political engagement, but as Morrison is profoundly concerned with relationships between individuals and how these relations are organized by social and political structures, it is not necessary to settle for the mere substitution of "personal" for "political." *Sula* traces the links between the personal and the political when the novel shows how Nel and Jude came together in the first place. Jude "wasn't really aiming to get married" (80)—until he was rejected by the men who selected workers for New River Road: "Jude himself longed more than anybody else to be taken. Not just for the good money, more for the work itself" (81). And the source of this work ethic? "More than anything he wanted the camaraderie of the road men: the lunch buckets, the hollering, the body movement that in the end produced something real, something he could point to. 'I built that road,' he could say" (82). Instead, Greeks and Italians are selected, and the mirror that might reflect Jude's potency, firmly in the hands of the white foremen, reflects nothing. So Jude decides to marry: "He chose the girl who had always been kind, who had never seemed hell-bent to marry, who made the whole venture seem like his idea, his conquest" (82–83). Nel becomes the perfect mirror for Jude's manhood—he "could see himself taking shape in her eyes" (83). In so doing Nel sacrifices all of her own aggression at the altar of Jude's manhood. As one character at the Time and a Half Pool Hall puts it, "all they want, man, is they own misery. Ax em to die for you and they yours for life" (83). Nel's lack of aggression is ultimately the determining factor in her life: "Except for an occasional leadership role with Sula, she had no aggression" (83).

Nel has no aggression because "Her parents had succeeded in rubbing down to a dull glow any sparkle or splutter she had" (83). This rubbing and polishing is in part an effort to remove blackness, as we see in this earlier scene of racial self-hatred:

> When Mrs. Wright reminded Nel to pull her nose, she would do it enthusiastically but without the least hope in the world.
>   "It hurts, Mamma."
>   "Don't you want a nice nose when you grow up?"
>   After she met Sula, Nel slid the clothespin under the blanket as soon as she got in the bed. And although there was still the hateful hot comb to suffer through each Saturday evening, its consequences—smooth hair—no longer interested her. (55)

Mrs. Wright wants Nel to have a European nose, not a flat African nose, and Nel desires these changes herself until she comes into contact with Sula's aggression. Sula's effects on Nel demonstrate the significance of emblematic action, which is a core of the Black Aesthetic as a political program.

Sula's aggression is, of course, not all good news. When she returns to Medallion after ten years at school and in various cities, she is accompanied by a magic-realist plague of robins. The community assumes she has been at parties for ten years, but Sula insists to Nel that she was at college; this is the beginning of Sula's reformation as a pariah. Perhaps because of her time away from the community, Sula puts Eva in a nursing home and disregards communal values in other ways as well. Morrison has insisted in the interview with Claudia Tate that putting elders in a nursing home is not something black people *do*, but in the novel Sula's aggressive actions are not interpreted as a sign of "whiteness." The chapter "1939" begins: "When the word got out about Eva being put in Sunnydale, the people in the Bottom shook their heads and said Sula was a roach" (112). All the worst stories about her are recycled, "But it was the men who gave her the final label, who fingerprinted her for all time. They were the ones who said she was guilty of the unforgivable thing—the thing for which there was no understanding, no excuse, no compassion. The route from which there was no way back, the dirt that could not ever be washed away. They said Sula slept with white men" (112). At a time when America was entering the omni-organization of World War II, an organization made possible by the hatred of enemy Germans and Japanese, the Bottom community has organized itself around its hatred of Sula. Though she has certainly flaunted her freedom, it is interesting to note that the facts of the matter are incidental to the need to construct the inner enemy: "It may not have been true [that Sula slept with white men], but it certainly could have been. She was obviously capable of it." Note that Sula is not accused of being white, only of giving herself to white men. The community will regard Sula as a roach, but, just as Morrison's black people do not "stone sinners," they do not literally cast her out or deny her blackness.

As Shadrack had to segregate the red from the brown from the white, the community organizes racial anger in a way that subjects all individual human relationships to community restrictions, a process that Sula ignores. The community in this one respect mirrors the racist whites who have sequestered the black population to the Bottom: "They insisted that all unions between white men and black women be rape; for a black woman to be willing was literally unthinkable. In that way, they regarded integration with precisely the same venom that white people did" (113). *All* white people? The assumption that all black people or all white people think in a certain way marks the communal/choric voice of *Sula*'s narrator. The effects of making Sula into the community pariah, thereby funneling all frustration into a single body that the community is free to hate without inhibition, are entirely salutary on the community as a whole: "Once the source of their personal misfortune was identified, they had leave to protect and love one another. They began to cherish their husbands and wives, protect their children, repair their homes and in general band together against the devil in their midst" (117). Whether or not it is moral, this shift in communal values is most certainly, in William James's famous phrase, an "equivalent of war." Sula "was a pariah, then, and she knew it." She does not become a pariah to save the community in a Christlike gesture of self-sacrifice, though her behavior is described as stemming from an inability to lie (121). There is even the suggestion that she is something of a sexual mystic, or perhaps a kind of blues artist (Dittmar 150)—an entirely honorific way of being understood within an African-American community, if anyone from the Bottom would have understood her that way.

Sula is entirely unappreciated. Her capacity for self-appreciation emerges in utterly solitary moments, cut off from any glimmer of communal recognition or forgiveness. In the quiet after sex, which to Sula is "not eternity but the death of time," Sula's grief emerges: "She wept then. Tears for the deaths of the littlest things: the castaway shoes of children; broken stems of marsh grass battered and drowned by the sea; prom photographs of dead women she never knew; wedding rings in pawnshop windows; the tidy bodies of Cornish hens in a nest of rice" (123). When Morrison speaks about *Sula* in interviews, she always speaks on the community's behalf, but it is moments like this one that complicate the community's monological assertion that Sula is evil whereas the people of the Bottom are purely good. We learn from this utterly private moment that Sula has compassion for the lost things that the rest of the community forgets in its struggle to organize its resources efficiently.

The movement into Sula's inner world prepares the reader for Sula's prophecy. Nel visits Sula on her deathbed not out of love, but out of duty. Nel-the-martyr, visiting her "friend": "I heard you was sick" (138). At this meeting Sula challenges Nel's conventional ordering of good and evil, asking, "How you know? [. . .] About who was good. How you know it was you?" (146). But this question is not likely to change Nel's mind, since Nel has already decided that "Talking to her about right and wrong was like talking to the deweys" (the three none-too-bright boy-men who grow up in Eva Peace's house; 145). Exasperated, Nel pulls out the community's ace-in-the-hole, the withdrawal of love: "You laying there in that bed without a dime or a friend to your name having done all the dirt you did in this town and you still expect folks to love you?" (145). Sula's answer, her prophecy, is the fruit of her identity quest in all its facets, and it is the hidden content of this prophecy alone that can salvage Sula's self-experiments from the waste-bin:

"Oh, they'll love me all right. It will take time, but they'll love me." The sound of her voice was as soft and distant as the look in her eyes. "After all the old women have lain with the teenagers; when all the young girls have slept with their old drunken uncles; after all the black men fuck all the white ones; when all the white women kiss all the black ones; when the guards have raped all the jailbirds and after all the whores make love to their grannies; after all the faggots get their mother's trim; when Lindbergh sleeps with Bessie Smith and Norma Shearer makes it with Stepin Fetchit; after all the dogs have fucked all the cats and every weathervane on every barn flies off the roof to mount the hogs [. . .] then there'll be a little love left over for me. And I know just what it will feel like." (145–46)

The magic-realist catalog may seem radically unlike anything that occurs in the Bottom, but the gist of the message is that when racialized sexual taboos give way, which is to say when the scapegoat is no longer available as a "community organizer," then Sula will be loved. Sula has an uncanny knowledge about scapegoating and community organization, but Nel does not recognize even a grain of truth in Sula's statement and so says, "Goodbye, Sula. I don't reckon I'll be back" (146).

The Loss of the Scapegoat

Before Sula dies she has a horrid dream in which she is overcome by the Clabber Girl Baking Powder lady who fills her eyes, nose, and throat with the choking white powder: death (or is it integration?) is a choking, stifling whiteness. Then Sula dies, thinking of Nel. Medallion's denizens could not be more pleased: "The death of Sula Peace was the best news folks up in the Bottom had had since the promise of work at the tunnel" (153). Once again, Sula is connected to the work and the building from which African-American men have been excluded. The community believes at first that the loss of their devil foreshadows wonderful things to come. Some of the Bottom even grieve at the loss of "the most magnificent hatred they had ever known" (173).

"The rumor that the tunnel spanning the river would use Negro workers became an announcement" (151). The political fortunes of the town are not on the rise, however, and all the ensuing problems develop directly after Sula's death. Sula dies in 1940. Things go bad in October of that year, and problems continue to develop into the spring of 1941, in which there were no auspicious marigolds. Without Sula, the Bottom is out of joint: "Still it was not those illnesses or even the ice that marked the beginning of the trouble, that self-fulfilled prophecy that Shadrack carried on his tongue. As soon as the silvering began, long before the cider cracked the jugs, there was something wrong. A falling away, a dislocation was taking place" (153). Lack of butter and the substitution of oleomargarine one morning during World War II leads Teapot to beat her child. The Canadian Negroes (who had never been slaves) begin to speak condescendingly to Southern-born residents of the Bottom, and white people who come into town bearing secondhand Christmas gifts receive clipped thanks in return. Without Sula as the lightning rod to draw all hatred and aggression through herself into the ground, aggression is on the rise in the Bottom.

Several traditional structures are eroded by Sula's death. When Shadrack sees Sula's body laid out, he loses faith in his own ritual National Suicide Day, and this loss of faith bespeaks a shift in the mood of the community as a whole. The willingness to endure what the narrator has called the weight of adult pain is beheld in a more skeptical manner than before. Under these conditions, Shadrack's bell "Called to them to come out and play in the sunshine—as though sunshine would last, as though there really was hope. The same hope that kept them picking beans for other farmers; kept them from finally leaving as they talked of doing; kept them knee-deep in other people's dirt; kept them excited about other people's wars; kept them solicitous of white people's children; kept them convinced that some magic 'government' was going to lift them up, out and away from that dirt, those beans, those wars" (160). The National Suicide Day parade of 1941 is presented as a childish shirking of adult pain—rather than as a revolt against decades of discrimination, or a refusal to continue to internalize self-hatred. In the sunshine there is an efflorescence of hope, but to the narrator's skeptical choric voice this hope is a delusion. Whether in her own name or through the narrative of *Sula*, Morrison has frequently voiced comparable attitudes, emphasizing the costs of assimilation and desegregation rather than the gains. As in Melville's *Moby-Dick*, the most revolutionary and progressive sentiments are contained by, perhaps even protected by, an essentially conservative narrative cloak.

The conservative as well as the liberal/progressive voices within Morrison's work must figure into an account of her significance as a political writer. Morrison has said in interviews that change and political struggle tend to be the material of white, male fantasies, not those of black women. In *Playing in the Dark*, as we have seen, she discounts the appeal of the politician in the African-American imagination, since the politician is an outsider ineradicably associated with political betrayal.

In interviews and in her criticism, she speaks uncritically on behalf of "the community," as though in partial observation of the Black Aesthetic priority of community needs over the niceties of art. Read page-by-page, Morrison's novel appears to present the Bottom's stoicism in the face of adversity without any hint of critical distance or ambivalence. With Sula's death comes the breakdown of stoicism, the rise in black pride, and the organized effort for social change.

Black pride is definitely on the rise in the Bottom of 1941, but this pride is at odds with the older forms of communal identity bespoken by the novel's first page. Ron Karenga, one of the theoreticians included in Gayle's *The Black Aesthetic*, begins his essay "Black Cultural Nationalism" with an assertion of the priority of political activism over art (and everything else in the black community): "Black art, like everything else in the black community, must respond positively to the reality of revolution" (32). It would appear, from the perspective of "1941" in any event, that Morrison is far from responding positively to the reality of Karenga's revolution. In the chapter entitled "1941" the men and women who attack the tunnel (because the promises of jobs for blacks have again fallen through) are almost as mindless as the headless soldier Shadrack saw die on the battlefield: "Like antelopes they leaped over the little gate—a wire barricade that was never intended to bar anything but dogs, rabbits and stray children—and led by the tough, the enraged and the young they picked up the lengths of timber and thin steel ribs and smashed the bricks they would never fire in yawning kilns, split the sacks of limestone they had not mixed or even been allowed to haul; tore the wire mesh, tipped over wheelbarrows and rolled forepoles down the bank, where they sailed out on the icebound river" (161). The riot—or should we say the rebellion?—destroys the New River Road tunnel, and gets a large number of people killed. To call it a riot is to identify with the communal perspective articulated by Morrison in interviews as well as by the narrative voice that addresses us in *Sula*. That perspective tends to be politically quietistic. It construes the destruction not as a political action but as a failure of communal art and ritual to redirect rage properly: "They didn't mean to go in, to actually go down into the lip of the tunnel, but in their need to kill it all, all of it, to wipe from the face of the earth the work of the thin-armed Virginia boys, the bull-necked Greeks and the knife-faced men who waved the leaf-dead promise, they went too deep, too far" (161). From the activist perspective of the Black Aesthetician, the tunnel is a monument to the racist hierarchies that keep the Bottom on the bottom of American society, but from the communal perspective with which we come to associate the narrative voice, the hatred and anger against the Greeks and other poor whites is a will-o'-the-wisp that steals the lives of young men and women. From this perspective National Suicide Day, the community's homegrown political pageant, finally becomes a self-fulfilling prophecy.

Sula's Apotheosis

There is another perspective possible, one that emerges suddenly at the close of the final chapter entitled "1965," a perspective that radically subverts the communal perspective that has been stable throughout *Sula*. The chapter begins with the sentence "Things were so much better in 1965" (163), but this admission of positive political change is immediately followed by a qualifier: "Or so it seemed." The positive changes include the integration of African Americans into a previously all-white work force. "And a colored man taught mathematics at the junior high school."

In 1965 Nel recounts the changes that have taken place since the war: "In the meantime the Bottom had collapsed. Everybody who had made money during the war moved as close as they could to the valley" (165). The events of 1965 include the Civil Rights Act of 1965 and the Watts riot of August 1965. Both events increased black pride,[21] so why does Morrison qualify the changes with "Or so it seemed"?

The sentiment is carefully balanced, lest the author be accused of nostalgia for Shadrack's toilet-water mirror, but the cost of assimilation into American society will not be ignored in this novel. The collapse of the Bottom and the flight out of black neighborhoods into the valley land is, from a pro-assimilationist perspective, a sign that African Americans are entering the mainstream of American society, but from the African-American communal perspective, the flight from the Bottom is a symbolic action akin to Nel's pulling her nose or straightening her hair. It is not only a flight to economic success, it is also a flight *from* blackness. The changes of 1965 are bittersweet, the narrator's tone almost mournful: "It was sad, because the Bottom had been a real place. These young ones kept talking about the community, but they left the hills to the poor, the old, the stubborn—and the rich white folks. Maybe it hadn't been a community, but it had been a place. Now there weren't any places left, just separate houses with separate televisions and separate telephones and less and less dropping by" (166). Insofar as we regard the events of 1965 from the communal perspective, the events are inextricably linked with the loss of the actual ground of African-American identity.

But insofar as this communal perspective is regarded as provincial, which it is by Sula when she returns from her years away from Medallion, the events of 1965 are akin to the very events in Sula's prophecy.

When black and white Americans work side by side, intermarriage becomes possible; all the taboos that Sula flaunted begin to lose their hold
on the community. Not all change is pleasant: 1965 is also the year of the
Watts riots and the assassination of Malcolm X. In Morrison's imaginary
world, all of these violent changes begin when Sula dies and the people
of the Bottom mourn over "the curved earth that cut them off from the
most magnificent hatred they had ever known" (173).

We know that Sula's prophecy has come true because "there is a little
love left over" for her in Nel's mind: "Leaves stirred; mud shifted; there
was the smell of overripe green things. A soft ball of fur broke and scattered like dandelion spores in the breeze" (173). This, the very grief Nel
could not manage to feel when Jude left, can only come (according to the
logic of Sula's prophecy) after the taboos have been up-ended, after the
Bottom has undergone a revolution of sorts. Nel's realization is signaled
by her Lear-like cry, "'O Lord, Sula,' she cried, 'girl, girl, girlgirlgirl'"
(174). Just as Eva had to put aside her hatred of BoyBoy until she could
afford it, Nel has to wait until 1965 to take in the "bottomless" sorrow
that concludes the novel: "It was a fine cry—loud and long—but it had
no bottom and it had no top, just circles and circles of sorrow." Nel's cry,
set as it is in 1965, at first appears to have only the most tangential relation to political events. But when we consider the magic-realist description of social revolution of Sula's prophecy, it becomes clear that political change, both in terms of cost and gain, is measured on every page of
this novel. It is not the sort of political novel that prior studies of the genre
willingly encountered, but to *not* revise our sense of the political in the
face of overwhelming political changes is to vacate the claims of community upon which those earlier studies were founded. *Sula* may not be
as subversive as some readers would claim, but there is much more to
political activity than subversion.

Notes

1. The quotation marks around "accident" are Walker's (387). Though Walker
does not spell it out in this way, the quotation marks around the word accident
suggest that she has received symbolic punishment for being a "tomboy" (386).
The first thing her brother says is that if she tells, "we will get a whipping" (386).
On "the politics of speech" in the work of Walker and Kingston, see Cheung.

2. Ellison wrote to Callahan that "My problem [. . .] is to affirm while resisting" (Callahan, "Frequencies" 89), a formulation that is very close to Hutcheon's
definition of the postmodern as "complicitous resistance." This formulation is

entirely consistent with the Invisible Man's conclusion at the end of Ellison's novel. Pondering the koan of his grandfather's deathbed advice, in which he was told to live with his head in the lion's mouth, the Invisible Man concludes that "we were to affirm the principle on which the country was built and not the men, or at least not the men who did the violence" (496).

3. Wright and Schaub (1988) both write about how the Invisible Man is torn between the roles of artist and politician.

4. For a critique of the Black Power position by a prominent African American no less critical of the movement's tendencies than Ellison, see King's "Black Power" (23–66).

5. The responses to Ellison's work have varied greatly, and those who are concerned with an African-American aesthetic have also had more varied responses to *Invisible Man* than the more polemical assessments would have us believe. Smith has an excellent summary of this range of positions: "The assumptions behind Ellison's formulations have jeopardized his credibility with more ideological writers and scholars. Black aestheticians such as Addison Gayle, Jr., argue that by emphasizing the universality of his work and vision, Ellison eschews the specific political responsibilities of the black writer. Offering a more subtle indictment, Donald B. Gibson demonstrates that although Ellison denies the political implications of his work *Invisible Man* is nonetheless 'a social document that supports certain values and disparages or discourages others, and as such it must take its place among other forces that seek to determine the character of social reality.' Perhaps most generously, Houston A. Baker, Jr., shows that although in his essays Ellison favors the tradition of Western literary art over folklore, his novel actually breaks down the distinction between the two modes of creative discourse and celebrates the black expressive tradition" (O'Meally 26).

6. Nadel notes that the New York policeman, who would ordinarily wear blue, wears a "black shirt" in this episode (157 n.4).

7. On the novel's epistemological skepticism, see "Romance as Epistemological Design: William Melvin Kelley's *A Different Drummer*" (in Brück and Karrer 103–22), in which Brück focuses on philosophical uncertainty to steer away from politics. His approach is, however, hardly incompatible with a political interpretation.

8. Commenting on what we might call a "white gaze," Morrison tells an interviewer: "The complaint is not being seen for what one is. That is the reason why my hatred for white people is justified and their hatred for me is not" ("Interview" 261). Double standards flourish. Imagine the critical response if a white writer were to say "My hatred of blacks is justified because . . . " to an interviewer. No one, to my knowledge, has acknowledged, never mind criticized, Morrison's justification of racial hatred.

9. We see another double-standard, this one not in Morrison's favor, at work in responses to child-murder in African-American literature. Charles Johnson criticizes Morrison's *Beloved* for sympathetically presenting Sethe's decision to

murder her child rather than permit the child to be recaptured ("Interview" 170–71). I have seen no criticism of the African's similarly motivated attempt at infanticide in *A Different Drummer*.

10. Note the parallel with *Moby-Dick:* neither the Dons of "The *Town-Ho's* Story" nor the men on the porch have the cultural literacy to understand accurately the political Other.

11. Karl objects to the "tacked on" conclusion, and Gayle also sees the departure from Tucker Caliban's story as unwarranted.

12. Kelley's novel came back into print in 1990 after many years "underground," but Kelley himself is indexed neither in *The Columbia Literary History of the United States* nor *The Columbia History of the American Novel*. The novel's critical invisibility may have something to do with its political pushiness, since *A Different Drummer* is at least as dubious of the reader's goodwill as *The Iron Heel*.

13. Gates provides a succinct analysis of the movement in "Tell Me, Sir, . . .What *Is* 'Black' Literature?" Gates writes: "The black arts movement, whose leading theoreticians were Amiri Baraka and Larry Neal, was a reaction against the New Criticism's formalism. The readings these critics advanced were broadly cultural and richly contextualized; they aimed to be 'holistic' and based formal literature firmly on black urban vernacular, expressive culture. Art was a fundamental part of 'the people'; 'art for art's sake' was seen to be a concept alien to a 'pan-African' sensibility, a sensibility that was whole, organic, and, of course, quite ahistorical. What was identified as European or Western essentialism—masked under the rubric of 'universality'—was attacked by asserting an oppositional black or 'neo-African' essentialism. In place of formalist notions about art, these critics promoted a poetics rooted in a social realism, indeed, on a sort of mimeticism; the relation between black art and black life was a direct one" (20).

14. While Kelley alluded to Thoreau to signal his protagonist's freedom from herd mentality, all of the Negroes in his imaginary southern state "boycott" at once; it is difficult *not* to read the novel as a blueprint for social protest—though some have tried. Davis criticizes Gayle's charges of superfluous art: "It is this aspect of the novel, born out of multiple points of view, that Gayle condemns as superfluous to Tucker Caliban's story, at best clouding the novel, at worst rendering it chaotic" (5).

15. On cosmology, see Montgomery's examination of the tensions between Western and African conceptions of time.

16. Mayfield asserts the priority of revolutionary change over "the niceties of art": "Wiping it clean from the very beginning as though it never happened: that is enough to occupy the rest of our lives. Let another generation deal with the niceties of beauty and art. This generation of black men and women has its work cut out for it" (31).

Morrison's generalizations about black people not wanting to change things or not running the pariah out of town appear—when read side by side with essays from *The Black Aesthetic*—to be more wishful thinking than observation. While there is one positive mention of Ellison in the collection (by Emanuel in "Blackness: A Quest for Aesthetics"), several of the contributors attempt to run Ellison out of town, as it were. In one essay Gayle argues that Ellison is only regarded as a major American novelist because he is convenient for the white vision of America, and in his conclusion, "The Function of Black Literature at the Present Time," Gayle damns Ellison for his supposed assimilationist negation of the black self. But Gayle reads askew to support this charge: "The narrator of *Invisible Man* . . . is—to be sure—a Rinehart, the identity he assumes near the end of the novel. A man without a distinctive identity, he is all things to all men" (414–15). The Invisible Man explicitly rejects both the fanatical selfhood of Brother Jack and the annihilation of self he perceives in Rinehart.

Though she parts ways from Karenga, Gayle, and Baraka in not creating literature that demands political action, Morrison, like other writers of the Black Aesthetic, enjoys making polemical generalizations. Even speaking as she does for the narrower group, black women, raises questions, however. What would Sonia Sanchez say about Morrison's claim that black women do not work for change? Alice Walker? To engage political questions is inevitably to traffic in such generalizations. Like Ellison and Kelley, Morrison denies politics for rhetorical and ultimately political reasons.

For a comprehensive discussion of Morrison's work as an "articulation of black Cultural Nationalism," see Heinz's *The Dilemma of Double-Consciousness: Toni Morrison's Novels*.

17. Ellison and King presumed a fallible American identity and did not conceive of Americanness in zero-sum terms. Their thinking is in line with that of American Studies scholars who have described the characteristics of the American self. In a preface to *The American Self: Myth, Ideology, and Popular Culture*, Sam B. Girgus acknowledges the dynamic nature of the American self: "before our national identity gets buried for good beneath continuing waves of faddish cynicism, it might be well to remember that much of American history and culture has been made out of the tension between our idealistic rhetoric of mission and the reality of our actions" (x).

18. On the sea-change in American literary criticism vis-à-vis African-American literature, see Gates's "What Is 'Black' Literature?"

19. In using the phrase "momentary gods" I am drawing on Max Müller's notions of the evolution of religious ideas as presented by Cassirer in *Language and Myth*, 17–22.

20. Students have asked, in frustration, "Why doesn't she cut *them*?" When we do not wish to identify with a person in trouble, we insist that the victim has more choices than she or he really does.

21. Sears and McConahay argue in *The Politics of Violence: The New Urban Blacks and the Watts Riot* that the Watts riot led to increased ethnic pride. See especially chapter 12, "Black Identity and Political Estrangement," 187–95.

CONCLUSION

Politics and Interpretation in America

The one thing about this universe of ours which intrigues me, which makes me realize that it *is* divine and beyond all knowing, is that it lends itself so easily to any and all interpretations.
—Henry Miller

One use of literature, especially in America, is to read the world as an infinite poetic text, to interpret it in innumerable ways, and thus to feel as though the elements of our world form a vast work of art. This utopian urge to escape all conditions is perhaps the chief pleasure of the Whitmanesque mode. The qualities of mystery and wonderment that Henry Miller praises in the quotation above bespeak a desire to leap beyond constraints into a realm of interpretive freedom. Politics checks the freedom of this interpreting self, which is one reason Americans hate politics.

Unconditioned existence, in which one can become like Emerson's "transparent eyeball," is often discussed as the essence of American selfhood, but Terence Martin reports in *Parables of Possibility: The American Need for Beginnings* that "what no longer informs American life at the end of the twentieth century is a *collective* sense of a beginning based on some benign form of transcendence" (215). Even if the American expectation of limitless possibilities has long been on a crash course with itself, we are still faced with a variation on the same old theme: the limitless individual is trapped within a shrinking, oppressive world.

The problems of writing and criticizing political fiction in America are compounded by the American need to see the world in relation to a transcendent or innocent individual, a need that ultimately brings individuals to minimize their own complicity with and capacity within power structures. The self as interpreter often displaces the self as political actor. Political action, while it is born out of interpretive judgment, requires an end or at least a suspension of interpretive wonder, and so we may conceive of politics and interpretation as each undoing the other: "conscience doth make cowards of us all." This difference between political action and interpretive speculation is at the heart of what we mean when we say that there is a difference between aesthetics and politics. This does not mean that political action and the production of literature are antithetical, just that the combination of these elements is an intricate business. Slogans such as "the personal is the political" and "everything is political" hardly do justice to the political novelist's task.

The political act itself requires the suspension of interpretation. One of the things literature often resents about politics is just this delimitation of a horizon of possibilities, an exclusion of *some* possibilities—which will frequently strike literary observers as "unimaginative." Politics, from a strictly literary point of view, opens the door to a flawed dimension of human existence. Literary study favors open-ended interpretation (the celebration of Bakhtin's heteroglossia), whereas politics tends toward a finality of meaning that is called monologic. A "reader-response politics" in which various communities of discourse decide who won the election and what a law might be would not be very useful. In the nonfictional world of elections and revolutions, political activity cannot be nearly as open-ended as the significance of a piece of literary text. Politics fulfills our need for a focused sense of communal vision by weeding out rather than understanding alternative visions.[1]

Politics and interpretation in American fiction are especially at odds, and so when we interpret a political novel it is usually quite difficult to endorse it simultaneously as both an aesthetic object and as a political action, since it probably has not been composed that way; American authors are more often guided by the assumption that politics and interpretation are activities permanently in conflict. One favored way to combine politics and interpretation in the United States is, in fact, to foreground the conflict between them. The novelist may affirm that there is an either/or logic dividing politics from literary art if the writer thematically incorporates this division into his or her work, as Melville did in his "two-book" novel *Moby-Dick,* and as Robert Penn Warren did in *All the King's Men.* Or the writer may devise a form through which to combine the antithetical impulses of politics and interpretation, as Margaret Atwood does in *The Handmaid's Tale.* It may be possible to understand a political novel as a thing of beauty without paying much attention to the question of how the author combines politics and aesthetics, but any analysis of an author's political action depends upon our understanding about how politics and interpretion have been combined. Do they negate one another, does the author deny any difference between political action and literary interpretation, or does the author offer these modes of language as complimenting each other? If we bear in mind the differences between politics and interpretation when considering a given novel, we can reliably distinguish the politically active work from that which takes politics as a subject matter but that makes no effort to, in Orwell's phrase, "push the world in a certain direction."

All the King's Men *as an Anti-Political Political Novel*

All the King's Men poses something of a mystery: Why is the most celebrated postwar American political novel the achievement of that most prominent of the New Critics, Robert Penn Warren? Is this the literary equivalent to "Only Nixon could go to China"? We can better understand the puzzle of this novel's success if we begin at its end, for in its end is its beginning: Jack Burden's expiatory review of his political history occurs after he has *left* politics, and so we track his interpretation of his experience. If the novel begins famously on a fatally sinewy southern road that all but determines a tragic end, we are reminded in each chapter that expedient political action is one option and that studied interpretation is its corrective.

We read the novel in part for the useful moral lessons it offers, but Warren sets the novel in opposition to pragmatic and worldly values whenever possible, such as when he rejected journalistic relevance as a positive value in his "Note to *All the King's Men*," published in *The Sewanee Review* in 1953. There, Warren did not so much deny as qualify and contain *All the King's Men*'s significance as a politically engaged text:

> One of the unfortunate characteristics of our time is that the reception of a novel may depend on its journalistic relevance. It is a little graceless of me to call this characteristic unfortunate, and to quarrel with it, for certainly the journalistic relevance of *All the King's Men* had a good deal to do with what interest it evoked. My politician hero, whose name, in the end, was Willie Stark, was quickly equated with the late Senator Huey P. Long, whose fame, even outside of Louisiana, was yet green in pious tears, anathema, and speculation. (479)

Warren went on to say that this political equation led to many too-quick interpretations of the work, veering either toward a defense of Huey

Long or a call for the assassination of dictators. Warren felt there was nothing much to be said to those who held the former view, since you cannot really answer such "innocent boneheadedness." The latter view, in which the novel was understood to be "a rousing declaration of democratic principles and a tract for the assassination of dictators," was, he claimed, "somewhat more congenial to my personal views" but, just the same, "almost as wide of the mark" (480). "Journalism" is not subject to interpretation to the degree that poetry is, and so Warren resisted such nonliterary ways of understanding his work. Journalistic relevance was regrettable for Warren because, he felt, such a view of events implied a radical simplification—the sort of expedient simplification, we might add, that is made every day by politicians, bureaucrats, lobbyists, and newspaper editors.

And sometimes by philosophers. If we are to consider Huey Long as a model for Willie Stark, Warren points out that "the scholarly and benign figure of William James" was also a model. What do Huey Long and William James have to do with one another? For Warren they were both figures "that stood in the shadows of imagination behind Willie Stark." Warren stressed that he was not as much concerned with this or that politician in America as he was "the kind of doom that democracy may invite upon itself." The novel, read in the way Warren would wish, is less an effort to have readers take sides in an immediate political struggle, and more a broad philosophical warning about the shortcomings of American pragmatism and expediency. "The book [. . .] was not intended to be a book about politics. Politics merely provided the framework story in which the deeper concerns, whatever their final significance, might work themselves out" (480). Politics for Warren is that which sharply limits the possibilities of interpretation, and this limitation of interpretive possibilities is what makes literature, unlike politics or journalism, the realm of "deeper concerns."

One might counter Warren's literary universalism by arguing that it is this timeliness, this mortality visited upon the body politic, that gives any transcendent notion of innocence its relative value. To say that politics merely provides the framework for any such notion is like saying that death merely provides the framework for life. The fatal clash of innocence and experience that Willie Stark traces back, in his own version of original sin, to "the stink of the didie" may very well exist as a transcendent theme to illuminate all human behavior, but this theme captures our communal attention in a singular way when we find that the theme has manifested itself in a shift in local social and political realities.

At the conclusion of *All the King's Men* Jack Burden's Olympian detachment is shattered by his hard-earned awareness of the threads of responsibility running through the world. He tells us that he and Anne Stanton will go back to Burden's Landing: "and soon now we shall go out of the house and go into the convulsion of the world, out of history into history and the awful responsibility of Time" (434). It is, he tells us, 1939. Even so it seems we are more going "out of history" than into it, and so Burden leaves politics. Even if he knows deeply that he can never wash his hands of it, he *can* cease to be an activist. He cannot avoid being a witness, but that role is more akin to the poet than the politician. Readers are secondary witnesses, and through Burden's narrative we experience his political world in exact terms, just as readers of *The Divine Comedy* experience hell exactly; neither experience is recommended. Burden says, of one of the precipitate ironies of his experience, that "the situation is too much like the world in which we live from birth to death, and the humor of it grows stale from repetition" (438). Even while he speaks in a poetically exasperated voice, Burden is perfectly mindful of the prosaic world that awaits him at this novel's end, but if he and Anne are about to go into the "convulsion of the world," it is not because they want to but rather because they have to. Praised as America's finest political novel, *All the King's Men* could just as well be praised as an antipolitical novel for the attitude it develops toward political action. *All the King's Men* may well be thought of as an antidote to political activism.

The Dialogue of Politics and Interpretation in The Handmaid's Tale

A novelist could combine political activism and literary art by questioning whether there is any difference whatsoever between the two uses of language. This mode of political art is, however, ultimately self-defeating, since the writer sacrifices both monological forcefulness and open-ended literariness through such an insistence. The writer requires the reader's recognition of differences between political and aesthetic intent in order to create an *activist* political novel. Specifically, a tension is required between political proposition and open-ended interpretation, and efforts to level any differences between them undermine both political resolve and aesthetic potential. Such a tension is maintained in the work of Canadian author Margaret Atwood, who has skillfully balanced politics and interpretation in a novel about the timeliest of American political issues, a woman's right to choose whether or not to bear an unwanted child. *The Handmaid's Tale* portrays a heroine's flight from political power, but this novel is not a flight from politics, since it encourages political activity in a way that *All the King's Men* does not.[2] One form of this encouragement is to make literary interpretation an anti-fundamentalist political weapon, thus creating tactical alliances between political action and literary interpretation.

As we have asked why the most highly regarded postwar political novel in America was written by one of the New Critics, we must ask another question: Why is the finest American political novel written during the Age of Reagan a Canadian import? Perhaps part of the advantage stems from the author not conceiving of herself as writing within the tradition of American Adamicism.

Structured around a young American woman's (apparent) escape to Canada, Atwood's *The Handmaid's Tale* expresses the flight from "Americanness," but, surprisingly, Atwood's own resistance to American culture has become increasingly dialogic: she resists fundamentalist notions of American identity even in an Orwellian critique of American political tendencies. Without a sense of opposition, of the world being divided into "sides," the political novel is difficult to recognize, and yet splitting the world into "us" and "them" is a risky maneuver for any novelist. Several such oppositions are at play in *The Handmaid's Tale*. There is a clash of world views represented by the Christian fundamentalists who have taken over America on the one hand, and there are, on the other, women like Offred who suffer the results of fundamentalist governance. There is also Atwood's intercultural theme of the United States in cultural opposition to Canada, which she expresses in gendered terms as well, characterizing American culture as predominantly masculine with Canadian culture as a more feminine or at least a more gender-balanced culture.[3] *The Handmaid's Tale* represents several kinds of political opposition but does not surrender to what Nietzsche called the metaphysician's fundamental "faith in opposite values" (10). Like *The Iron Heel*, Atwood's novel designates an enemy, but *The Handmaid's Tale* does not denounce a metaphysical opposite or "essential" enemy. Rather than name the enemy in Adamic fashion as the eternal enemy of all, Atwood carefully presents the political quest of a non-Adamic namer, one who is aware of the contingencies of her views and language at all times. In so doing, she designates an enemy without sacrificing the possibility of multiple interpretations.

The political novel must name an enemy, be it those who practice patriarchy or political correctness, fascism or Stalinism, Gingrichism or

Shirley Chisholm. For a literary artist the association with political hatred is an awkward matter, and for a feminist writer this "otherization" is especially tricky, since feminist thought has strongly criticized such "otherization" as a characteristic of patriarchal ideology.[4] Atwood's novel is carefully structured to avoid such a simplistic division of good and evil, even while it positions itself in opposition to political ideologies such as those advanced by America's Christian Right.

At the beginning of this novel, Atwood's heroine Offred is a prisoner of a Christian fundamentalist regime that has violently overthrown the constitutional government of the United States and has renamed the country "Gilead." The novel dramatizes the clash of ideologies by focusing mainly on Offred's everyday struggles for sanity and survival and by concluding with her attempt to escape, which may or may not have succeeded. The novel is clearly opposed to the political effects of religious fundamentalism, but it fashions its resistance in a manner that avoids becoming what I call "counter-fundamentalism," an equal-and-opposite rectitude and disregard for the rights of the political Other; a kind of political tunnel vision formed as a direct result of one's resistance to fundamentalism. When Nietzsche claimed that "He who fights too long against dragons becomes a dragon himself," he was warning that in struggle we risk becoming just like our enemy.[5] For the feminist political novel, and for the feminist struggle as it extends beyond the covers of a novel, one key problem has been to resist patriarchal discourse and policy without recreating it in feminist form. Atwood's political novel fights a dragon without becoming one.

The Handmaid's Tale closes with the notes to a futuristic counterpart to a Modern Language Association or American Studies Association conference. Our interpretation of the main fictional narrative is held up for comparison against that of a fictional group of intellectuals who study Offred's time and the decades after the fall of Gilead. Do the Historical Notes give us an exit from politics, or does the final section return us to political questions in some final way?

In this future, Offred's story has become a text, a verbal object of study, open to multiple interpretations. As one politically trenchant article on Atwood's novel makes clear, multiplicity of interpretation and the fact of political engagement are at odds with one another within literary texts. Arnold E. Davidson argues that the Historical Notes function as Atwood's indictment of academic critics who enjoy word play but are obtuse to political consequences when studying literature. Davidson interprets the Historical Notes as a scholarly apparatus in such a way as to decrease the number of politically acceptable interpretations. Davidson's main point is that the Historical Notes do not, in terms of political responsibility, let readers off the hook.

Some readers might feel that the jokes in the Historical Notes are there to restore an everyday level of comfort after enduring an imaginary experience of totalitarian society. The notes, by this way of reading, tell us that the nightmare is over, that we are "off the hook." However, the double entendre humor in the notes, Davidson argues, has not been included to let academics off the hook but instead unmasks the sexism of everyday society. In academic communities as elsewhere, sexism, even in the form of jokes, can work to prepare the way for Gilead, yet if academics who make sexist jokes are *on* the hook, then the novel operates like the Wall on which abortionists are hung in Atwood's imagined future.[6] There are serious problems with this reading. If the novel were punitive in the way Davidson suggests, it would itself be a fundamentalist (or totalitarian, or monologic) political novel because of its intolerance of opposition. If we follow Offred's story closely, we see that Offred carefully avoids the vengeful or otherwise narrowly dualistic attitudes indicated by Davidson.

Davidson sees the fictional academic proceedings as marked by institutional oppression and patriarchal sexism, such as when the fictional Professor Pieixoto commits double entendre in his keynote address. Davidson writes, "A most dubious note it is. His joke turns upon a bad pun conjoining the 'charming Arctic char' that 'we all enjoyed' last night at dinner and the current 'charming Arctic Chair' that 'we are [now] enjoying.'" Through word play, Pieixoto suggests that the group is sexually enjoying the chair of the session, Professor Maryann Crescent Moon. Davidson correctly points out that the remarks are sexual. Perhaps they are also in questionable taste, but to argue that Pieixoto's reconstruction of Offred's story "duplicat[es] the suppression her society inflicted on her" (120) is to succumb to the interpretive strictness of the Gileadean functionary Aunt Lydia, "who was in love with either/or" (8). Davidson, in restrictively interpreting the meaning of the speaker's jokes, is stripping language of its play. Even if we agree with Davidson's political purposes, supposing them to include feminist goals such as equal rights for women, resistance to the idea that literary study should be apolitical, and so forth, we need not acquiesce to the implication that all sexual humor is sexist or that all sexism is equally bad.

Context is all. We should be able to recognize that Pieixoto's "chair" jokes do not make him a sexist of the Commander's ilk. We need not be "in love with either/or." His desire to know more about the Commander than about Offred can be interpreted as institutional sexism, but to totalize his after-dinner remarks as Gileadean in tendency is to ignore the freedom of the post-Gileadean world. The problems with Davidson's form of political interpretation far outweigh the possible gains. Are we to condemn Offred as "sexist" for not being as committed a feminist as was her mother (who burned fashion magazines and pornography alike)? Did Offred's political laxity bring on the Gileadean world? Such a reading, it seems to me, requires that the critic ignore those parts of the novel that warn us about ideological hardening of the arteries, and there are many such passages in *The Handmaid's Tale*, a novel that consistently refuses the temptations of counter-fundamentalism. Consider, in this context, Offred's own "chair" meditation:

> I sit in the chair and think about the word *chair*. It can also mean the leader of a meeting. It can also mean a mode of execution. It is the first syllable in *charity*. It is the French word for flesh. None of these facts has any connection with the others.
> These are the kinds of litanies I use, to compose myself. (110)

These are the litanies through which she observes her own language, preserving its pre-Gileadean interpretive spaces. Offred does not rename the world in Adamic fashion, in a way that would signify her otherness from society. She is as politically opposed to the society that controls her every move as she can be, but she learns that she must not make the mistake of perceiving that world in a final, totalized way. Even at its political worst, the world lends itself to interpretation, at least for those who wish to preserve the difference between public and private space.

In the privacy of her room, in the "Night" sections of the novel, Offred "takes back the night" through imaginative word play. The slack in the language that she discovers, this play in the system of meaning, is certainly what repressive functionaries such as the Aunts, the Angels, and the Commanders struggle to eliminate when they deprive Offred of freedom of speech and movement. Granted: different contexts give the same pun different meanings, and so Pieixoto's word play is not an act of resistance against oppression in the manner of Offred's chair meditation, but this does not make him a totalitarian. "Chair" means different things in different contexts, and Atwood connects various contexts through the common node "chair" to dramatize the relational nature of meaning. This novel is a warning about the dangers of those who do not respect the importance of context, and so it is ironic that Davidson sees the Historical Notes as "fundamentally" sexist. To equate the Gileadean repression of Offred's voice with Pieixoto's reconstruction of it is to narrow the set of possible meanings too much. Because he who fights a dragon may become one, political actors must resist being absorbed by the world view they have chosen to oppose.

The Gileadean world view, following as it does from a fundamentalist approach to language, differs in extraordinary ways from Pieixoto's sometimes wry scholarly view: the idea of a plurality of competing voices is inimical to the fundamentalist mode of interpretation. Gileadean geography, or world-writing, is similarly a monologic discourse. Other ways of mapping the world are forcefully repressed within Gilead, as are voices from beyond the Gileadean border. The Montreal satellite station is blocked, and the Commander is irritated when Radio Free America's broadcast gets through: "Damn Cubans, he says. All that filth about universal daycare" (209). The Commander's moral geography demonizes voices that challenge the Gileadean claims to righteousness: talk of daycare is filth and Cubans are damned.

Offred, it is true, loathes the Gileadean world view and so does not wish to reproduce it. Her desire for biological reproductive choice is directly paralleled by this desire for ideological reproductive choice. Though she is initially moved to deny she is part of this world, she learns to "place" herself within this political context. Near the beginning of her narrative Offred says "not *my* room, I refuse to say *my*" (8), but by ultimately accepting the limited space that she is allowed as *her* space, Offred's commitment to survival deepens. The idea of "home," or rather the Gileadean Ideology of the Home, is a mockery to Offred, but she gradually learns that she must resist this ideology from some *place*. In an ironic amendment to Woolf's "A Room of One's Own," she says, "My room, then. There has to be some space, finally, that I claim as mine, even in this time" (50). Offred's acceptance of personal space is, in the Gileadean context, a political act.

Enclosed by her Handmaid wings, and by the repressive social structure that controls all her movements, Offred must exercise her mind through scattered and seemingly insignificant observations. Much of her private word play in the "Night" sections is subversive of both Gileadean morality and geography. When Moira escapes, Offred is pleased to think that she is now a "loose woman" (133). She is also a "gender traitor" (a bi- or homosexual) and, therefore, morally "loose." When she is *on the loose*, she is violating the Gileadean laws that physically imprison women. *Loose* undergoes a transformation in the novel, since the restrictive, mor-

alistic epithet comes to mean *free*. Offred's word play is the inner
coefficient of Moira's outer movement. Offred's word play makes readers aware of the external language, the general language bordering all
our thoughts, a language that has moralistic and political values built into
it. In the context of Offred's pun, her sense of Moira as "loose woman"
confronts the assumption built into our language that any woman without a male companion is morally questionable. While Offred's word play
is not as daring as Moira's escape, it is integral to her survival plans that
she keep her mind free, or perhaps we should say "loose."

In her resistance to the mind-constricting designs of Gileadean fundamentalism, Offred consciously avoids what I have been calling
counter-fundamentalism. It occurs when one's resistance to a fundamentalism, religious or political, becomes an equal and opposite form of fundamentalism. In *The Handmaid's Tale* the solution to this problem is to
reveal the shallowness of moral geography, especially regarding the
United States/Canadian border (see Schlueter). The binary opposition
of Canada-the-victim oppressed by the brutal Evil Empire to the south
frequently surfaces in Atwood's work, certainly in *The Handmaid's Tale*.
The binary opposition is reproduced but also called into question. In the
fictional Historical Notes Pieixoto speculates on the question of Offred's
escape: "Was she smuggled over the border of Gilead, into what was
then Canada, and did she make her way thence to England? This would
have been wise, as the Canada of that time did not wish to antagonize
its powerful neighbor, and there were roundups and extraditions of such
refugees" (310). Atwood complicates her moral geography by refusing
a bi-polar world of moral absolutes. This is why Offred's tapes are discovered in an attic in Bangor, Maine, rather than on the Canadian side
of the border: the novel subverts the facile heroic codes that would
present a dashingly successful escape to free Canada. By refusing a form
of closure that resolves all political tensions within the novel, *The
Handmaid's Tale* responds to very current political contexts, and, furthermore, engages in political struggles in a style that maintains the possibility of multiple interpretations.[7] We may enjoy the belief that we have
inherent rights, but we can only hold such truths self-evident so long
as there is no strong challenge from within our community to those
rights. (Just as we do not know how Offred's struggle ends, reproductive rights such as abortion are currently up for grabs in the United
States.)

In a sense the novel does allow for an escape to Canada. Recall that
the Historical Notes provide a fictional transition from Gileadean totali-

tarianism to a post-Gileadean free (or freer) world. Although the escape into the "Twelfth Symposium on Gileadean Studies [. . .] held at the University of Denay, Nunavit" (299) is hardly dashing, the shift into the Historical Notes does retrieve the reader from the wretched situations about which dystopian writers like Atwood warn us.[8] The denial function of this Canadian happy ending is signaled by the Swiftian place name "Nunavit" and also by the name "Denay," which we might pronounce "deny."[9] Still, it has to be admitted that this ending is really janiform, since the denial function is counterbalanced by the plain fact that researchers Pieixoto and Wade are, like Offred, dedicated to the reconstruction of the past. They are not regenerating Gilead, even if the main purpose of their meeting is to study it. Atwood is *not* proposing that academics model future MLA proceedings on the Nuremberg Trials. Rather, the Historical Notes undermine any remaining potential for counter-fundamentalism by showing that not all sexism is equal. Insisting that Atwood's futuristic, multicultural academics are sexist in the same way as the Commander completely overlooks her suggestion that we need not create a demon when designating a political opponent. We can choose to admit that we are composed of motives and histories in some ways similar to those that make up our opponents, and this meditation on the substance of our "enemy" can only temper our more hateful tendencies. Through its dialogic approach to communication, *The Handmaid's Tale* designates political opponents without declaring total war on them.

It is undoubtedly the case that Offred does not escape the Commander's house by word play alone. I do not suggest that Atwood wishes readers to substitute crossword puzzles for political action. Even so, the Historical Notes satirize academics who make professional capital out of the suffering of others while the notes simultaneously celebrate the freedom to study odd topics and to make bad jokes.

Word play may be worth struggling for, but it is not the equivalent of political action. Within the world of the novel, political activity is risky in a way we should not underestimate. Offred is never certain whom she can trust (with the exception of Moira), and the regular betrayal of trust in the Gileadean world is part of what makes the *inner* world of imaginative freedom attractive to her. It is a world over which she has control. Political literature, in bringing about a confrontation between our inner freedoms and the outer world, surrenders some of this freedom and thus undertakes risks that parallel the risks of political activism. As a woman in Gileadean society may be pronounced an Unwoman and sent to "the colonies" (slave labor camps), a political novel in our world may be pronounced Unliterature. Atwood is one of those writers who is willing to put her imaginary world in jeopardy for the difference it might make to readers in the real world.

Atwood's nonfundamentalist moral map is a way of knowing the world that refuses absolutist statements about that world, but is it based also upon a moral-political uncertainty principle? That is to say, in addition to being a form of communication, does dialogism also imply a political philosophy, if not a set of policies? One answer to this question is to argue that dialogism is a means but can never be an end.[10] At several junctures in her narrative, Offred does not even say what happened but rather offers a variety of reconstructions "because what you say can never be exact, you always have too many parts, sides, crosscurrents, nuances" (134). If "what you say can never be exact," then you cannot name the world. Taken to an extreme, this uncertainty principle would make it impossible to designate a moral or political danger. The intersubjectivity of dialogism subverts notions of a "simple genuine self against the whole world." This is all to the good when, for strategic purposes, one wishes to challenge individualist ideologies, but, taken to an extreme, dialogism as an end in itself subverts the capacity to oppose even if it privileges the formation of an oppositional voice.

Politics, Dialogism, and the American Self

The conflict between political action and dialogic interpretation does not prevent the writing of political novels, though an understanding of this built-in problem can greatly enhance our ability to appreciate them adequately. In art we may conceive of dialogue as an end in itself, but in politics dialogue cannot exist solely as an end. It will sooner or later reveal itself to be a means to an end, and so political novelists are taking very different kinds of risks when they choose to marshall literary strategies for a political cause. American literary criticism has favored those novelists who write *about* politics over those who have combined politics with literary purpose, largely because politically intransitive writing does not restrict readerly interpretation in the way that writing infused with monologic purpose must. To resolve this problem by invariably celebrating heteroglossia and denigrating monologia makes perfect sense just so long as one believes in an American dream of endless frontiers and limitless possibilities. One alternative to the way of "the simple, genuine self against the whole world" would be to admit the political facets of life as a necessary aspect of interdependent being and to conceive of political cooperation and compromise as something more than a fall from individual purity. In the short run this means critics must read American fiction with an eye to their own prejudices against political necessity, and in the long run it means that the American self requires reform no less frequently than do American political structures. To reinvent one is to reinvent the other.

Notes

1. Literary folk can of course interpret a political event until the cows come home, and there is also a form of political attack that masks itself as interpretation when in fact the interests motivating the interrogators have already determined conclusions to those "questions." Conservatives such as Rush Limbaugh have been "interpeting" President Clinton since he entered office.

2. *The Handmaid's Tale* shows up at Pro-Choice rallies and is a useful dystopian statement to political actors who wish to resist the growth of, say, Christian right-wing fundamentalists in America. This is not to say Atwood is a politician rather than a writer. In response to Linda Sandler's questions about her political activism, Atwood was quick to draw lines between what she does and what actual politicians do: "Activism isn't very good for the writer, and I'm not very good at it. I believe in saying what I think, and that's no way to be a politician" (*Conversations* 56). Political activity demands stricter limits on free expression and interpretation, and Atwood is *relatively* more active than Warren along these lines.

3. When Joyce Carol Oates asked Atwood about similarities between *Surfacing* and James Dickey's novel *Deliverance*, Atwood responded by stressing gendered cultural differences between American and Canadian writing: "There's a relationship of sorts, but for me it's one of opposites. For the central figure in Dickey's book, as I recall, nature is something wild, untamed, feminine, dangerous and mysterious, that he must struggle with, confront, conquer, overcome. Doing this involves killing. For me, the works cognate with Dickey's are Mailer's *Why Are We in Vietnam?*, Faulkner's *Bear*, Hemingway's 'Short Happy Life of Francis Macomber,' and, if you like, *Moby Dick*, though Ahab was not seen by Melville as having chosen the right path. The books cognate with mine are Canadian and probably unknown in the United States; Howard O'Hagan's *Tay John* is one of them" (*Conversations* 76).

4. In *This Sex Which Is Not One*, Irigaray articulates the feminist apprehension in which fighting the dragon of patriarchy only causes the feminist agent to be turned into a dragon: "what is important is to disconcert the staging of representation according to *exclusively* 'masculine' parameters, that is, according to phallocratic order. It is not a matter of toppling that order so as to replace it— that amounts to the same thing in the end—but of disrupting and modifying it, starting from an 'outside' that is exempt, in part, from phallocratic law" (quoted

in Rigney 1). In my discussion Atwood avoids demonizing Offred's fundamentalist captors in an absolute way because she is aware that such demonization, ultimately, "amounts to the same thing in the end."

5. Even violence committed in self-defense can have brutalizing effects. Orwell quotes Nietzsche in an "As I Please" column on the cruel treatment of collaborators after France was liberated from Nazi domination: "He who fights too long against dragons becomes a dragon himself: and if thou gaze too long into the abyss, the abyss will gaze into thee" (3:230–31). Orwell claimed to understand the French anger at Nazi collaborators, but he interprets "too long" in this passage to mean "after the dragon has been beaten."

6. Davidson allows for the possibility of not being on the hook: either we read uncritically along sexist lines, or we condemn such a mode of cultural discourse. No middle ground exists.

7. Offred's narrative was discovered on cassette tapes. Did she record *over* Elvis Presley (implying that we must change/challenge popular culture in our resistance to Gilead), or does her narrative hide *under* the lyrics of the King (implying that popular culture aids and abets our struggles from freedom)? In the case of the former, the point would go to Davidson, but I believe Atwood is, in the particular instance of the cassette tapes, offering an interpretive ambiguity.

8. The dual perspective created by the Historical Notes is similar in effect to that in *The Iron Heel* (1908), an effect also achieved by the Newspeak Appendix in Orwell's *Nineteen Eighty-Four*.

9. Or Atwood could be hinting that universities ought to "deny none of it."

The novel is rife with suggestive names. Offred is of course the handmaid "offered" in the biblical passage, but she is also "afraid." Moira is more "merry" than most, and Aunt Lydia is an example of how church "laity" function in a fundamentalist theocratic society.

10. Brian Walker argues that "Bakhtin's polyphonic vision does not by itself constitute a moral viewpoint" (121), and Lentricchia makes similar complaints about American pragmatism in *Criticism and Social Change* (1–5).

Works Cited and Consulted

Aaron, Daniel. *Writers on the Left: Episodes in American Literary Communism.* New York: Harcourt, Brace and World, 1961.

Adams, Henry. *The Education of Henry Adams.* New York: Houghton Mifflin, 1918.

Adams, Laura. *Existential Battles: The Growth of Norman Mailer.* Athens: Ohio University Press, 1976.

Alter, Robert. *Motives for Fiction.* Cambridge, Mass.: Harvard University Press, 1984.

———. *The Pleasures of Reading in an Ideological Age.* New York: Simon and Schuster, 1989.

Arac, Jonathan. *Critical Genealogies: Historical Situations for Postmodern Literary Studies.* New York: Columbia University Press, 1989.

Attwater, Donald. *A Dictionary of Saints.* Harmondsworth, U.K.: Penguin Books, 1965.

Atwood, Margaret. *The Handmaid's Tale.* Boston: Houghton Mifflin, 1986.

———. *Margaret Atwood: Conversations.* Ed. Earl G. Ingersoll. Princeton, N.J.: Ontario Review Press, 1990.

Auden, W. H. *The Collected Poetry of W. H. Auden.* New York: Random House, 1945.

Bakhtin, M. M. *The Dialogic Imagination.* Ed. Michael Holquist. Trans. Caryl Emerson and Michael Holquist. Austin: University of Texas Press, 1981.

Barbour, James. "'The *Town-Ho*'s Story': Melville's Original Whale." *ESQ* 2 (1975): 111–15.

Beckett, Samuel. "Dante . . . Bruno . Vico . . Joyce." In *Our Exagmination Round His Factification for Incamination of Work in Progress.* 1929. Rpt., Norfolk, Conn.: New Directions, 1962. 3–22.

Bellamy, Edward. *Looking Backward, 2000–1887*. Boston: Ticknor, 1888.

Bennett, Tony. *Formalism and Marxism*. London: Methuen, 1979.

Bercovitch, Sacvan, and Myra Jehlen, eds. *Ideology and Classic American Literature*. New York: Cambridge University Press, 1986.

Blotner, Joseph. *The Modern American Political Novel, 1900–1960*. Austin: University of Texas Press, 1966.

———. *The Political Novel*. Garden City, N.Y.: Doubleday, 1955.

Booth, Wayne. "Introduction." In *Problems of Dostoevsky's Poetics*. Ed. and trans. Caryl Emerson. Minneapolis: University of Minnesota Press, 1984. xiii–xxvii.

Boyers, Robert. *Atrocity and Amnesia: The Political Novel since 1945*. New York: Oxford University Press, 1985.

Braudy, Leo, ed. *Norman Mailer: A Collection of Critical Essays*. Englewood Cliffs, N.J.: Prentice-Hall, 1972.

Breasted, James Henry. *A History of Egypt*. New York: Charles Scribner's Sons, 1905.

Bromwich, David. *Politics by Other Means: Higher Education and Group Thinking*. New Haven, Conn.: Yale University Press, 1992.

Brück, Peter, and Wolfgang Karrer, eds. *The Afro-American Novel since 1960*. Amsterdam: B. R. Gruner, 1982.

Buckler, Steve. *Dirty Hands: The Problem of Political Morality*. Aldershot: Avebury, 1993.

Burke, Kenneth. "Literature as Equipment for Living." In *The Philosophy of Literary Form: Studies in Symbolic Action*. New York: Vintage Books, 1957. 253–62.

———. *A Rhetoric of Motives*. Berkeley: University of California Press, 1969.

Callahan, John. "Frequencies of Eloquence: The Performance and Composition of *Invisible Man*." In O'Meally, 55–94.

———. *In the African-American Grain: The Pursuit of Voice in Twentieth-Century Black Fiction*. Urbana: University of Illinois Press, 1988.

Carroll, Joseph. "Matthew Arnold." In *The Johns Hopkins Guide to Literary Theory and Criticism*. Ed. Michael Groden and Martin Kreiswirth. Baltimore: Johns Hopkins University Press, 1994. 45–48.

Casas, Bartolomé de Las. *The Heath Anthology of American Literature*. Ed. Paul Lauter et al. Lexington, Ky.: D. C. Heath, 1990. 70–80.

Cassirer, Ernst. *Language and Myth*. Trans. Susanne K. Langer. New York: Harper and Bros., 1946.

Cheung, King-Kok. "'Don't Tell': Imposed Silences in *The Color Purple* and *The Woman Warrior*." *PMLA* 103:2 (1988): 162–74.

Chomsky, Noam. "The Manufacture of Consent." In *The Chomsky Reader*. New York: Pantheon Books, 1987. 121–36.

Conn, Peter. *The Divided Mind: Ideology and Imagination in America, 1898–1917*. New York: Cambridge University Press, 1983.

Cowan, Michael. "The Americanness of Norman Mailer." In Braudy, 143–57.

Crews, Frederick. "Whose American Renaissance?" *New York Review of Books* 35 (27 Oct. 1988): 68–81.

Davidson, Arnold E. "Future Tense: Making History in *The Handmaid's Tale*." In *Margaret Atwood: Vision and Forms.* Ed. Kathryn VanSpackeren and Jan Garden Castro. Carbondale: Southern Illinois University Press, 1988. 113–21.

Davis, Charles E. "W. M. Kelley and H. D. Thoreau: The Music Within." *Obsidian II* 2:1 (Spring 1987): 2–13.

Deleuze, Gilles, and Felix Guattari. *Anti-Oedipus: Capitalism and Schizophrenia.* Trans. Robert Hurley, Mark Seem, and Helen R. Lane. Minneapolis: University of Minnesota Press, 1983.

Des Pres, Terrence. *Praises and Dispraises: Poetry and Politics, the 20th Century.* New York: Penguin Books, 1989.

Didion, Joan. *After Henry.* New York: Simon and Schuster, 1992.

Dionne, E. J., Jr. *Why Americans Hate Politics.* New York: Touchstone, 1992.

Dittmar, Linda. "'Will the Circle Be Unbroken?': The Politics of Form in *The Bluest Eye*." *Novel* 23 (1990): 137–55.

Doctorow, E. L. "E. L. Doctorow, Novelist." Interview by Bill Moyers. In *A World of Ideas: Conversations with Thoughtful Men and Women about American Life Today and the Ideas Shaping Our Future.* Ed. Betty Sue Flowers. New York: Doubleday, 1989. 83–95.

Douglass, Frederick. "Narrative of the Life of Frederick Douglass, an American Slave." In *The Norton Anthology of American Literature.* Ed. Nina Baym et al. New York: W. W. Norton, 1989. 1874–938.

Duban, James. "Chipping with a Chisel: The Ideology of Melville's Narrators." *Texas Studies in Literature and Language* 31 (1989): 341–85.

———. *Melville's Major Fiction: Politics, Theology, and Imagination.* DeKalb: Northern Illinois University Press, 1983.

———. "'A Pantomime of Action': Starbuck and the American Whig Dissidence." *New England Quarterly* 3 (1982): 432–39.

Dyson, Michael Eric. *Making Malcolm: The Myth and Meaning of Malcolm X.* New York: Oxford University Press, 1995.

Eagleton, Terry. *Literary Theory: An Introduction.* Minneapolis: University of Minnesota Press, 1983.

Egan, Philip J. "Time and Ishmael's Character in 'The *Town Ho's* Story' and *Moby-Dick*." *Studies in the Novel* 4 (1982): 337–47.

Ehrenreich, Barbara. "Foreword." In *Male Fantasies.* Klaus Theweleit. Vol. 1. Trans. Stephen Conway. Minneapolis: University of Minnesota Press, 1987.

Elliott, Emory, gen. ed. *Columbia History of the American Novel.* New York: Columbia University Press, 1991.

———. *Columbia Literary History of the United States.* New York: Columbia University Press, 1988.

Ellison, Ralph. *Going to the Territory.* New York: Vintage, 1987.

———. *Invisible Man.* New York: Signet Books, 1952.

———. *Shadow and Act.* New York: Random House, 1966.

Emanuel, James A. "Blackness: A Quest for Aesthetics." In Gayle, 192–223.

Feifer, George. *Tennozen: The Battle of Okinawa and the Atomic Bomb.* Boston: Houghton Mifflin, 1992.

Fisher, Philip. *Hard Facts: Setting and Form in the American Novel.* New York: Oxford University Press, 1985.

———, ed. *The New American Studies: Essays from Representations.* Berkeley: University of California Press, 1991.

Folena, Lucia. "Philologists, Witches, and Stalinistas." In *The Violence of Representation: Literature and the History of Violence.* Ed. Nancy Armstrong and Leonard Tennenhouse. London: Routledge, 1989. 219–38.

Foley, Barbara. *Radical Representations: Politics and Form in U.S. Proletarian Fiction, 1929–1941.* Durham, N.C.: Duke University Press, 1993.

Foner, Philip S. "Introduction." In *Jack London, American Rebel: A Collection of His Social Writings.* New York: Citadel Press, 1947. 3–130.

Foster, Charles H. "Something in Emblems: A Reinterpretation of *Moby-Dick.*" *New England Quarterly* 1 (1961): 3–35.

Franklin, H. Bruce. "Introduction." In *The Iron Heel* by Jack London. Chicago: Lawrence Hill Books, 1980. i–vi.

Fraser, John. *Violence in the Arts.* New York: Cambridge University Press, 1974.

Freud, Sigmund. *The Interpretation of Dreams.* Trans. James Strachey. New York: Avon Books, 1965.

Fussell, Paul. *The Great War and Modern Memory.* New York: Oxford University Press, 1975.

Gair, Christopher. "Looking Forward/Looking Backward: Romance and Utopia in *The Iron Heel.*" In *The Critical Response to Jack London.* Ed. Susan M. Nuernburg. Westport, Conn.: Greenwood Press, 1995. 150–65.

Gates, Henry Louis, Jr. "Tell Me, Sir, . . . What Is 'Black' Literature?" *PMLA* 105:1 (1990): 11–22.

Gayle, Addison, Jr., ed. *The Black Aesthetic.* Garden City, N.Y.: Doubleday, 1971.

Geiger, Don. "Melville's Black God: Contrary Evidence in 'The *Town-Ho's* Story.'" In *Discussions of Moby-Dick.* Ed. Milton R. Stern. Boston: D. C. Heath, 1968. 93–97.

Gibson, Donald B. *The Politics of Literary Expression: A Study of Major Black Writers.* Westport, Conn.: Greenwood Press, 1981.

Gilbert, Sandra S., and Susan Gubar. *The War of the Words.* Vol. 1 of *No Man's Land.* New Haven, Conn.: Yale University Press, 1988.

Gilmore, Michael. *American Romanticism and the Marketplace.* Chicago: University of Chicago Press, 1985.

Girgus, Sam B. "Preface: The American Self Today." In *The American Self: Myth, Ideology, and Popular Culture.* Ed. Sam B. Girgus. Albuquerque: University of New Mexico Press, 1981. ix–x.

Gordimer, Nadine. *The Essential Gesture: Writing, Politics, and Places.* Ed. Stephen Clingman. New York: Penguin Books, 1989.

Graff, Gerald. "American Criticism Left and Right." In Bercovitch and Jehlen, 91–121.

Grant, Robert. "Absence into Presence: The Thematics of Memory and 'Missing' Subjects in Toni Morrison's *Sula*." In *Critical Essays on Toni Morrison*. Ed. Nellie McKay. Boston: G. K. Hall, 1988. 90–103.

Hassan, Ihab. *Radical Innocence: Studies in the Contemporary Novel*. New York: Harper and Row, 1961.

Hayford, Harrison. "Unnecessary Duplicates: A Key to the Writing of *Moby-Dick*." In *New Perspectives on Melville*. Ed. Faith Pullin. Kent, Ohio: Kent State University Press, 1978. 128–61.

Heimert, Alan. "*Moby-Dick* and American Political Symbolism." *Arizona Quarterly* 4 (1963): 498–534.

Heinze, Denise. *The Dilemma of "Double-Consciousness": Toni Morrison's Novels*. Athens: University of Georgia Press, 1993.

Herbst, Josephine. Letter to Alfred Kazin, 7 Feb. 1966. Herbst Collection, Beinecke Library, Yale University, New Haven, Conn.

Horsley, Lee. *Political Fiction and the Historical Imagination*. Houndmills: Macmillan, 1990.

Howard, Leon. *Herman Melville, A Biography*. Berkeley: University of California Press, 1951.

Howe, Irving. *Politics and the Novel*. Rev. ed. New York: New American Library, 1987.

Hutcheon, Linda. *The Politics of Postmodernism*. London: Routledge, 1989.

"Jack London: A Sketch of His Life and Work." New York: Macmillan, 1905. Huntington Library 262252. San Marino, Calif.

"Jack London: His Life and Literary Work." New York: Macmillan, ca. 1910. Huntington Library 434989. San Marino, Calif.

"Jack London: His Life and Literary Work." New York: Macmillan, 1972. Huntington Library 435917. San Marino, Calif.

Jacoby, Russell. *The Last Intellectuals: American Culture in the Age of Academe*. New York: Basic Books, 1987.

James, C. L. R. *Mariners, Renegades, and Castaways: The Story of Herman Melville and the World We Live In*. 1957. Rpt., New York: Allison and Busby, 1985.

Jameson, Fredric. *Marxism and Form: Twentieth-Century Dialectical Theories of Literature*. Princeton, N.J.: Princeton University Press, 1971.

———. *The Political Unconscious: Narrative as a Socially Symbolic Act*. Ithaca, N.Y.: Cornell University Press, 1981.

———. "Postmodernism and Consumer Society." In *The Anti-Aesthetic: Essays on Postmodern Culture*. Ed. Hal Foster. Seattle: Bay Press, 1983. 111–25.

———. *Signatures of the Visible*. New York: Routledge, 1990.

Jay, Gregory S. "The End of 'American' Literature: Toward a Multicultural Practice." *College English* 3 (1991): 264–81.

Jaynes, Julian. *The Origin of Consciousness in the Breakdown of the Bicameral Mind*. New York: Penguin Books, 1976.

Johnson, Charles. "The Color Black." *New York Times Review of Books*, 23 May 1993, 16.

———. "An Interview with Charles Johnson." By Jonathan Little. *Contemporary Literature* 34 (1993): 159–81.

Johnson, Samuel. *Samuel Johnson: Rasselas, Poems, and Selected Prose.* 3d ed. Ed. Bertrand H. Bronson. San Francisco: Rinehard Press, 1971.

Johnston, Carolyn. *Jack London—An American Radical?* Westport, Conn.: Greenwood Press, 1984.

Kaiser, Ernest. "The Failure of William Styron." In *William Styron's Nat Turner: Ten Black Writers Respond.* Ed. John Henrik Clarke. Boston: Beacon Press, 1968. 50–65.

Karcher, Carolyn L. *Shadow over the Promised Land: Slavery, Race, and Violence in Melville's America.* Baton Rouge: Louisiana State University Press, 1980.

Karl, Frederick. *American Fictions, 1940–1980.* New York: Harper and Row, 1983.

Kavanagh, James H. "Ideology." In *Critical Terms for Literary Study.* Ed. Frank Lentricchia and Thomas McLaughlin. Chicago: University of Chicago Press, 1990. 306–20.

Kazin, Alfred. Letter to Josephine Herbst, 4 Feb. 1966. Herbst Collection, Beinecke Library, Yale University, New Haven, Conn.

Kelley, William Melvin. *A Different Drummer.* New York: Bantam Books, 1962.

King, Martin Luther, Jr. "Black Power." In *Where Do We Go from Here: Chaos or Community?* New York: Harper & Row, 1967. 23–66.

———. "I Have a Dream." In *Black Writers of America: A Comprehensive Anthology.* Ed. Richard Barksdale and Keneth Kinnamon. New York: Macmillan, 1972. 871–73.

Kosok, Heinz. "Ishmael's Audience in 'The *Town-Ho's* Story.'" *Notes and Queries* 14 (1967): 54–56.

Kostelanetz, Richard. *Politics in the African-American Novel.* Westport, Conn.: Greenwood Press, 1991.

Kucherawy, Dennis. "Reign of Terror." *Maclean's Magazine* 104 (12 Aug. 1991): 43.

Labor, Earle, and Jeanne Campbell Reesman. *Jack London.* Rev. ed. New York: Twayne, 1994.

Labor, Earle, and Robert C. Leitz III. "Jack London on Alexander Berkman: An Unpublished Introduction." *American Literature* 61 (1989): 447–56.

Lacan, Jacques. *Écrits: A Selection.* Trans. Alan Sheridan. New York: W. W. Norton, 1977.

———. *The Four Fundamental Concepts of Psycho-Analysis.* Trans. Alan Sheridan. New York: W. W. Norton, 1978.

Lauret, Maria. *Liberating Literature: Feminist Fiction in America.* London: Routledge, 1994.

LeClair, Tom, and Larry McCaffery, eds. *Anything Can Happen: Interviews with Contemporary American Novelists.* Urbana: University of Illinois Press, 1988.

Leeds, Barry. *The Structured Vision of Norman Mailer*. New York: New York University Press, 1969.

Lennon, J. Michael, ed. *Conversations with Norman Mailer*. Jackson: University Press of Mississippi, 1988.

Lentricchia, Frank. "The American Writer as Bad Citizen—Introducing Don DeLillo." *South Atlantic Quarterly* 89 (1990): 239–44.

———. *Criticism and Social Change*. Chicago: University of Chicago Press, 1983.

Levine, Robert S. "Fiction and Reform I." In Elliott, *Columbia History*, 130–54.

Lewis, R. W. B. *The American Adam: Innocence, Tragedy, and Tradition in the Nineteenth Century*. Chicago: University of Chicago Press, 1955.

London, Jack. Ephemera: Scrapbooks. Huntington Library JL 517, v. 9. San Marino, Calif.

———. "The Iron Heel." Author's manuscript. 1906. Huntington Library JL 834. San Marino, Calif.

———. *The Iron Heel*. New York: Macmillan, 1908.

———. *The Iron Heel*. New York: Macmillan, 1919.

———. *The Iron Heel*. New York: Arcadia House, 1950.

———. *The Iron Heel*. Chicago: Lawrence Hill Books, 1980.

———. *Jack London: American Rebel*. Ed. Philip S. Foner. New York: Citadel Press, 1947.

———. "The Jungle." Notes for and manuscript of review. Huntington Library JL 1115 and 1116. San Marino, Calif.

———. *The Letters of Jack London*. 3 vols. Ed. Earle Labor, Robert C. Leitz III, and I. Milo Shepard. Stanford, Calif.: Stanford University Press, 1988.

Lutts, Ralph H. *The Nature Fakers: Wildlife, Science, and Sentiment*. Golden, Colo.: Fulcrum, 1990.

Mailer, Norman. *Advertisements for Myself*. New York: G. P. Putnam's Sons, 1959.

———. *Ancient Evenings*. Boston: Little, Brown, 1983.

———. *The Executioner's Song*. Boston: Little, Brown, 1979.

———. "Foreword." In *The Best of Abbie Hoffman*. Ed. Daniel Simon with Abbie Hoffman. New York: Four Walls Eight Windows, 1989. vii–ix.

———. *Harlot's Ghost*. New York: Random House, 1991.

———. "His Punch Is Better Than Ever." Interview by Bonnie Angelo. *Time Magazine*, 30 Sept. 1991, 68–70.

———. "Homage to Faulkner" (poem). *The New Yorker*, 11 Dec. 1995, 42.

———. "Introduction." In *Soon to Be a Major Motion Picture*. Abbie Hoffman. New York: Berkley Books, 1980. xiii–xv.

———. *Of a Fire on the Moon*. New York: New American Library, 1971.

———. *Pieces and Pontifications*. Boston: Little, Brown, 1982.

Mailloux, Steven. *Rhetorical Power*. Ithaca, N.Y.: Cornell University Press, 1989.

Maltby, Paul. *Dissident Postmodernists: Barthelme, Coover, Pynchon*. Philadelphia: University of Pennsylvania Press, 1991.

Martin, Jay. *Harvests of Change: American Literature, 1865–1914.* Englewood Cliffs, N.J.: Prentice-Hall, 1967.

Martin, Terence. *Parables of Possibility: The American Need for Beginnings.* New York: Columbia University Press, 1995.

Marx, Karl. *The Viking Portable Karl Marx.* Ed. Eugene Kamenka. New York: Penguin Books, 1983.

Marx, Leo. *The Machine in the Garden.* New York: Oxford University Press, 1964.

Maude, H. E. *Slavers in Paradise: The Peruvian Slave Trade in Polynesia, 1862–1864.* Stanford, Calif.: Stanford University Press, 1981.

Mayfield, Julian. "You Touch My Black Aesthetic and I'll Touch Yours." In Gayle, 24–31.

McHale, Brian. *Postmodernist Fiction.* New York: Methuen, 1987.

Melville, Herman. *Moby-Dick.* Ed. Harrison Hayford and Hershel Parker. New York: W. W. Norton, 1967.

———. "The Paradise of Bachelors and the Tartarus of Maids." In *The Norton Anthology of American Literature.* Vol. 1. Ed. Nina Baym et al. New York: W. W. Norton, 1989. 2208–24.

Miller, Henry. *A Devil in Paradise.* New York: Signet Books, 1956.

Miller, J. D. B. *The Nature of Politics.* Harmondsworth, U.K.: Penguin Books, 1961.

Millet, Kate. *Sexual Politics.* Garden City, N.Y.: Doubleday, 1970.

Milne, Gordon. *The American Political Novel.* Norman: University of Oklahoma Press, 1966.

Montgomery, Maxine Lavon. "A Pilgrimage to the Origins: The Apocalypse as Structure and Theme in Toni Morrison's *Sula.*" *Black American Literature Forum* 23 (1989): 127–37.

The Monthly List of New Macmillan Books. #109, Jan.–Feb. 1908. New York: Macmillan, 1908. Huntington Library JL 517. San Marino, Calif.

Morrison, Toni. Interview by Claudia Tate. In *Black Women Writers at Work.* Ed. Claudia Tate. New York: Continuum, 1983. 117–31.

———. Interview by Susan Stamburg. NPR (National Public Radio), Morning Edition, 10 Oct. 1993 (Far East Network 89.1 FM, Okinawa, Japan).

———. "Interview with Toni Morrison." By Tom LeClair. In LeClair and McCaffery, 252–61.

———. *Playing in the Dark.* New York: Vintage Press, 1992.

———. *Song of Solomon.* New York: New American Library, 1977.

———. *Sula.* New York: Plume, 1973.

———. "Unspeakable Things Unspoken: The Afro-American Presence in American Literature." *Michigan Quarterly Review* 28:1 (Winter 1989): 1–34. Rpt. in *Toni Morrison.* Ed. Harold Bloom. New York: Chelsea House, 1990. 201–30.

Murray, Albert. "Something Different, Something More." In *Anger and Beyond: The Negro Writer in the United States.* Ed. Herbert Hill. New York: Harper and Row, 1966. 112–37.

Nadel, Alan. *Invisible Criticism: Ralph Ellison and the American Canon.* Iowa City: University of Iowa Press, 1988.

National Endowment for the Humanities. *Overview of Endowment Programs: January 1992.* Washington, D.C.: Office of Publications and Public Affairs, 1992.

Nietzsche, Friedrich. *Beyond Good and Evil: Prelude to a Philosophy of the Future.* Trans. Walter Kaufmann. New York: Vintage Books, 1966.

Olson, Charles. *Call Me Ishmael.* New York: Reynold & Hitchcock, 1947.

O'Meally, Robert, ed. *New Essays on Invisible Man.* New York: Cambridge University Press, 1988.

Orwell, George. *The Collected Essays, Journalism, and Letters of George Orwell.* Vols. 1–4. Ed. Sonia Orwell and Ian Angus. New York: Harcourt Brace Jovanovich, 1968.

Paul, Sherman. "Melville's 'The *Town-Ho's* Story.'" In *Discussions of Moby-Dick.* Ed. Milton R. Stern. Boston: D. C. Heath, 1968. 87–92.

Pease, Donald E. "Citizen Vidal and Mailer's America." *Raritan* 11 (1992): 72–98.

———. "Introduction." In *New Americanists: Revisionist Interventions into the Canon.* Special edition of *boundary 2* 17 (1990): 1–37.

———. "Melville and Cultural Persuasion." In Bercovitch and Jehlen, 384–417.

Perloff, Marjorie. Book review. *Modern Language Quarterly* 56:4 (1995): 519–23.

Pettit, Alexander. Book review. *Modern Language Quarterly* 56:4 (1995): 511–13.

Pietz, William. "The 'Post-Colonialism' of Cold War Discourse." *Social Text* 19/20 (1988): 55–75.

Poirier, Richard. *A World Elsewhere.* New York: Oxford University Press, 1966.

———. *Norman Mailer.* New York: Viking Press, 1972.

Porter, Carolyn. *Seeing and Being: The Plight of the Participant Observer in Emerson, James, Adams, and Faulkner.* Middletown, Conn.: Wesleyan University Press, 1981.

Post-Lauria, Sheila. "'Philosophy in Whales . . . Poetry in Blubber': Mixed Form in *Moby-Dick.*" *Nineteenth-Century Literature* 45 (1990): 300–316.

Putnam, Robert D. "Bowling Alone: America's Declining Social Capital." *Journal of Democracy* 1 (1995): 65–78. Rpt. *Current*, June 1995, 3–9.

Radford, Jean. *Norman Mailer: A Critical Study.* London: Macmillan, 1975.

Railton, Stephen. *Authorship and Audience: Literary Performance in the American Renaissance.* Princeton, N.J.: Princeton University Press, 1991.

Reed, T. V. *Fifteen Jugglers, Five Believers: Literary Politics and the Poetics of American Social Movements.* Berkeley: University of California Press, 1992.

Reising, Russell. *The Unusable Past: Theory and the Study of American Literature.* New York: Methuen, 1986.

Rideout, Walter. *The Radical Novel in the United States, 1900–1954.* Cambridge, Mass.: Harvard University Press, 1956.

Rigney, Barbara Hill. *The Voices of Toni Morrison.* Columbus: Ohio State University Press, 1991.

Rodden, John. *The Politics of Literary Reputation: The Making and Claiming of "St. George" Orwell.* New York: Oxford University Press, 1989.

Rogin, Michael Paul. *Subversive Genealogy: The Politics and Art of Herman Melville.* New York: Alfred A. Knopf, 1983.

Rollyson, Carl. *The Lives of Norman Mailer.* New York: Paragon House, 1991.

Rorty, Richard. *Contingency, Irony, and Solidarity.* New York: Cambridge University Press, 1989.

Rose, Edward J. "Annihilation and Ambiguity: *Moby-Dick* and 'The *Town-Ho's* Story.'" *New England Quarterly* 4 (1972): 541–59.

Sachs, Viola. *The Game of Creation: The Unlettered Primeval Language of "Moby-Dick; or, The Whale."* Saint-Denis, France: University Press of Vincennes, 1982.

Said, Edward. "Opponents, Audiences, Constituencies and Community." In *The Anti-Aesthetic: Essays on Postmodern Culture.* Ed. Hal Foster. Seattle: Bay Press, 1983. 135–59.

Schaub, Thomas H. *American Fiction in the Cold War.* Madison: University of Wisconsin Press, 1990.

———. "Ellison's Masks and the Novel of Reality." In O'Meally, 123–56.

Schlueter, June. *Margaret Atwood's Vision and Form.* Carbondale: Southern Illinois University Press, 1988.

Scully, James. *Line Break: Poetry as Social Practice.* Seattle: Bay Press, 1988.

Sears, David O., and John B. McConahay. *The Politics of Violence: The New Urban Blacks and the Watts Riot.* Boston: Houghton Mifflin, 1973.

Seelye, John. *Melville: The Ironic Diagram.* Evanston, Ill.: Northwestern University Press, 1970.

Sherman, Joan R. *Jack London: A Reference Guide.* Boston: G. K. Hall, 1977.

Shoemaker, Steve. "Norman Mailer's 'White Negro': Historical Myth or Mythical History?" *Twentieth Century Literature* 37:3 (Fall 1991): 343–60.

Siebers, Tobin. *Cold War Criticism and the Politics of Skepticism.* New York: Oxford University Press, 1993.

Slotkin, Richard. "Myth and the Production of History." In Bercovitch and Jehlen, 70–90.

Smiley, Jane. "Say It Ain't So, Huck: Second Thoughts on Twain's 'Masterpiece.'" *Harper's Magazine* 293 (Jan. 1996): 61–67.

Smith, Valerie. "The Meaning of Narration in *Invisible Man.*" In O'Meally, 25–54.

Solano, Diana. "*Historia Nervosa:* Diagnosing Historians' Literary Anxieties." *Southern Review* (Monash University) 28:2 (July 1995): 226–39.

Spanos, William V. *The Errant Art of Moby-Dick: The Canon, the Cold War, and the Struggle for American Studies.* Durham, N.C.: Duke University Press, 1995.

Speare, Morris Edmund. *The Political Novel: Its Development in England and in America.* New York: Oxford University Press, 1924.

Spofford, William K. "Melville's Ambiguities: A Reevaluation of 'The *Town Ho's* Story.'" *American Literature* 2 (1969): 264–70.

Steel, Ronald. *Pax Americana*. New York: Viking Press, 1970.

Steele, Shelby. *The Content of Our Character*. New York: Harper Perennial, 1990.

Stern, Milton R. "Melville, Society, and Language." In *A Companion to Melville Studies*. Ed. John Bryant. New York: Greenwood Press, 1986. 433–79.

———. "*Moby-Dick*, Millennial Attitudes, and Politics." *ESQ: Journal of the American Renaissance* 54 (1969): 51–60.

Stewart, George R. "The Two Moby-Dicks." *American Literature* 4 (1954): 417–48.

Stowe, Harriet Beecher. *Uncle Tom's Cabin*. New York: New American Library, 1981.

Suleiman, Susan. *Authoritarian Fictions: The Ideological Novel as a Literary Genre*. Princeton, N.J.: Princeton University Press, 1993.

Tannen, Deborah. *You Just Don't Understand: Women and Men in Conversation*. New York: Ballantine Books, 1990.

Taylor, Gordon O. "Of Adams and Aquarius." *American Literature* 46 (1974): 68–82.

Theweleit, Klaus. *Male Fantasies*. Vol. 1. Trans. Stephen Conway. Minneapolis: University of Minnesota Press, 1987.

Tompkins, Jane P. *Sensational Designs: The Cultural Work of American Fiction, 1790–1860*. New York: Oxford University Press, 1985.

Trivedi, Harish, ed. *The American Political Novel: Critical Essays*. New Delhi: Allied, 1984.

Vaihinger, Hans. *The Philosophy of "As If": A System of the Theoretical, Practical, and Religious Fictions of Mankind*. Trans. C. K. Ogden. London: Routledge and Kegan Paul, 1949.

Van Leer, David. "Society and Identity," in *The Columbia History of the American Novel*, ed. Emory Elliot. New York: Columbia University Press, 1991. 485–509.

Vincent, Howard P. *The Trying-Out of Moby-Dick*. Boston: Houghton Mifflin, 1949.

Walker, Alice. *In Search of Our Mothers' Gardens*. San Diego: Harcourt Brace Jovanovich, 1983.

Walker, Brian. "John Rawls, Mikhail Bakhtin, and the Praxis of Toleration." *Political Theory* 23:1 (Feb. 1995): 101–27.

Warren, Robert Penn. *All the King's Men*. 1946. Rpt., New York: Bantam Books, 1951.

———. "A Note to *All the King's Men*." *Sewanee Review* 61 (Summer 1953): 476–80.

Wenke, Joseph. *Mailer's America*. Hanover, N.H.: University Press of New England, 1987.

West, Anthony. *Principles and Persuasions*. New York: Harcourt, Brace, and Company, 1957.

White, Hayden. *Metahistory: The Historical Imagination in Nineteenth-Century Europe*. Baltimore: Johns Hopkins University Press, 1974.

Whitfield, Stephen J. *The Culture of the Cold War*. Baltimore: Johns Hopkins University Press, 1991.

Wilding, Michael. *Political Fictions*. Boston: Routledge and Kegan Paul, 1980.

Wolin, Sheldon. *Politics and Vision: Continuity and Innovation in Western Political Thought*. Boston: Little, Brown, 1960.

Wright, John S. "The Conscious Hero and the Rites of Man: Ellison's War." In O'Meally, 157–86.

Yamamoto, Tsunetomo. *Hagakure: The Book of the Samurai*. Trans. William Scott Wilson. Tokyo: Kodansha International, 1979.

Zinn, Howard. *A People's History of the United States*. New York: Harper and Row, 1980.

Zoellner, Robert. *The Salt-Sea Mastodon: A Reading of "Moby-Dick."* Berkeley: University of California Press, 1973.

Index

JOHN WHALEN-BRIDGE, a visiting professor of English at the University of the Ryukyus in Japan, is working on a book about Asian influences on American culture.